The Law Relating to Schools

Fourmat Publishing

The Law Relating to Schools
by Neville S. Harris, LL.M, Ph.D,
Senior Lecturer in Law, Liverpool Polytechnic

ISBN 1 85190 093 4

First published 1990

All rights reserved

© 1990 Neville S. Harris
Published by Fourmat Publishing, 133 Upper Street, London N1 1QP

Printed in Great Britain by
Billing & Sons Ltd, Worcester

Preface

This book aims to provide a comprehensive account of the law relating to schools in England and Wales. It includes all relevant parts of the Education Reform Act 1988, which is introducing sweeping reforms to the public sector of education—in the curriculum (especially the National Curriculum), school admissions, local financial management of schools (or "LMS") and grant-maintained schools. It also includes the many statutory instruments which have followed in the wake of the Act—around forty relating to schools in 1989 alone! Their range and volume reflect the wide powers given to the Secretary of State under the 1988 Act.

The education system has entered a new era, and it is one of regulation. For those working in the field of education, or otherwise having an interest in it, knowledge of the increasingly complex legal framework is becoming supremely important. Thus the book has aimed to include not only the new regime laid down by the 1988 Act, but also the many other legal provisions generally considered to be of particular importance to the running of schools—covering areas such as school government, special educational needs, school attendance, care and supervision of pupils and discipline. Management themes, such as staffing and schools' budget shares under LMS, feature prominently. Other themes, such as parental involvement and equal opportunities, run through many parts of the book.

The implementation of education reform has been guided by the extensive literature emanating from the Department of Education and Science and others. The various circulars, reports, codes of practice and recommendations, are not the law. But they are important as sources of information and guides to practice. I have referred to them wherever appropriate. I have also cited relevant case law.

Many areas of the law relating to schools are complex and

the language used in the legislation and by the judges is frequently technical. The Education Reform Act 1988 is a particularly intricate piece of legislation. I have attempted to state the law as clearly as its substance allows. I hope that the end product proves comprehensible and will serve the needs of its intended wide-ranging readership—lawyers; education inspectors, advisers, administrators and welfare officers; head teachers and other teachers; governors; and perhaps also parents.

I have endeavoured to state the law as it stood on 31 March 1990. Certain legal provisions which, at the time of going to press, were due to become law after this date, have also been included.

Since the text of the book went to press, the Secretary of State's fresh decision to allow Beechen Cliff school in Bath to acquire grant-maintained status following the quashing of the original decision in February 1990 (see page 16), was upheld by the Court of Appeal in a judgment delivered on 15 May 1990.

The decision in *R* v *Secretary of State for Education and Science ex parte ILEA* (1990), discussed on page 37, has been upheld by the Court of Appeal (The Times, 17 May 1990).

Neville S Harris

Contents

		page
Chapter 1:	**Schools and their resources**	1
1.	Introduction	1
2.	Duty of LEAs to secure the provision of primary and secondary schools	2
3.	Primary, secondary, middle and special schools	8
4.	Categories of school	10
5.	Nursery education	26
6.	Changes to educational provision—general requirements under ERA 1988	27
7.	Establishment of schools	30
8.	Alteration of schools	33
9.	Closure and amalgamation of schools	36
10.	Finance: local management of schools	40
11.	The education of travellers and displaced persons	58
Chapter 2:	**Teachers and other staff**	59
1.	Introduction	59
2.	Staffing levels in schools	60
3.	Qualification for employment as a teacher	61
4.	Appointment of staff	71
5.	Discipline and dismissal of staff	80
6.	School teachers' pay and conditions	90
7.	Pay and conditions of non-teaching staff	98
8.	Local education authority training grants and education support grant schemes	100
9.	Appraisal schemes	102

Chapter 3:	**School government**	103
	1. Introduction	103
	2. Instrument and articles of government	104
	3. Composition of governing bodies	106
	4. Elections	111
	5. Appointment	113
	6. Governorship	113
	7. Governors' meetings	116
	8. Delegation	123
	9. Accountability and liability of governors	128
	10. Disputes with the LEA	130
	11. Expenses	132
	12. Information and training	132
	13. Control of school session times and term and holiday dates	133
Chapter 4:	**Parents as consumers: information and choice of school**	135
	1. Information	135
	2. Admissions	148
Chapter 5:	**Equal opportunities**	160
	1. Sex Discrimination Act 1975	161
	2. Race Relations Act 1976	168
	3. Assistance for the financially disadvantaged	172
Chapter 6:	**Pupils—attendance and discipline**	177
	1. Registration	177
	2. School attendance	178
	3. Discipline	187
Chapter 7:	**The curriculum**	196
	1. Introduction	196
	2. Basic principles	196
	3. Control of the secular curriculum	197
	4. Statements of curricular policy (secular)	198
	5. The "basic curriculum"	198
	6. The National Curriculum	199
	7. Political issues	206
	8. Sex education	207

	9. Homosexuality	210
	10. Collective worship and religious education	212
	11. External qualifications and examinations	218
	12. Charging for education	219
	13. Complaints	222
	14. Copyright law	223
Chapter 8:	**Special educational needs**	231
	1. Introduction to the legislation	231
	2. Definitions	232
	3. Integration	233
	4. Identification and assessment of needs	234
	5. Statementing	237
	6. Reassessment at parents' request	240
	7. Appeals and other forms of challenge	240
	8. Special needs and the National Curriculum	242
	9. Special needs in opted-out schools	243
	10. LMS and special needs provision	243
	11. Staff training	244
Chapter 9:	**Negligence, health and safety**	245
	1. Introduction	245
	2. Negligence in the care and supervision of pupils	246
	3. School premises and environment	264
Appendix 1:	Procedure for acquisition of grant-maintained status	277
Appendix 2:	DES Circular 7/88 Education Reform Act: Local Management of Schools (Annex A)	281
Appendix 3:	Conditions of employment of teachers	286
Appendix 4:	DES Circular 7/87 The Conduct of Governor Elections (Annex 9)	298
Index		303

Table of cases

A v Liverpool City Council [1982] AC 363 (HL) 186
Affutu-Nartoy v Clarke and ILEA [1984] The Times
  9 February 255
Associated Provincial Picture Houses Ltd v Wednesbury
  Corporation [1948] 1 KB 223 (CA) 4, 158

Baker, Re [1961] 3 All ER 276 (CA) 186
Barking and Dagenham L B C v Camara [1988] The Times
  18 July (EAT) 73
Barnes v Bromley LBC [1983] The Times 16
  November 251, 254
Barnes v Hampshire County Council [1969] 1 WLR 1563
  (HL) 259
Bates v Parker [1954] 1 All ER 768 (CA) 266
Beaumont v Surrey County Council (1968) 66 LGR
  580 .... 250, 257
Black v Kent County Council [1983] The Times 23
  May 252
Blyth v Birmingham Waterworks Co (1856) 11 Exch
  781 248
Bolam v Friern Hospital Management Committee [1957]
  2 All ER 118 249
Bostock v Kay [1989] The Times 20 April 120
Bovey v Board of Governors of the Hospital for Sick
  Children [1978] IRLR 241 (EAT) 90
Bradbury v Enfield London Borough Council [1967] 3 All
  ER 434 .... 5, 28
Brown v Board of Education (1954) (US) 160
Brunyate v ILEA [1989] 2 All ER 417 (HL) 116, 129
Butt v Cambridgeshire and Ely County Council (1970) 68
  LGR 81 252

Campbell and Cosans v UK (1982) 4 EHRR 293 193
Caparo Industries plc v Dickman [1990] 1 All ER 568
  (HL) 248
Carmarthenshire County Council v Lewis [1955] AC 549, 1
  All ER 565 260

xi

Chattopadhay v Headmaster of Holloway School [1981] IRLR 487 (EAT) 73
Chilvers v London County Council (1916) 80 JP 246 249
Ching v Surrey County Council [1910] 1 KB 736 269
Clark v Monmouthshire County Council (1954) 52 LGR 246 (CA) 257
Commission for Racial Equality v Dutton [1989] IRLR 8 (CA) 169
Coney v Choyce [1975] 1 WLR 422 30
Conrad v ILEA (1967) 65 LGR 543 .... 249, 255
Council of Civil Service Unions v Minister for the Civil Service [1985] AC 374, [1984] 3 All ER 935 (HL) 28
Crouch v Essex County Council (1966) 64 LGR 240 253
Crump v Gillmore (1969) 68 LGR 56 (DC) 184
Cumings v Birkenhead Corporation [1972] Ch 12, [1971] 1 WLR 1458 .... 4, 153

D, Re (1988) 86 LGR 442 (CA) 242
Daborn v Bath Tramways Motor Co Ltd [1946] 2 All ER 333 (CA) 250
Dawkins v The Crown Suppliers (1990) 16(2) New Community 296 (IT) 169
De Souza v Automobile Association [1986] IRLR 103 (CA) 80, 162
Debell and Teh v Bromley LBC [1984] The Guardian 13 November 166
Donoghue v Stevenson [1932] AC 562 (HL) 248
DPP v K [1990] 1 All ER 331 (DC) 275

Edwards v National Coal Board [1949] 1 KB 704 272
Ellis v Sayers Confectioners Ltd (1963) 61 LGR 299 (CA) 263
Enfield LBC v Forsyth (1987) 85 LGR 526, [1987] 2 FLR 126 180
Equal Opportunities Commission v Birmingham City Council [1989] 1 All ER 769 (HL) 4, 5, 162, 163, 165, 167
Fitzgerald v Northcote (1865) 4 F & F 656 .... 194, 195
Ford v Warwickshire County Council [1983] IRLR 126 .. 85
Fryer v Salford Corporation [1937] 1 All ER 617 ..... 249, 254

Gardiner v Newport County Borough Council [1974] IRLR 262 86

Table of cases

George v Devon County Council [1988] 3 All ER
 1002 .... 174, 184
Gibbs v Barking Corporation [1936] 1 All ER 115
 (CA) 255
Gillick v West Norfolk and Wisbech Area Health
 Authority [1985] 3 All ER 402 (HL) 209, 210, 252
Gillmore v London County Council [1938] All ER 31
 (DC) 265
Good v ILEA (1980) 10 Fam Law 213 (CA) 259
Griffiths v Smith [1941] AC 170 265

Hampson v Department of Education and Science [1990]
 2 All ER 25 (CA) 73, 170
Happe v Lay (1977) 76 LGR 313 (DC) 184
Harvey v Strathclyde Regional Council [1989] Public Law
 160 .... 40, 154
Hinchley v Rankin [1961] 1 All ER 692, [1961] 1 WLR
 421 179
Home Office v Dorset Yacht Co [1970] AC 1004, [1970] 2
 All ER 294 (HL) 248
Home Office v Holmes [1984] IRLR 299 (EAT) 89
Honeyford v Bradford City Metropolitan Council [1986]
 IRLR 32 (CA) 80, 131
Hudson v Governors of Rotherham Grammar School
 [1938] LCT 303 251

ILEA v Nash [1979] ICR 229 (EAT) 89

Jacques v Oxfordshire County Council (1967) 66 LGR
 440 263
James v Eastleigh Borough Council [1989] The Times 1
 July (CA) 161
Jarman v Mid-Glamorgan Education Authority (1985)
 82 LS Gaz 1249 (DC) 181, 184
Jeffrey v London County Council (1954)
 52 LGR 521 .... 251, 259
Jenkins v Howells [1949] 2 KB 218, [1949] 1 All ER 942
 (DC) 181

Kidd v DRG (UK) Ltd [1985] ICR 405 89

Lambeth LBC v Commission for Racial Equality
 [1990] The Times 24 April (CA) 72
Lee v Department of Education and Science (1968) 66
 LGR 211 28

xiii

Legg v ILEA [1972] 3 All ER 177 30
Lockett v Croydon LBC [1986] The Times 6 August
  (CA) 119
Lyes v Middlesex County Council (1962) 61 LGR 443 .. 250

McGoldrick v Brent LBC [1987] IRLR 67 .... 80, 131
Mandla v Dowell Lee [1983] 1 All ER 1062 (HL) .. 73, 169,
                                                                              170
Martin v Middlesbrough Corporation (1965) 63 LGR
  385 (CA) 249
Mays v Essex County Council [1975] The Times 11
  October 258
Meade v Haringey London Borough Council [1979] 2 All
  ER 1016, [1979] 1 WLR 637 (CA) 3, 4, 5, 60
Moore v Hampshire County Council (1981) 80 LGR 481
  (CA) 256
Morris v Caernarvon County Council [1910] 1 KB 858 269
Murphy v Epsom College [1985] ICR 80 (CA) 87

Nichol v Gateshead MBC (1989) 87 LGR 435 (CA) 40
Noble v ILEA (1984) 83 LGR 291 (CA) 121
Noonan v ILEA [1974] The Times 14 December 253
Norfolk County Council v Bernard [1979] IRLR 220
  (EAT) 87
Nyasi v Ryman (1988) 367 IRLIB 15 (EAT) 168

Ojutiku v MSC [1982] ICR 661 (CA) 170

Perera v Home Office [1980] IRLR 233 (EAT) 73
Pettican v Enfield LBC [1970] The Times 22 October .. 257
Porcelli v Strathclyde Council [1985] ICR 177 81
Porter v City of Bradford Metropolitan Council [1985] 14
  January Lexis 246, 262
Price v Civil Service Commission (No 2) [1978] IRLR 3 .. 73

R v Brent LBC ex parte Assegai [1987] The Times 18
  June, (1987) 151 LG Rev 891 (DC) 115
R v Brent LBC ex parte Gunning (1985) 84 LGR 211 .. 28,
                                                                              39
R v Chief Constable of Gwent (1989) 139 NLJ 1754
  (HL) 128
R v Croydon LBC ex parte Leney (1987) 85 LGR 466
  (DC) 2
R v Gilchrist [1961] The Times 11 July 193

Table of cases

R v Governors of Haberdashers' Aske's School ex parte ILEA (*see* Brunyate v ILEA (1989)) 116
R v Governors of Small Heath School ex parte Birmingham City Council [1989] The Times 14 August, [1989] The Guardian 19 September 120
R v Greenwich LBC ex parte Governors of John Ball Primary School [1989] The Times 16 November (DC) 154, 156
R v Grey [1666] Kel J 64, [1666] ER 1082 193
R v Hampshire Education Authority ex parte J (1985) 84 LGR 547 .... 175, 232, 233
R v Hereford and Worcester LEA ex parte Wm Jones [1981] 1 WLR 768 (DC) 3, 219
R v Hertfordshire County Council ex parte George (1988) Lexis CO/856/87 (DC) 29
R v Hopley (1860) 2 F & F 202 .... 193, 194
R v ILEA ex parte Ali [1990] The Times 21 February 4, 5, 159
R v Kirklees MBC ex parte Molloy (1988) 86 LGR 115, [1987] The Times 17 August (CA) 40
R v Lancashire County Council ex parte CM [1989] 2 FLR 279 (DC and CA), [1989] The Times 27 March (CA) 232
R v Liverpool City Council ex parte Ferguson; Same v Same ex parte Grantham [1985] The Times 20 November 4, 5
R v London Borough of Sutton ex parte Hamlet (1986) 26 March (unreported) (DC) 28
R v Manchester City Council ex parte Fulford (1984) 81 LGR 292 (DC) 194
R v Northampton County Council ex parte Gray [1986] The Times 10 June (DC) 2, 113, 159
R v Oxfordshire Education Authority ex parte W [1986] The Times 12 November (DC) 232
R v Rahman [1985] The Times 5 June (CA) 195
R v Secretary of State for Education and Science ex parte Avon County Council [1990] The Times 13 March (DC) 16, 29
R v Secretary of State for Education and Science ex parte Birmingham City Council (1985) 83 LGR 79 40
R v Secretary of State for Education and Science ex parte Collins (1983) 20 June (unreported) (DC) 28

R v Secretary of State for Education and Science ex parte
Davis [1988] The Guardian 12 December (DC) 241
R v Secretary of State for Education and Science ex parte
Hardy [1988] The Times 28 July, Lexis CO/354/88
(DC) 31
R v Secretary of State for Education and Science ex parte
ILEA and Anr [1990] The Times 3 March (DC) 37
R v Secretary of State for Education and Science ex parte
Keating (1985) 84 LGR 469, [1985] The Times 3
December 5, 164, 165
R v Secretary of State for Education and Science ex parte
Lashford [1988] 1 FLR 72 (CA) 238
R v Secretary of State for Education and Science ex parte
Talmud Torah Machzikei Hadass School Trust [1985]
The Times 12 April (DC) 24
R v Secretary of State for Wales ex parte Hawkins (1982)
28 May (unreported) (CA) 28
R v Secretary of State for Wales ex parte Russell (1983)
28 June (unreported) (DC) 28
R v South Glamorgan Appeals Committee ex parte Evans
(1984) 10 May Lexis CO/197/84 155
R v Spratt [1990] The Times 14 May (CA) 275
R v Surrey County Council ex parte H (1985) 83 LGR 219
(CA) 241
R v Surrey Quarter Sessions Appeal Committee ex parte
Tweedie (1963) 107 SolJ 555, (1963) 61 LGR 464
(DC) 179
R v Trustee of the Roman Catholic Diocese of Westminster ex parte Andrews [1989] The Times 18 August (CA),
sub nom Mars (1987) 86 LGR 507 (DC) 116
Rainey v Greater Glasgow Health Board [1987] IRLR 26
(HL) 170
Raval v DHSS [1985] ICR 685 (EAT) 72
Ravenscroft v Herbert [1980] RPC 193 226
Reffell v Surrey County Council [1964] 1 All ER 743,
(1964) 62 LGR 186 269
Rich v London County Council [1953] 1 WLR 895 249
Ricketts v Erith Borough Council (1943) 42 LGR 471 .. 257
Rogers v Essex County Council [1986] 3 All ER 321
(HL) 174, 184
Ryan v Fildes [1938] 3 All ER 517 (CA) 193

Table of cases

S (A Minor) (Care Order: Education), Re [1977] 3 All
  ER 582, [1977] 3 WLR 575 185
Saunders v Scottish National Camps [1980] IRLR 174
  (Ct S) 88
Secretary of State for Education and Science v Tameside
  Metropolitan Borough Council [1976] 3 All ER 665
  (HL) 4, 158
Shrimpton v Hertfordshire County Council (1911) 104 LT
  145 263
Simkiss v Rhondda Borough Council (1983) 81 LGR 460
  (CA) 251
Smerkinich v Newport Corporation (1912) 76 JP 454 ... 252
Smith v ILEA [1978] 1 All ER 411 (CA) 4, 153
Smith v Martin and Kingston-upon-Hull Corporation
  [1911] 2 KB 775 247
Snowball v Gardner Merchant Ltd [1987] ICR 719, [1987]
  IRLR 397 81
Spiers v Warrington Corpn [1954] 1 QB 61 184
Staley v Suffolk County Council and Dean Mason (1986)
  26 November (unreported) (DC) 251
Steel v Union of Post Office Workers [1978] ICR 181 ... 170
Surrey County Council v Lewis [1987] 3 All ER 641
  (HL) 86

Tabor v Mid-Glamorgan County Council [1982] COIT
  1165/7 86
Taylor v Kent County Council [1969] 3 WLR 156 87
Tillotson v Harrow Borough Council (1984) (unreported)
  (DC) 256

Van Oppen v Clerk to the Bedford Charity Trustees
  [1989] 3 All ER 389 (CA), [1989] 1 All ER 273
  (DC) 250, 253, 254
Vaughan v Solihull MBC [1982] The Times 25 May
  (CA) 33
Vogler v Hertfordshire County Council [1975] The
  Times 7 and 8 November 87

W v Hertfordshire County Council [1985] AC 791
  (HL) 186
Ward v Hertfordshire County Council (1969) 114 Sol J 87
  (CA) 258, 265
Watkins v Birmingham City Council [1975] The Times 1
  August (CA) 247

xvii

Watt v Kesteven County Council [1955] 1 All ER 473
   (CA) 5, 153
Webb v Essex County Council [1954] Times Educational
   Supplement 12 November 246
West Bromwich Building Society v Townsend [1983] ICR
   257 .... 272, 274
Wheat v E Lacon Ltd [1966] 1 All ER 582 (HL) 265
Williams v Cardiff Corporation [1950] 1 All ER 250 266
Williams v Eady (1893) 10 TLR 41 (CA) 249, 250
Wilsher v Essex Area Health Authority [1988] 1 All ER
   871 (HL), [1986] 3 All ER 801 (CA) 249
Wiseman v Salford City Council [1981] IRLR 202 86
Woodward v Mayor of Hastings [1944] 2 All ER 505
   (CA) 265
Wright v Cheshire County Council [1952] 2 All ER 789
   (CA) 249, 255
Wood v London Borough of Ealing [1967] Ch 346 153

Table of Statutory Instruments

Control of Substances Hazardous to Health Regulations 1988 SI 1988 No 1657
Copyright (Librarian and Archivists) (Copying of Copyright Material) Regulations 1989 SI 1989 No 1212
Direct Grant Schools Regulations 1959 SI 1959 No 1832
Disabled Persons (Services, Consultation and Representation) Act (Commencement No 4) Order 1988 SI 1988 No 51
Education (Abolition of Corporal Punishment) (Independent Schools) Regulations 1987 SI 1987 No 1183
Education (Abolition of Corporal Punishment) (Independent Schools) (Amendment) Regulations 1989 SI 1989 No 1233
Education (Abolition of Corporal Punishment) (Independent Schools) (Prescribed Categories of Persons) Regulations 1989 SI 1989 No 1825
Education (Approval of Special Schools) Regulations 1983 SI 1983 No 1499
Education (Assisted Places) (Incidental Expenses) Regulations 1989 SI 1989 No 1237
Education (Assisted Places) Regulations 1989 SI 1989 No 1235
Education (Financial Delegation to Schools) (Mandatory Exceptions) Regulations 1989 SI 1989 No 1352
Education (Grant-Maintained Schools) (Finance) Regulations 1989 SI 1989 No 1287
Education (Grant-Maintained Schools) (Publication of Proposals) Regulations 1989 SI 1989 No 1469
Education (Grant-Maintained Schools) (Termination of Power to Determine a Period of Suspension) Order 1988 SI 1988 No 1981
Education (Grants and Awards) Regulations 1984 SI 1984 No 1098
Education (Grants) (City Colleges) Regulations 1987 SI 1987 No 1138
Education (Inner London Education Authority) (Transitional and Supplementary Provisions) Order 1989 SI 1989 No 46
Education (Inner London Education Authority) (Transitional and Supplementary Provisions) (No 2) Order 1989 SI 1989 No 1135
Education (Middle Schools) Regulations 1980 SI 1980 No 918
Education (Modification of Enactments Relating to Employment) Order 1989 SI 1989 No 901
Education (National Curriculum) (Attainment Targets and Programmes of Study in Mathematics) Order 1989 SI 1989 No 308
Education (National Curriculum) (Attainment Targets and Programmes of Study in Science) Order 1989 SI 1989 No 309
Education (National Curriculum) (Attainment Targets and Programmes of Study in English) Order 1989 SI 1989 No 907
Education (National Curriculum) (Attainment Targets and

Programmes of Study in English) (No 2) Regulations 1990 SI 1990 No 423
Education (National Curriculum) (Exceptions) (Wales) Regulations 1989 SI 1989 No 1308
Education (National Curriculum) (Modern Foreign Languages) Order 1989 SI 1989 No 825
Education (National Curriculum) (Temporary Exceptions for Individual Pupils) Regulations 1989 SI 1989 No 1181
Education (Parental Ballots for Acquisition of Grant-Maintained Status) Regulations 1988 SI 1988 No 1474
Education (Particulars of Independent Schools) Regulations 1982 SI 1982 No 1730
Education (Pre-Scheme Financial Statements) (Amendment) Regulations 1989 SI 1989 No 1288
Education (Pre-Scheme Financial Statements) Regulations 1989 SI 1989 No 370
Education (Prescribed Public Examination) Regulations 1989 SI 1989 No 377
Education (Provision of Clothing) Regulations 1980 SI 1980 No 545
Education (Publication of Proposals for Reduction in Standard Number) Regulations 1988 SI 1988 No 1515
Education (Publication of Schemes for Financing Schools) Regulations 1989 SI 1989 No 2335
Education (Publication of School Proposals) (No 2) Regulations 1980 SI 1980 No 658
Education (School Curriculum and Related Information) Regulations 1989 SI 1989 No 954
Education (School Curriculum and Related Information) (Amendment) Regulations 1989 SI 1989 No 1136
Education (School Government) Regulations 1987 SI 1987 No 1359
Education (School Government) Regulations 1989 SI 1989 No 1503
Education (School Information) Regulations 1981 SI 1981 No 630
Education (School Premises) (Amendment) Regulations 1989 SI 1989 No 1277
Education (School Premises) Regulations 1981 SI 1981 No 909
Education (School Records) Regulations 1989 SI 1989 No 1261
Education (School Teachers' Pay and Conditions) (Amendment) Order 1989 SI 1989 No 1453
Education (School Teachers' Pay and Conditions) Order 1989 SI 1989 No 904
Education (Schools and Further Education) Regulations 1981 SI 1981 No 1086
Education (Special Education Needs) Regulations 1983 SI 1983 No 29
Education (Teachers) Regulations 1982 SI 1982 No 106
Education (Teachers) Regulations 1989 SI 1989 No 1319
Education (Training Grants) (Amendment) Regulations 1988 SI 1988 No 355
Education (Training Grants) (Amendment) Regulations 1989 SI 1989 No 366
Education (Training Grants) Regulations 1987 SI 1987 No 96
Education Reform Act (Commencement No 1) Order 1988 SI 1988 No 1459
Education Reform Act (Commencement No 4) Order 1988 SI 1988 No 2271
Education Reform Act (Commencement No 5) Order 1989 SI 1989 No 164
Education Reform Act (Commencement No 6) Order 1989 SI 1989 No 501

Table of statutory instruments

Education Support Grant (Amendment) (No 2) Regulations 1988 SI 1988 No 2037
Education Support Grant (Amendment) Regulations 1989 SI 1989 No 2446
Health and Safety (Training for Employment) Regulations 1988 SI 1988 No 1222
Health and Safety (Youth Training Scheme) Regulations 1983 SI 1983 No 1919
Health and Safety Information for Employees Regulations 1989 SI 1989 No 682
Magistrates' Courts (Children and Young Persons) Rules 1988 SI 1988 No 913
Pupils' Registration (Amendment) Regulations 1988 SI 1988 No 1185
Pupils' Registration Regulations 1956 SI 1956 No 357
Reporting of Injuries, Diseases and Dangerous Occurrences Regulations 1985 SI 1985 No 2023
Safety Representatives and Safety Committees Regulations 1977 SI 1977 No 500
Scholarships and Other Benefits Regulations 1977 SI 1977 No 1443
Sex Discrimination (Designated Institutions) Order 1975 SI 1975 No 1902
Sex Discrimination (Designated Institutions) Order 1980 SI 1980 No 1860

Abbreviations

CA	Court of Appeal
DES	Department of Education and Science
EA	Education Act (eg EA 1944 = Education Act 1944)
E(No 2)A 1986	Education (No 2) Act 1986
EPCA 1978	Employment Protection (Consolidation) Act 1978
ERA 1988	Education Reform Act 1988
EWO	Education Welfare Officer
FE	further education
GM	grant-maintained
HL	House of Lords
HMI	Her Majesty's Inspectors
ILEA	Inner London Education Authority
LEA	local education authority
NC	National Curriculum
QBD	Queen's Bench Division
SEAC	School Examinations and Assessment Council
SEN	special educational needs
SI	statutory instrument(s) (as in SI 1989 No 907)

Chapter 1

Schools and their resources

1. Introduction

The categories of school in the public sector of education in England and Wales are still broadly those established by the Education Act 1944 ("EA 1944"), although the Education Reform Act 1988 ("ERA 1988") has added an important further category—"grant-maintained" schools. Although there is a flourishing private sector of education, the public sector is by far the more important, at least in numerical terms. According to Department of Education and Science ("DES") statistics, its 26,000 schools provide education for some nine million pupils. By contrast there are some 2,300 private and independent fee-paying schools with 600,000 pupils.

Schools in the public sector are generally referred to in current legislation as "maintained". For the most part this means wholly or partly financed by local education authorities ("LEAs"). The LEAs in England and Wales are the county councils, district councils in former metropolitan counties, and the outer and (from 1 April 1990 when the Inner London Education Authority ("ILEA") is abolished) inner London boroughs (EA 1944 s 6 as amended; ERA 1988 ss 162 and 163). (Transitional arrangements were made for the transfer of certain of ILEA's functions to the inner London councils: the Education (Inner London Education Authority) (Transitional and Supplementary Provisions) Order 1989 and (No 2) Order 1989. See DES Circular 6/88 *The Transfer of Responsibility for Education in Inner London*.) LEAs are required to have education committees, which must include persons with experience of education and local education conditions (EA 1944 Sch 1 paras 1 and 2; see *R* v *Croydon LBC ex parte Leney* (1986)). They must also appoint chief education officers to be responsible for the administration of the education service in the authority's area (EA 1944 s 88).

The new grant-maintained schools are maintained by the Secretary of State rather than LEAs. City Technology Colleges and Colleges for the Technology of the Arts (ERA 1988 s 105—see below, page 22) are not classed as "maintained" for the purposes of current legislation.

Public education in England and Wales must be organised into "three progressive stages": "primary education, secondary education and further education" (EA 1944 s 7). LEAs must, so far as their powers allow:

> "contribute towards the spiritual, moral, mental and physical development of the community by securing that efficient education throughout those stages shall be available to meet the needs of the population of their area" (EA 1944 s 7).

"Efficient" in this context has not been defined, but seems to include, for example, making adequate curricular provision, although the "basic curriculum" and "National Curriculum" laid down in ERA 1988 and certain regulations made thereunder are independent requirements (see Chapter 7).

In any event, the vagueness of much of EA 1944 s 7 suggests that it is extremely unlikely that the section could be enforced in the courts. Moreover, a parent has generally to request the Secretary of State to use his/her powers to give directions to LEAs and governors under ss 68 and 99 of the same Act before the court will entertain an application for judicial review (*R* v *Northamptonshire County Council ex parte Gray* (1986); see further pages 158–159). In any event, there are more specific duties in s 8.

2. Duty of LEAs to secure the provision of primary and secondary schools

LEAs must ensure that there are available in their area "sufficient schools" for *primary* and *secondary* education (EA 1944 s 8(1)).

(a) "Sufficient schools"

The 1944 Act states that the schools for an area must be sufficient in:

> "number character and equipment to afford for all pupils opportunities for education offering such variety of instruction and training as may be desirable in view of their different ages, abilities, and aptitudes, and of the different periods for which they may be expected to remain at school, including practical instruction and training appropriate to their respective needs" (s 8).

(In fulfilling this duty LEAs must, *inter alia*, ensure that special educational provision is made for those with special educational needs.)

The pace of educational reform, and the increasing financial pressures on LEAs in recent years, have created tensions between the various parties with an interest in the education system. Many of the legal disputes which have arisen have concerned the extent of the duty imposed on LEAs by s 8(1).

This duty in s 8(1) is deliberately couched in broad and general terms to allow LEAs to have regard for a wide range of considerations which might affect their performance (eg financial constraints: *R v Hereford and Worcester LEA ex parte Jones* (1981)). So, in *Meade v Haringey London Borough Council* (1979), the Court of Appeal considered that a LEA might not be in breach of s 8 by taking a decision to close its schools during a caretakers' strike, if the authority was seeking to minimise the longer term disruption to pupils' education which could result from a deterioration in industrial relations. There would, in the words of Eveleigh LJ, have to be a "just and reasonable excuse" for any such emergency closure.

Although the argument that this part of s 8 reveals an "absence of a clear-cut definition of any essential minimum standard and content of the education which must be provided in schools" (P Meredith, *Individual Challenge to Expenditure Cuts in the Provision of Schools* (1982) JSWL 344) is still valid, the new curriculum requirements of Chapter I of ERA 1988 (see Chapter 7) have made the scope of the duty more clear. Nevertheless, so far as the organisation of education is concerned, the fact remains that the general duty in s 8 to provide "sufficient schools" is regarded as no more than a target duty, which leaves LEAs a "broad discretion to choose what in their judgment are the means best suited to their area for providing . . . instruction" (*Secretary of State for Education and Science ex parte Tameside MBC* (1976), per Lord Diplock at 695b). So, in *Cumings* v *Birkenhead Corporation* (1972), a LEA's policy of allocating places at Roman Catholic secondary schools to pupils who had attended Roman Catholic primary schools did not put the authority in breach of s 8 (nor of s 76 of the same Act, which lays down a general condition that pupils are to be educated in accordance with the wishes of their parents). Moreover, this broad discretion means that a LEA can fulfil its duty to provide schools "sufficient in . . . character" by, for example, providing comprehensive or selective schools or both (*Smith* v *Inner London Education Authority* (1978) CA; *Equal Opportunities Commission* v *Birmingham City Council* (1989) (HL) per Lord Goff at 775c).

Although it is clear that the s 8(1) duty extends not only to the provision of buildings and equipment, but also to teachers and other essential personnel (*Meade* v *Haringey LBC* (1979); *R* v *Liverpool City Council ex parte Ferguson and Others; Same* v *Same, ex parte Grantham and Others* (1985)), it has to be understood that the duty is not considered absolute. The High Court recently held that a temporary failure to comply fully with the standard set by s 8(1), arising out of a situation beyond the control of the authority (in this case shortage of teachers due to difficulties in recruitment in inner London), would not put the LEA in breach of its duty (*R* v *ILEA ex parte Ali* (1990)).

What would put a LEA in breach of its duty to provide "sufficient schools" (enabling intervention by a court or the Secretary of State under s 68) would be a decision which was unreasonable in the sense that no reasonable authority would have taken it (*Secretary of State for Education and Science* v *Tameside MBC* (1976) per Viscount Dilhorne at 678d; *Associated Provincial Picture Houses Ltd* v *Wednesbury Corporation* (1948)). Judicial intervention by way of review would also be possible if a decision was *ultra vires* in other ways—for example where relevant considerations were not taken into account or irrelevant ones were. The Court of Appeal in *Meade* v *Haringey LBC (op cit)* made it clear that if it was established that the LEA's decision to close schools had been taken for purely political reasons, it would have been unlawful. It would also be unlawful if the LEA took a decision which "fl[ew] in the face of" the s 8(1) duty (per Denning MR) or acted "in total disregard of its responsibilities as an Education Authority" (per Watkins LJ in *R* v *Liverpool City Council ex parte Ferguson, op cit*).

It is probable that the Secretary of State alone could be the judge, under s 99 of the 1944 Act, of an alleged *simple* failure in respect of the s 8(1) duty; the remedy offered by that section (directions to the LEA/governors, enforceable via *mandamus*) would be regarded as exclusive (see *Watt* v *Kesteven CC* (1955); *Bradbury* v *Enfield LBC* (1967)). The court would not be able to intervene, because Parliament did not intend to make the s 8(1) duty to be owed to individuals personally (see HWR Wade, *Administrative Law,* 6th ed (1988) page 749). In *R* v *ILEA ex parte Ali (op cit)*, Woolf LJ emphasised that s 8(1) was "intended to enure for the public in general and not intended to give the individual litigant a cause of action". (This was fatal to Mr Ali's claim for damages in respect of the LEA's failure to provide his son with a school place.) The default powers in ss 68 and 99 are discussed further at pages 158–159 below.

LEAs must also comply with s 23 Sex Discrimination Act 1975, which requires LEAs to carry out their various functions under the Education Acts, including those under EA 1944 s 8, without practising sex discrimination (*R* v *Secretary of State for Education and Science ex parte Keating* (1985), *per* Taylor J). (There are other duties, under ss 22 and 25 of the 1975 Act—see further Chapter 6.) But in a case of alleged sex discrimination under s 23, it is not necessary to show that the LEA is in breach of s 8 (*Equal Opportunities Commission* v *Birmingham City Council, op cit,* at 776).

(b) Primary education

As stated above, LEAs must ensure that there are available in their areas sufficient schools for primary education. Primary education is defined as:

"full-time education suitable to the requirements of junior pupils who have not attained the age of ten years and six months, and full-time education suitable to the requirements of junior pupils who have attained that age and whom it is expedient to educate together with junior pupils who have not attained that age" (EA 1944 s 8(1)(a)).

Junior pupils are pupils aged under twelve years (EA 1944 s 114(1)). Education provided to pupils aged between two and five years is nursery education, which LEAs may provide, but are under no duty to do so (see page 26). It may be noted that the division of the primary stage into two segments, "infants" and "juniors" has become common practice but is not, in itself, a statutory requirement.

(c) Secondary education

LEAs must also ensure that there are sufficient schools for secondary education. Secondary education is defined as:

"full-time education suitable to the requirements of senior pupils, [and full-time education suitable to the requirements of junior pupils who have attained the age of ten years and six months and whom it is expedient to educate together with senior pupils]" (s 8(1)(b) as amended by the Education (Miscellaneous Provisions) Act 1948 s 3 and ERA 1988 s 120(6)(a)).

A "senior pupil" is one who is aged at least twelve and under nineteen.

In fulfilling their duty to ensure that sufficient schools for secondary education are available, LEAs must have regard, *inter alia*, to any facilities for full-time education for senior pupils at any futher education institutions maintained by the authority in the exercise of its functions under EA 1944 s 41 (EA 1944 s 8(3), added by ERA 1988 s 120(6)(b)).

(d) Further education

Secondary education provided to those aged sixteen or over must be distinguished from further education. The Education Reform Act 1988 has given LEAs more clear-cut responsibilities concerning the provision of further education ("FE") than those which existed previously. LEAs must make sure that there are "adequate facilities" for FE in their areas (EA 1944 s 41 substituted by ERA 1988 s 120(2)). In fulfilling this duty LEAs are required to take account of:

(i) the education provided by universities, institutions funded by the Polytechnics and Colleges Funding Council (see ERA 1988 s 132) and other bodies (EA 1944 s 41(9)); and
(ii) the requirements of those with learning difficulties (see below).

"Further education" is defined as:

(i) full- and part-time education for persons over compulsory school age ("including vocational, social, physical and recreational training"); and
(ii) "organised leisure-time occupation [defined in s 41(7)] provided in connection with the provision of such education" (EA 1944 s 41(2)).

Full-time education for those aged sixteen or over, which is of a kind given in schools, will not be classed as FE if it "is or is to be provided by an institution which does not provide part-time senior education or post-school age education to a significant extent" (s 41(4)). Part-time senior education here means part-time education for sixteen to eighteen year olds, and "post-school age education" means full- or part-time education for persons aged nineteen or over (s 41(5)). Unfortunately, neither full-time nor part-time is defined— nor is "significant extent". If a question arises as to whether the education referred to in s 41(4) is given to a "significant extent", that question is to be determined by the Secretary of State (EA 1944 s 67(4A) added by ERA 1988 s 120(7)).

Thus it is the institution in which the education takes place, rather more than the particular type of education, which is the determinant of whether a particular post-sixteen pupil is in further or secondary education. This contrasts with the distinction between FE and higher education. The latter is defined for the purposes of s 41 with reference to the provision of particular *courses* (ERA 1988 s 120(1) and Sch 6). LEAs are under no duty to provide facilities for higher education (ERA 1988 s 120(1)), but may do so or may arrange for such education to be provided (EA 1944 s 41(3)). LEAs may also secure the provision of FE for persons living outside their areas (s 41(8)).

The lack of educational provision for those aged sixteen or over with special educational needs has been a cause of criticism. In some cases only considerably local pressure and threatened legal action has persuaded LEAs to offer such provision (Newell, *Further education: the legal basis* (1983) 9 (3) *Special Education: Forward Trends,* pages 6–7). The extent of LEAs' responsibilities in this area has not been clear, and the Education Act 1981 (see Chapter 8) does not specifically deal with this age group, although in any event it is almost certainly covered by the broad duties in EA 1944 s 8 (above). Now, however, in determining whether there are "adequate facilities" for FE for their areas, LEAs must consider the requirements of those above compulsory school age who have learning difficulties, as defined in s 41(11):

"(a) . . . a significantly greater difficulty in learning than the majority of persons of his age; or
(b) . . . a disability which either prevents or hinders him from making use of facilities of a kind generally provided by the local education authority concerned in pursuance of their duty [to secure that FE is provided]".

(Note: a person does not have a learning difficulty solely because the language or form of language in which he is taught differs from that which has at any time been spoken in his home: s 41(12).)

3. Primary, secondary, middle and special schools

Having defined what is meant by primary and secondary education (and distinguished the latter from further education) we can consider the schools in which such provision is to be made. *Primary* schools are those providing primary eduation, although when the school is for two to five year olds it is a "nursery school" (see page 26). *Secondary* schools are those providing secondary education. In fulfilling their duty to provide "sufficient schools" in their areas, LEAs must have regard, *inter alia,* to the need for securing that primary and secondary education are provided in separate schools (s 8(2)(a)). However, "middle schools", providing education to pupils of primary and secondary school age, may be created, on the approval of the Secretary of State (EA 1964 s 1; Education (Middle Schools) Regulations 1980 (SI 1980 No 918)). Such schools will officially be designated as primary or secondary schools, depending on whether the majority of their pupils are to be of primary or secondary school age.

Special schools are schools which are "specially organised to make special educational provision for pupils with special educational needs and which are for the time being approved by the Secretary of State" (EA 1944 s 9(5) as substituted by EA 1981 s 11(1)). Approval will be in accordance with regulations made under EA 1981 s 12 (see Education (Approval of Special Schools) Regulations 1983). Special schools are specifically excepted by EA 1944 s 8(2) from the requirement that primary and secondary education should be provided in separate schools (above), although approval may, in individual cases, be subject to the school's offering only one or the other stage of education. In the case of special schools for pupils with emotional and behavioural difficulties ("EBD schools"), the DES considers that, wherever possible, separate "primary" stage and "secondary" stage schools should be available (DES Circular 23/89, *Special Schools for Pupils with Emotional and Behavioural Difficulties*). A survey by HMI (Report 62/89) resulted in the conclusion that all-age schools for EBD pupils are less successful.

The provision of special schools may be one way in which a LEA complies with its duty to secure that there are sufficient schools for providing special educational provision for pupils who have special educational needs (EA 1944 s 8(2)(c)). (See further Chapter 8: *Special educational needs*.) In fact, provision may be also arranged in an ordinary school or, for example, a non-"maintained" special school; under EA s 8(1) LEAs only have to ensure that sufficient schools are *available*. But a LEA may not arrange for provision to be made at an independent school for a child in respect of whom it maintains a statement as to his special educational needs under EA 1981 s 7(1) unless:

    (i) the school is approved (under EA 1981 s 13 and in

accordance with any regulations made thereunder—none have so far been made) by the Secretary of State as suitable for the admission of such children; or
(ii) the Secretary of State consents to the child being educated at the school in question.

4. Categories of school

One of the reasons that parts of education law dealing with schools are so complex is that there are so many types of what are referred to as "maintained" schools. In particular, there are county schools, voluntary aided and controlled schools and special agreement schools, which categories were established by the 1944 Act (ss 9(2) and 15(1)). There are also grant-maintained schools. Independent schools (discussed at pages 23 to 26) are not classed as "maintained".

As it has been the intention that the various categories of school should enjoy differing levels of self-government and autonomy from their LEAs (the governors of voluntary aided schools, for example, have traditionally had more control over staff appointments and the use of premises than governors of county or controlled schools (see below)), separate legal provisions covering each category appear at various places in the legislation. Nevertheless, it may be observed that "for the most part LEAs and voluntary schools form a harmonious and indivisible entity and see themselves very clearly as working under the same umbrella within the maintained sector" (D Nice (ed), *Education and the Law* (1986), page 61).

When reading the ensuing paragraphs explaining the different categories of school, readers are asked to bear in mind that so far as the financial arrangements for maintaining schools and meeting running costs are concerned, substantial changes will occur once local financial management is introduced under ERA 1988 (see page 40 *et seq*).

(a) County schools

County schools are the major providers of education in

Schools and their resources

England and Wales: approximately 75 per cent of pupils in the maintained sector attend them. The majority of secondary schools in this sector are comprehensives, although there is no legal duty to establish such schools. (A legal duty to establish comprehensives was introduced by the last Labour government under the Education Act 1976, but was subsequently removed under the incoming Conservative administration's Education Act 1979 (s 1); the impetus for the wholesale introduction of these schools came from DES Circular No 10 of 1965 (10/65), which urged re-organisation along comprehensive lines.)

County schools (see EA 1944 s 9(2)) are maintained wholly by LEAs, who own them and employ staff to work in them. The upkeep of the school premises and the cost of alterations or improvements have traditionally been the responsibility of the LEA, although significant alterations are generally financed by the DES. The LEA also controls the use of premises—although (since September 1988) such control is only during "any school session, or break between sessions on the same day" (E(No 2)A 1986 s 42(a)). At all other times use of the school premises is to be under the control of the governing body. Such control by the governors must be exercised "subject to any direction given to them by the [LEA]" and with due regard being given to making the premises available to the community served by the school, when they are not required by the school (s 42(b)). A recent survey has shown that many LEAs have not yet handed over control under s 42 and that, in some of the areas where they have, the directions issued have been so restrictive as virtually to "nullify the whole purpose of s 42" (*Hire purpose*, Times Educational Supplement, 2 June 1989).

County schools will, of course, gain a considerable degree of independence from their LEAs under the arrangements for financial delegation (see page 40 *et seq*).

(b) Voluntary schools

Over twenty per cent of pupils in the maintained sector attend voluntary schools, of which approximately two-thirds are Church of England and most of the remaining third are

Roman Catholic. There is also a small number of schools with a Jewish foundation. Voluntary schools fall into three categories—controlled, aided or special agreement (EA 1944 ss 9(2) and 15). In this section of the book we shall be concerned solely with distinguishing between these categories, with reference to their chief characteristics, as with county schools above. More specific legal provisions relevant to them—such as those dealing with governing bodies and the appointment and dismissal of teachers—are discussed elsewhere in the book.

The classification of a particular voluntary school will depend, *inter alia*, on whether certain maintenance expenses may be borne by the governors (with a contribution from the Secretary of State) (EA 1944 s 15). If the Secretary of State is satisfied the expenses can be so borne, the school will be an aided or special agreement school; if not, the school will be controlled.

(i) Voluntary controlled schools

There are around 3,000 voluntary controlled schools in England and Wales. A voluntary school will be classed as controlled if the Secretary of State is not satisfied that the governors are able and willing to meet (with the help of a contribution from the Secretary of State) certain maintenance costs (set out in s 15(3)—see *voluntary aided schools*, below) (EA 1944 s 15(2)). The 1944 Act, with the creation of the controlled category, has enabled voluntary bodies to exert a certain amount of influence over a school without the burden of paying for its maintenance and running costs— which must be borne by the LEA (see s 15(3)). The foundation (basically the body which established the school) will own the building(s)—although the LEA has legal rights if the property is sold or if the school is discontinued (see EA 1944 s 14, as amended by EA 1946, and page 37). The LEA retains ownership of playing fields.

Significant enlargements (as defined in EA 1944 s 114(1)) to school premises will require the Secretary of State's approval (EA 1980 ss 13 and 14).

Generally speaking, the governors have control over the use of voluntary school premises (EA 1944 s 22(3))—although, subject to certain exceptions, LEAs may give directions as to their use (EA 1944 s 22(1) as amended by EA 1980 Sch 1).

As will be seen below, the governing bodies of controlled schools enjoy no greater powers under the E (No 2) A 1986 over staff appointments and dismissals than governors of county schools. Under pre-financial delegation arrangements which that Act covers, LEAs appoint teachers and other staff for controlled schools and pay their salaries. Note that for schools with up to and including 599 pupils, the numbers of LEA and foundation governors on a controlled school's governing body are equal—a gain for foundations compared with the previous legislation. In larger schools the LEA has one more governor than the foundation (see Chapter 3).

(ii) Voluntary aided schools

There are nearly 5,000 voluntary aided schools. Aided schools have always enjoyed considerable independence from their LEAs with the voluntary body exerting overall control. Aided status is particularly favoured by certain religious denominations because the school is controlled almost exclusively by the governing body, on which the foundation governors must be in the majority (E (No 2) A 1986 s 4) (see Chapter 3). The school must be conducted in accordance with the terms of its trust deed (as modified by the Secretary of State because of any inconsistency between those terms and the school's instrument or articles of government: EA 1944 s 17(4)).

The chief advantage of aided status is that the school gains this independence at the cost of only a relatively small contribution towards the cost of alterations and repairs for which the governors are responsible, *viz*:

> "such alterations to the school buildings as may be required by the local education authority for the purpose of securing that the school premises should conform to the prescribed standards, and . . . repairs to the school buildings . . . [other than those to] the interior of the school buildings, or for repairs to those buildings necessary in consequence of the use of the school premises, in

pursuance of any direction or requirement of the authority, for purposes other than those of the school" (EA 1944 s 15(3)).

This means, *inter alia*, that the LEA is responsible for the interior of the school buildings, the playground and playing fields. The LEA is also responsible for provision and upkeep of equipment and payment of teachers' and other staff salaries. The governors are responsible for most repairs to the actual buildings, although they are entitled to a contribution towards the cost (EA 1944 s 102) (see below). (All of this is affected by financial delegation schemes when in force; see page 40.) Note that s 15(3) also makes the governors responsible for meeting liabilities incurred by them, or by former governors or trustees, in connection with the provision of premises or equipment for the purposes of the school. The governors are also responsible for meeting the cost of a significant enlargement of premises and of new premises where a school moves to a new site or when a new school is established (but the LEA is responsible for the site, grounds, playing field etc). In such cases the governors can claim a contribution from the Secretary of State (see below).

The rate of contribution required from the governors (with the Secretary of State paying the rest) was originally set at fifty per cent. But the 1944 Act was subsequently amended so that the governors' contribution became fifteen per cent, at which rate it still stands (EA 1944 s 102). Fifteen per cent is also the required contribution towards the cost of any significant enlargement of the school premises, including the provision of a new site.

LEAs' rights concerning the use of voluntary aided schools' premises are limited. Provided that a LEA requires the use of the premises for any purposes in connection with education or the welfare of the young and is satisfied that there is no other suitable accommodation for the purpose in the area, it may require the governors to allow it to use the premises free of charge on any week day (up to a maximum of three in any week) at times when they are not required for school purposes (EA1944 s 22(2)).

(iii) Special agreement schools

This category effectively dates back to the Education Act 1936 and it currently numbers around 100 schools, all of which are in the secondary sector. Special agreement schools are so called because of the special agreement under which the LEA will pay a contribution grant of between 50 and 75 per cent of the cost of building a voluntary school or enlarging an existing one. Note that on repayment of the grant the governors may apply to the Secretary of State for voluntary aided status (see EA1944 s 15(5)).

For the purposes of ss 15 (maintenance, repairs etc), 22 (use of premises) and 102 (85 per cent DES contribution in respect of certain costs), special agreement schools are bracketed together with aided schools (see above). The only difference of any substance in status between the two categories is related to the appointment of staff (but see below).

(c) Grant-maintained schools

Under local financial management (see page 40 *et seq*) LEAs will lose a great deal of control over schools in their area as schools acquire greater autonomy. The possibility of a school becoming grant-maintained is stated to provide "an additional route to autonomy" and lend "a new and powerful dimension to the ability of parents to exercise choice within the publicly provided sector of education" (DES *Grant-maintained schools: Consultation Paper* July 1987). More recently it has been claimed that the establishment of these schools will "prove to be a stimulus for higher standards at all schools" (DES Circular 10/88, para 2), although there have been claims that such schools will be perceived as "better resourced and elitist" and that their existence will promote "greater divisiveness" in the education system (P Meredith, *Educational Reform* (1989) 52 MLR 215, 228).

Whatever the arguments, grant-maintained status has arrived, and the first batch of schools to attain this status left local authority control on 1 September 1989. A further six schools joined these eighteen on or by 1 April 1990.

Acquisition of grant-maintained ("GM") status is dependent

upon parental endorsement under a secret, postal ballot (see below) and approval by the Secretary of State—which may be given "only if the Secretary of State is satisfied, on the basis of the evidence before him, that this is an appropriate step for the governors to take" (DES Circular 10/88, para 2). The High Court, in February 1990, upheld a claim by Avon County Council that the Secretary of State had acted unlawfully in conferring GM status on Beechen Cliff, a boys' school in Bath (*R* v *Secretary of State for Education and Science ex parte Avon County Council* (1990)). The Secretary of State's decision had thrown the LEA's secondary school reorganisation plans for Bath into chaos. The court held that the Secretary of State, in turning down the LEA's reorganisation plans, (as he has to do if he approves GM status: ERA 1988 s 73(5)—see page 29) had failed to give proper consideration to the effect of allowing one school to acquire GM status —"disruption, delay and prolonged uncertainty for the majority of children and their parents in Bath" (per Hutchinson J).

In some cases parents perceive opting out as a way of preserving the character of a school which may be under threat.

For example, the parents of Bacup and Rawtenstall Grammar School, which became a GM school on 1 September 1989, were apparently reluctant to see the school become a comprehensive school (*The Guardian*, 29 August 1989). In contrast, parents of pupils at two comprehensive schools at Milton Keynes contemplated opting out to frustrate LEA plans to reintroduce grammar schools to the area (*The Times*, 13 November 1989).

(i) Eligibility for grant-maintained status

Any county or voluntary school is eligible to be considered for GM status (ERA 1988 s 52(5)), with the exception of:

    (a) primary schools with fewer than 300 registered pupils (s 52(6))—the Secretary of State may vary this figure by Order (s 52(7));
    (b) county or voluntary schools which have received permission from the Secretary of State to close, on application of the LEA (s 52(8));

(c) voluntary schools in respect of which the governors have given notice of intention to discontinue the school (s 52(9)).
(d) nursery schools (s 52(5));
(e) special schools (*ibid*).

(ii) Property

GM schools have property rights (and liabilities) transferred to them from the LEA (but generally not in respect of property held on trust) (ERA 1988 s 74). Loan obligations incurred by the LEA and premature retirement payments to former staff remain the LEA's responsibility (s 74(3)). Transferred property is held by the governing body for the lifetime of the school (see s 57(3)); any transfer of the school to a new site will be treated as a continuation of the school for this purpose (s 101). The governors are able to dispose of premises only with the consent of the Secretary of State (s 57(3) and (4)(b)). The Secretary of State could order that some or all of the proceeds of sale go to the LEA.

Property not used for school purposes is not transferred. Property with joint community/school use will, so far as possible, be apportioned (Sch 10 para 1).

Responsibility for ensuring that property is transferred to the governors by the required date rests with the Education Assets Board (s 198(3)). Appointments to the Board are made by the Secretary of State, and selection must be made from persons with experience in property management, local government or education (s 197(3)). The Board must act in accordance with the powers and procedures laid down in Sch 8 to the 1988 Act. The Board's principal functions are spelt out fully in ss 198–201 of, and Sch 10 to, the Act. The Secretary of State has to consult the Board over a variety of matters relating to the determination of property value where a grant-maintained school is discontinued (under ss 94–99) (s 200).

Restrictions prevent LEAs from disposing of property liable to be transferred on a school's becoming grant-maintained and incorporated as such (s 74(1)). The restrictions apply once the LEA has been informed that the governors are to consider balloting parents on a change to GM status or when

parents have made a valid written request for such a ballot (s 76(3)). The restriction ends:
  (i) if the governors fail, within the next 42 days, to resolve to hold a ballot of parents; or
  (ii) if a parents' ballot fails to secure the necessary majority; or
  (iii) if the ballot is in favour of opting out but the proposals are rejected by the Secretary of State or withdrawn (s 76(4)).

The effect of the restriction is that the LEA will require the governors' consent (and Secretary of State's consent if the value of the property exceeds a set sum—currently £6,000) to dispose of property used wholly or partly for the purposes of the school (s 77(2)).

(iii) Staff

The position concerning transfer of staff can conveniently be dealt with here. All staff employed to work wholly at the school, including meals staff preparing meals for consumption on the premises, will be transferred to the governing body's employ:

> "The contract of employment between a person to whom this section applies and the former employer shall have effect from the transfer date as if originally made between him and the governing body of the grant-maintained school" (ERA 1988 s 75(6)).

All the previous employer's rights, duties, powers and liabilities under the contract of employment with the employees shall vest in the governing body of the GM school on the transfer date (s 75(7)). The employee cannot treat the change of employer as a "substantial change . . . to his detriment in his working conditions" such as would be sufficient to give him/her a right to terminate his/her contract of employment (s 75(8)). A teacher's pay and conditions will not be adversely affected by the transfer and will continue to be governed by the School Teachers' Pay and Conditions Document in force at the time (Sch 12 para 25 amending EA 1980 s 27).

The appointment, dismissal and withdrawal of staff by the

LEA will be restricted once the application for GM status is in progress. Parallel provisions to those governing transfer of property, outlined above, will apply (DES Circular 10/88, para 52; ERA 1988 s 78).

(iv) Funding

The Secretary of State is under a legal duty to maintain grant-maintained schools (ERA 1988 s 52(2)). The payments are to take the form of annual "maintenance grants", paid to the governing body (s 79(1)). Despite this, LEAs' rate support grant payments from central government will reflect a notional need to spend on providing education for *all* pupils resident in their areas and attending maintained schools, including GM schools. The maintenance grant paid by the Secretary of State to the governors of GM schools will thus be recouped from LEAs, either through direct payments to the Secretary of State (and into the Consolidated Fund) or by deduction from rate support grant or other grant(s) (s 81(1)–(8); see DES Circular 21/89, *Grant-Maintained Schools: Financial Arrangements*, paras 17–21). Note: a small percentage of the annual maintenance grant may be carried over by the school at the end of the financial year (*ibid*, para 52).

The amount of the maintenance grant is to be determined under regulations. The Education (Grant-Maintained Schools) (Finance) Regulations 1989—in force from 1 September 1989 were replaced by 1990 Regulations of the same name on 1 April 1990. Guidance is contained in Circular 21/89.

The government's stated intention on the funding of GM schools is that:

> "the acquisition by a school of grant-maintained status should not change the financial position either of the school or of local ratepayers in the LEA which previously maintained the school" (DES Circular 10/88, para 53).

This financially neutral effect flows from the fact that, on the one hand, GM schools will not receive support services from the LEA (other than those bought-in), and so would actually be entitled to a larger grant than that paid to LEA-funded schools under financial delegation arrangements; and on the other, the fact that administrative costs and the cost of support services will have to be borne by the school. (See, further, DES Circular 10/88, para 66, and Maclure, *Education Reformed* (1988), page 69.) LEAs will have certain continuing responsibilities towards GM schools after opting out (see page 21).

The actual funding arrangement where a financial delegation scheme is in force in the authority is that the Secretary of State determines as the level of the school's grant the amount that the school would have received as its budget share from its former maintaining authority *plus* a school's share of expenditure by the LEA on items falling outside the delegated budget *plus* the cost of school meals (Education (Grant-Maintained Schools) (Finance) Regs 1990 reg 4). If the school's incorporation date does not coincide exactly with the start of the funding year, apportionment is to be made (reg 7). Requirements which may be attached to the payment of the maintenance grant are spelled out in the regulations (reg 9 and Sch 4). Transitional arrangements for the calculation of the maintenance grant for the year ending 31 March 1989 have been laid down (reg 3).

The 1988 Act states that provision may also be made, via regulations, for "special purpose grants" and "capital grants" (s 79(3)).

Special purpose grants may cover expenditure in connection with a prescribed educational purpose, or in respect of special educational needs (see Education (Grant-Maintained Schools) (Finance) Regulations 1990 reg 11 and Sch 6). These grants will cover such items as in-service training and expenditure for the purposes for which ESGs are payable (see pages 101–102). (Section 11 funding, that is, grants made under s 11 Local Government Act 1966 for the education of pupils of New Commonwealth origin, will also be available to GM schools: ERA 1988 s 211.) Special purpose grants may also cover expenses, of a class or description specified in the regulations, which "it appears to the Secretary of State the governing bodies of such schools cannot reasonably be expected to meet from maintenance grant" (s 79(3)). Requirements may be attached to the provision of these grants (reg 12 and Sch 4).

Capital grants, of 100 per cent of the costs they are to cover (s 79(5)), may be made in respect of prescribed categories of expenditure of a capital nature (s 79(3)(b) and (6) and the Education (GM Schools) (Finance) Regulations 1990, *op cit*, Sch 5). The Secretary of State will "consider each application for capital grant on its merits and in the light of the total resources available nationally for building projects and other capital expenditure at all maintained schools" (DES Circular 10/88, para 60).

Various requirements, with which governing bodies will be under a duty to comply, may be attached to special purpose and capital grants, including a requirement to repay all or part of them (s 79(7)–(11)). In fact, a repayment of excess maintenance grant received can also be ordered if an overpayment (defined in s 80(5) as the amount paid in grants less the amount payable in accordance with the grant regulations) is made to the governing body in any financial year (s 80(3)). Repayments of either of these types may take the form of deductions from further grants (s 80(4)).

It is for the Secretary of State to decide when, and at what intervals, maintenance, special purpose and capital grants shall be paid (s 80(1)).

(v) LEAs' continuing responsibilities

After a school has acquired GM status, a LEA will remain responsible for, *inter alia*:

(a) its duties under the Education Act 1944 relating to the availability of "sufficient schools", the enforcement of school attendance, and the provision of free transport;
(b) its duties under the Education Act 1981 towards pupils with special educational needs (see Chapter 8).

LEAs will be under a duty (ERA 1988 s 100(1)) to ensure that pupils in GM schools receive no less favourable treatment in respect of (a) and (b) above than pupils in schools they maintain. LEAs will continue to have a duty to provide a careers service (Employment and Training Act 1973 s 8)—which must be made available to pupils in GM schools.

GM schools will receive no allowance in their annual maintenance grant for certain LEA central services like careers. But many other such services do not have to be provided by LEAs to GM schools. Services which the LEA will not be obliged to provide include school meals and milk and the advisory services. The governors of GM schools will have legal responsibility for the provision of free school meals to eligible pupils. The maintenance grant provided to the governors will contain an allowance for such provision. Governors may contract with outside bodies, including the LEA, for the provision of such services—ERA 1988 s 57(3)(c) and Sch 12 paras 11 and 24 (amending Local Government (Goods and Services) Act 1970 and EA 1980 s 22, respectively). Local authorities may also provide cleaning services, but only if they have first taken part in competitive tendering for such provision (Local Government Act 1988 Part I).

For the opting out procedure, see Appendix 1.

(d) City technology colleges and city colleges for the technology of the arts

The government originally intended that about twenty of these "centres of excellence" would be established, with the help of considerable injections of private capital. Public money, which it now seems is required in greater amounts than had previously been thought necessary, may also be provided (ERA 1988 s 105(1) and (4); see also the Education (Grants) (City Colleges) Regulations 1987).

City colleges must be located in an "urban area" (the first was set up in Solihull). They must cater for pupils aged eleven to eighteen with "different abilities" who are wholly or mainly drawn from that area (ERA 1988 s 105(2)(a) and (b)). There must be a "broad curriculum", but with an emphasis on science and technology (in the case of city technology colleges); or on technology in its application to the performing and creative arts (city colleges for the technology of the arts) (s 105(2)(c)). The requirements of ERA 1988 relating to the National Curriculum, religious education and collective worship do not apply to these city colleges because they are not "maintained schools" for the purposes of the Chapter I of the Act; in s 105(1) they are referred to as "independent schools". Corporal punishment may not be administered in these city colleges (Education (Abolition of Corporal Punishment) (Independent Schools) Regulations 1987, reg 2(c) and (d) added by Amendment Regulations 1989 with effect from 1 September 1989).

(e) Independent schools

(i) Definition

An independent school is defined in law as:

"any school at which full-time education is provided for five or more pupils of compulsory school age (whether or not such education is also provided for pupils under or over that age), not being a school maintained by a local education authority, a grant-maintained school or a special school not maintained by a local education authority" (EA 1944 s 114(1) as amended).

(ii) Registration

For the operation of an independent school to be lawful, it must be entered on the register kept (under EA 1944 s 70(1)) by the Registrar of Independent Schools. In most cases, where a person operates an independent school which is neither registered nor provisionally registered (under EA 1944 s 70(1)(b)) that person may be liable on summary conviction to a fine and, in the case of any further offence, up to three months' imprisonment (s 70(3) and (3A)).

(iii) Controls

Independent schools enjoy a considerable degree of autonomy, especially in relation to financial matters. They are frequently registered as charities, but may also be run as businesses with a view to profit. They are free from the requirements concerning the provision of information and the National Curriculum (see Chapter 6). (They are required by the Education (Assisted Places) Regulations 1989 to publish details of their assisted places scheme—see below.) There are, however, certain controls which may be exercised by the Secretary of State, and the schools may be inspected by Her Majesty's Inspectorate of Schools.

The proprietors must submit to the Registrar (above) annual particulars concerning such matters as pupils enrolled and examinations for which pupils are being prepared (Education (Particulars of Independent Schools) Regulations 1982).

The Registrar must also be notified of changes in the management personnel and in the name and location of the school. If these requirements are not met, the Secretary of State may, after giving two months' notice of the specific shortcomings, order that the school be removed from the Register of Independent Schools (*ibid*). Moreover, the Secretary of State is under a duty to serve on the proprietor of a registered or provisionally registered school a notice of complaint if satisfied that the school is "objectionable" on certain grounds. These grounds (the apposite one(s) of which should be specified by the Secretary of State in his notice) refer to the unsuitability of the school premises or parts thereof, the inadequacy or unsuitability of the accommodation, any lack of efficient and suitable instruction, and the unsuitability of a teacher or proprietor for their position (EA 1944 s 71(1)). Any teacher considered unsuitable is entitled to receive a copy of the notice (s 71(2)). In one case the court held that where a school caters for the special traditions and characteristics of a particular sect, it is "suitable" if it primarily equips children for a place in the community in which they live, rather than in the wider community, so long as it leaves the children with the option of adopting some other way of life in the future if they so choose: *R* v *Secretary of State for Education and Science ex parte Talmud Torah Machzikei Hadass School Trust* (1985).

In every case the notice of objection must specify a time, of not less than one month, in which the complaint may be referred to the Independent Schools Tribunal (s 71(3)). The Tribunal, which is to be constituted in accordance with EA 1944 Sch 6, has various powers when determining the appeal —including annulment of the complaint, ordering that the school be struck off the register or struck off unless certain problems are rectified, and disqualification of a teacher or proprietor from holding that particular position (EA 1944 s 72(2)). (In the last case, it is an offence for the person concerned to continue in that position after being disqualified: s 73(2) and (3).) It is possible subsequently to have the disqualification removed by the Secretary of State, or on appeal from his refusal, by the Independent Schools Tribunal (s 74).

Independent (non-special) schools providing accommodation for up to fifty pupils will be "children's homes" controlled by ss 63–65 Children Act 1989.

(iv) The assisted places scheme

The assisted places scheme was introduced under the Education Act 1980, with effect from 1 October 1980. It aims to enable pupils "who might otherwise not be able to do so to benefit from education at independent schools" (s 17). The scheme provides for:

(a) the remission of school fees by "participating schools" (that is, independent schools with which the Secretary of State has entered into a "participation agreement") (EA 1980 s 17(2)); and
(b) the reimbursement of the school concerned by the Secretary of State (s 17(1)).

In 1989, the average cost of fees at independent schools was £2,887 per year, and the average assisted place contribution from the government was £2,264 (*The Times*, 27 November 1989).

The fees covered by the scheme are tuition and other fees which are required in order to be able to attend the school, but excluding boarding fees and any others excluded by the participation agreement (s 17(3)(a)). Also covered are entrance fees for public examinations paid for by the school (s 17(3)(b)). Certain incidental expenses, relating to such things as school uniform and transport, are also covered (Education (Assisted Places) (Incidental Expenses) Regulations 1989).

Schedule 4 to the 1980 Act makes provision for the termination of participation agreements by either party if certain conditions are met. Three years' notice is needed, unless the Secretary of State is terminating the agreement because educational standards are not being maintained at the school, or because a condition under the agreement or relevant regulations (see below) is not being met.

Eligibility for assistance under the scheme, and other aspects of the scheme's operation, are governed by regulations (currently the Education (Assisted Places) Regulations 1989), which must be reviewed, following consultation, every two years (EA 1980 s 17(9)). The conditions of eligibility refer to such matters as residence in the British Isles, age, and parental income. Income scales are periodically amended. The extent of any remission of fees hinges on the level of income as determined under the regulations.

Around 34,000 assisted places are financed by the government at present. That figure might be higher, but for the less than complete take-up of the scheme (around 88 per cent across England and Wales: *The Times*, 27 December 1989).

5. Nursery education

There was always uncertainty about whether the Education Act 1944 had imposed a duty on LEAs to provide nursery education. Under that Act, a primary school could be a nursery school if mainly concerned with the provision of education to two, three and four year olds (EA 1944 s 9(4)). Moreover, LEAs were required to ensure that there were sufficient schools (s 8(1)(a)) offering primary education— full-time education suitable to the requirements of *junior pupils*, defined in s 114(1) simply as pupils below the age of twelve. But the Education Act 1980 (s 24(2)) states that LEAs' duty under s 8(1)(a) of the 1944 Act does not apply in respect of pupils below the age of five years.

The *power* of LEAs to maintain or assist schools providing nursery education was stated to be preserved (EA 1944 s 9(2); EA 1980 s 24(2)), and LEAs are empowered to establish nursery schools, to maintain such schools whether established by them or not, and to assist any such school not established by them (EA 1980 s 24(1)). The prohibition against charging parents for the admission of their child to a maintained school, or in respect of provisions made (subject to exceptions—see Chapter 7, pages 219–221), seems to apply to nursery schools.

The requirements of Part I of ERA 1988 covering the National Curriculum, collective worship and religious education apply neither to a nursery school nor to a "nursery class in a primary school" (ERA 1988 s 25(2)). Moreover, there is no duty to provide the National Curriculum to *any* child below the age of five (ERA 1988 s 2(1)(b)), even one in a reception class in an infants' school. (The first "key stage" in relation to an individual pupil runs from the date the pupil reaches compulsory school age (ERA 1988 s 3(3)(a)—see Chapter 6, page 178). In practice, of course, an under five year old would almost certainly be taught the National Curriculum if others in the class who were aged five were.

A nursery school will be neither a county nor a voluntary school (EA 1944 s 9(2)). Most nursery schools are maintained and funded in the same way (although obviously not on the same basis) as county schools and are covered by the same procedure on the proposed cessation of LEA maintenance of the school (EA 1980 s 12(1)). Some nursery schools are independent; the Secretary of State has a power to pay a grant direct to such schools, in accordance with regulations (EA 1944 s 100, as amended; Direct Grant Schools Regulations, SI 1959 No 1832). Nursery schools are not within the categories of school specified in ERA 1988 s 52 which can become grant-maintained, nor are they entitled to delegated budgets.

6. Changes to educational provision— general requirements under ERA 1988

The law on establishment, enlargement and closure of county and voluntary schools is discussed below. Before dealing with the specific provisions, mention must be made of certain general provisions introduced under ERA 1988. These are concerned with ensuring that before certain changes to a school are made, via procedures in EA 1980 ss 12 and 13, the governors are given an opportunity to apply for grant-maintained ("GM") status. The rules may be summarised thus:

(a) Before formulating any proposals for ceasing to maintain, making significant changes to the character of, or significantly enlarging a school which might be eligible for GM status, the LEA must *consult the governing body of the school* (ERA 1988 s 73(1)).

Consultation is a pre-requisite to many changes in educational administration and organisation. Failure to consult, where such consultation is a mandatory requirement, will amount to procedural *ultra vires*: the decision will have been taken unlawfully and may be quashed by the courts (see *Bradbury v Enfield LBC* (1967); *Lee v DES* (1968)). In fact, even where there is no statutory requirement to consult there may still be a public law duty to do so. In *R v Brent LBC ex parte Gunning* (1985) the LEA had decided, on 12 July 1984, to make proposals for the amalgamation and closure of secondary schools. The decision was held to be *ultra vires* because the authority had failed to consider a report from its education committee. A similar failure had occurred in respect of its decision on 10 May 1984 to consult interested parties on the draft proposals. The authority had not consulted parents. Although the court did not infer a duty *per se* to consult parents, Hodgson J felt that parents had a legitimate expectation to be consulted and, accordingly, "they had the same legal right to consultation as if such a right had been expressly conferred on them by statute". (In *R v London Borough of Sutton ex parte Hamlet* (1986) Webster J said that it was wrong to talk of a legal right to consultation; there was a right, on the grounds of unfairness or procedural impropriety, to judicial review of a decision made without consultation (cited in Leill and Saunders, *The Law of Education* 9th ed F[7]).) This concept of *"legitimate expectation"* is of growing importance in public law, and affects decision-making by LEAs and other public bodies. In one of the leading authorities, Lord Fraser explained that "legitimate, or reasonable, expectation may arise either from an express promise given on behalf of a public authority or from the existence of a regular practice which the claimant can reasonably expect to continue" (*Council of Civil Service Unions v Minister for the Civil Service (1985)*). It may be noted that successive circulars since 1980 dealing with school changes have emphasised the importance of consulting parents. In a number of unreported cases, successful challenges against a failure to consult over school closure have been made (*R v Secretary of State for Wales ex parte Hawkins* (1982) (CA); *R v Secretary of State for Education and Science ex parte Collins* (1983) (QBD); *R v Secretary of State for Wales ex parte Russell* (1983) (QBD); all cited in P Meredith, *Falling Rolls and the Re-organisation of Schools* (1984) JSWL 208, 218 n 69). Once an adequate consultation period has expired, there is normally no obligation on the LEA to consult further (*R* v *Hertfordshire County Council ex parte George* (1988) (QBD)).

The statutory requirement in s 73(1) to consult the governing body of the school is mandatory. But, as we have seen above in any event, such consultation may well have been necessary before ERA 1988. Whatever the source of the requirement, the above new provision has been introduced for a specific purpose, as DES Circular 10/88 (para 33) makes clear:

> "This provision will allow the governing body time to consider whether the LEA's plans are such that the parents' views should be sought on the advisability of preparing an application for grant-maintained status".

Its effect, therefore, is to encourage schools to consider opting out of LEA control.

(b) No proposals concerning the establishment, significant alteration or closure of a county school (under EA 1980 s 12) or establishment or alteration of a voluntary school (*ibid*, s 13) may be published in respect of a school which has been given approval to become grant-maintained (ERA 1988 s 73(2)).

(c) If an EA 1980 s 12 or s 13 proposal (see (b) above) has already been published, an application for the acquisition of GM status will be treated as a statutory objection to the proposals—with the result that the Secretary of State's approval of the proposals, which might not have been necessary (see below), will be required (s 73(4)(a)).

(d) If an application for GM status is made while s 12 or s 13 proposals are awaiting approval, both sets of proposals will be considered together "on their merits" (DES Circular 10/88, para 37 and see *R* v *Secretary of State for Education and Science ex parte Avon County Council* (1990), discussed at page 16 above), but the Secretary of State must not consider the proposals until he has made his decision about GM status (ERA 1988 s 73 (4)(b)). If the Secretary of State approves GM status the s 12 or s 13 proposals must be rejected (s 73(5)).

(e) Between 4 August and 30 November 1988, consideration of any s 12 or s 13 proposals was suspended by the Secretary of State, under the power to suspend contained in

ERA 1988 s 73(6). This was another move designed to "allow eligible schools the opportunity to decide whether they wish to apply for grant-maintained status" (DES Circular 10/88, para 38). Further periods of suspension, in respect of proposals published before 31 December 1988, were also ordered (Education (Grant-Maintained Schools) (Termination of Power to Determine a Period of Suspension) Order 1988).

7. Establishment of schools

(a) County schools

LEAs must act within the strict framework laid down in EA 1980 s 12 (and ERA 1988 s 73(2)–(12), discussed above), if they wish to establish a county school or maintain as a county school any school which is not such a school.

The first stage, after consultation with the governors of the school and formulation of proposals, is publication. Proposals have to be published in a local newspaper and must be posted in at least one conspicuous place in the area. They must also be posted at or near the main entrance of the school to which they relate (Education (Publication of School Proposals) (No 2) Regulations 1980). (Non-compliance with this requirement may not necessarily invalidate the procedure as a whole; in *Coney* v *Choyce* (1975) the court held that non-compliance with such a requirement (then contained in 1968 regulations) did not affect the legality of the authority's subsequent action, because no person had suffered any substantial prejudice and the requirement could only be said to be "directory" rather than "mandatory".) The published proposals must also be sent to the Secretary of State (EA 1980 s 12(1)). Adequate and accurate details of what is proposed must be stated (*Legg* v *ILEA* (1972)). Particulars of the admissions total for the school and the time or times at which it is intended to implement the proposals are to be stated (s 12(2), as amended by ERA 1988, Sch 13 Part I). The published proposals must also explain rights concerning objections to the proposals (*ibid*).

If, at any time within two months after publication of the

proposals, ten or more local government electors for the area submit an objection to them to the LEA, the LEA must transmit such objection to the Secretary of State within one month of receipt (s 12(3)). Note that an application for GM status is treated as a statutory objection (above).

The next stage is approval or otherwise by the Secretary of State (see DES Circular 3/87). Approval is necessary if either:

(i) the Secretary of State gives notice to that effect to the LEA within two months of receipt by him of the proposals; or
(ii) if objections have been made under s 12(3) (s 12(5)).

(Secretary of State approval for the maintenance as a county school of a school which is currently a voluntary school is always required (s 12(4))). The main reason the 1980 Act was drafted in such a way as to allow LEAs to proceed with certain changes (more especially closures) mostly without seeking Secretary of State approval was to cut down on delays resulting from administrative pressures on DES staff. These were likely to increase during a period of falling rolls from 1980 onwards. Even in cases where approval may not be necessary, the LEA will still have to "determine whether the proposals should be implemented"—within four months of submission of the proposals to the Secretary of State (s 12(7)). Such determination must be notified to the Secretary of State (s 12(8)).

If the proposals *do* require the approval of the Secretary of State, he may reject them, approve them without modification, or, after consultation with the LEA, approve them with such modification as he thinks desirable (s 12(6)). (On the formalities of giving approval etc under s 12(6) for establishment, significant alteration or closure, see *R* v *Secretary of State for Education and Science ex parte Hardy* (1988).) The LEA *must* implement the proposals as approved under s 12(6) or, where approval was not necessary, as determined by the LEA under s 12(7) (above) (s 12(9)).

(b) Voluntary schools

Proposals for the establishment of a voluntary school, to be maintained as such by a LEA, must also be published (s 13(1)). However, the responsibility for publication rests with the persons wishing to establish the school rather than with the LEA. Before publishing their proposals, those persons must consult the LEA (*ibid*). A copy of the published proposals must be sent to the Secretary of State (*ibid*). Similar provision to that in s 12 (see above) is made for objection to the proposals by local government electors (s13(2) and (3)). An application for GM status counts as a statutory objection, as in the case of county schools. Such differences as there are in the procedures flow mainly from the fact that there is an extra party involved when a voluntary school is proposed. Thus, for example, when the Secretary of State decides to approve proposals with modification, both the LEA *and* the proposers must be consulted (s 13(4)).

All proposals for the establishment of a voluntary school require the approval of the Secretary of State; he may approve or reject them outright or approve them with modification (*ibid*). The LEA and proposers *must* implement approved proposals (s 13(5)). The LEA has a separate duty to provide any playing fields or buildings (other than school buildings) required by virtue of the approved proposals (s 13(6)). Subsequent modification by the Secretary of State of proposals to be implemented is possible (s 13(7)).

(c) Approval of school premises

Where proposals are made for the establishment of a county or voluntary school, the persons making the proposals must submit particulars relating to the premises or proposed premises to the Secretary of State for approval. Such particulars must be given at such time and in such form and manner as the Secretary of State may direct (EA 1980, s 14(1)). If a voluntary school is being proposed, the proposers must consult the LEA before submitting particulars of premises to the Secretary of State (s 14(2)). Once approved, the particulars must be implemented (s 14(3)).

When the plans are submitted to him, the Secretary of State is empowered to grant exemption from certain legal requirements concerning the erection of buildings required for the purposes of a school (EA 1944 s 63(2)). Such buildings are not subject to building regulations under Part II of the Building Act 1984.

(d) Grant-maintained schools

The provisions governing the establishment of a GM school, and in particular the arrangements for a ballot of parents, are set out in Appendix 1.

8. Alteration of schools

(a) Significant changes

The procedures in EA 1980 ss 12 and 13, and ERA 1988 s 73, all of which were discussed earlier, also apply to a "significant change in the character, or significant enlargement of the premises of" a school which is a county or voluntary school (ss 12(1)(d) and 13(1)(b) (respectively)). (ERA 1988 s 89 deals with such changes when they are to be made to a GM school.)

(i) Change of character

A change of character shall:

> "include, in particular, changes in character resulting from education beginning or ceasing to be provided for pupils above or below a particular age, for boys as well as girls or for girls as well as boys, or from the making or alteration of arrangements for the admission of pupils by reference to ability or aptitude" (EA 1980 s 16(2)).

(ERA 1988 s 104(1)(d) uses exactly the same definition for the purpose of significant changes to GM schools under s 89 of that Act; see also s 104(1)(c).) It appears, therefore, that an increase in the size of the intake would not, of itself, constitute a change of character for this purpose. In *Vaughan v Solihull Metropolitan Borough Council* (1982) Lawton LJ referred to a "long-standing administrative practice which regarded a change of twenty per cent in unit totals as a guide to what constituted a reorganised school";

but this was in the context of the Burnham rules for determining head teachers' pay with reference to the size of a school. The twenty per cent figure has, until recently, been relevant in the case of reductions in school places (EA 1980 s 15(1) – now repealed).

(ii) Significant

The question of whether a change is "significant" in this context is one for the Secretary of State to decide (EA 1944 s 67(4), as amended by ERA 1988 Sch 12 para 4(3) to include changes to grant-maintained schools).

(iii) Significant changes to GM schools

Proposals for a significant change in the character, or a significant enlargement in the premises of a GM school must be published by the governors under requirements very similar to those for county and voluntary schools (ERA 1988 s 89). The governors' decision to publish proposals will be invalid unless affirmed at a further meeting held not less than twenty-eight days after the first (s 89(11)). When publishing their proposals, the governors must state the time or times of their proposed implementation and the number of pupils to be admitted to the school following the changes (s 89(3)). They must also publish a statement "describing any effect the implementation would have on provision at the school for pupils who have special educational needs" (s 89(5)(a)). Any changes affecting the religious character of the school require the consent in writing of the trustees of the school (if any) (s 89(2)).

The proposals must be posted at or near the main entrance to the school and in at least one conspicuous place in the area. They must be available for inspection by the public at the school or other place in the area to which members of the public might conveniently have access (eg a public library). As soon as possible thereafter, details must be published in a local newspaper circulating in the area served by the school (Education (Grant-Maintained Schools) (Publication of Proposals) Regulations 1989 reg 4).

As with proposed significant changes to county and voluntary schools, provision is made for objections to be made (direct to the Secretary of State) within two months of publication of the proposals (s 89(6)). The right to lodge objections has to be notified in the published proposals (s 89(5)(b)). Objections may be made by any ten or more local government electors, the governing body of any school "affected by the proposals" (ie, other schools in the district) and *any* LEA concerned (ie, not just the one in whose area the school is situated) (s 89(6)).

The Secretary of State's powers to approve, approve with modifications or reject the proposals, and the governors' duty to implement the proposals if approved, are equivalent to those applicable to county and voluntary schools, discussed earlier (ERA 1988 s 89(7) and (8)). See pages 30 and 32.

(b) Approval of school premises on significant changes to school

Where proposals are submitted to the Secretary of State under EA 1980 ss 12 or 13 for the making of a significant change in the character of a county or voluntary school, or a significant enlargement of its premises, approval for the premises or proposed premises must be sought, under EA 1980 s 14, in the same way as when a school is established (see page 32). When such changes are proposed for a grant-maintained school, Secretary of State approval must be sought in like manner (ERA 1988 s 90).

(c) Transfer of site

If it is proposed that a school should be moved to a new site, Secretary of State approval will be required (see EA 1944 s 16, as amended, in the case of county and voluntary schools, and ERA 1988 s 91 in the case of GM schools). It will be necessary to show that the premises will meet required standards. Conditions relating to the transfer may be imposed. (See, further, DES Circular 3/87 Annex 3.)

(d) Reductions in school places

The procedure in the Education Act 1980 (s 15) governing reductions in school places at county or voluntary schools has gone (s 15 repealed by ERA 1988 Sch 13 Part II).

Reductions in admissions limits are now governed by ERA 1988 s 28 and SI 1988 No 1515. This is discussed in Chapter 4 (see pages 148 to 159). It continues to be the government's policy that LEAs should rationalise provision and remove surplus school places (see DES Circular 3/87, *Providing for Quality: The Pattern of Organisation to Age 19*). The view is encapsulated in a statement by an education minister to the House of Commons:

". . . there are limits to what the country can afford to spend on education. What we spend must be spent constructively and not wasted on keeping open empty classrooms and buildings" (J Dunn MP, HC Debs 20 December 1983).

9. Closure and amalgamation of schools

Falling rolls in secondary schools in particular, and in urban areas such as Liverpool, where the number of primary school children has fallen by thirty per cent in the past decade, have led to a significant number of closures or amalgamations in the 1980s as LEAs have reorganised their schools provision. (Note that there is "no statutory procedure for 'amalgamation' as such"; the situation where two schools are amalgamated is said to be "analysed legally as closing one or both schools down and establishing a new one" (P Meredith, *Falling Rolls and the Reorganisation of Schools* (1984) JSWL 208, 213 and n 45).) As we have seen, the government's policy is that LEAs should take steps to eliminate over-capacity. Over the next few years further reorganisations are likely as LEAs look to amalgamations as a means of providing the National Curriculum in their schools effectively and efficiently.

(a) County, voluntary and nursery schools

The provisions, referred to earlier, governing proposals for the establishment of county schools, including those relating to Secretary of State approval and the right of objection within two months of publication of the proposals, apply also to decisions to "cease to maintain" any county,

Schools and their resources

voluntary or nursery school (EA 1980 s 12(1)(c) and (e)). Note that where a closure is concerned, s 12 also applies to voluntary schools, and the governors have a right to object (s 12(3)). These provisions were described in some detail on page 30. The governors may resolve to discontinue a voluntary school, and must serve on the LEA and Secretary of State two years' notice of their intention to do so (EA 1944 s 14(1)). But when expenditure on the school has been incurred by central government or the LEA, the Secretary of State's leave for discontinuance is required and he may attach such conditions for repayment of expenditure as he considers just. In *R* v *Secretary of State for Education and Science ex parte ILEA and Anr* (1990) the LEA challenged the Secretary of State's refusal, on granting leave for discontinuance, to attach conditions for repayment of sums spent by the LEA on improving Haberdashers' Aske's Schools at Hatcham. The schools were to be turned into a city technology college (CTC). The application for judicial review was denied. The court held that while the purpose of the leave requirement (with conditions) is to protect the public interest where an educational asset has been created partly out of public funds, the Secretary of State has been granted a wide discretion by Parliament and is entitled to take into account various factors when deciding what requirements, if any, are just. In this case he was entitled to have regard for the fact that, first, the CTC would cater for pupils drawn from the same catchment area as before, and secondly, that the LEA would not have to make replacement provision if the school became a CTC.

(b) Grant-maintained schools

Similar provisions apply in the case of a decision by the governors to discontinue a GM school (ERA 1988 s 92 and Education (Grant-Maintained Schools) (Publication of Proposals) Regulations 1989), although the procedure is more drawn out, presumably in order to minimise the chances of such schools deciding to discontinue. The Secretary of State expects the discontinuance of a GM school to be "exceptional" (DES Circular 10/88, para 69). He actually has the power to cease maintaining such a school (ERA 1988 s 93(1)). This might be exercised if he considers a school's deficiencies to

be "irredeemable" (DES Circular 10/88, para 72) – because:
> (i) the number of registered pupils at the school has become too small for sufficient and suitable instruction to be provided for them at reasonable cost (s 93(3)(a)); or
> (ii) the governing body has failed to comply with the curriculum requirements of Chapter I of ERA 1988 (s 93(3)(b)); or
> (iii) "the governing body have been guilty of substantial or persistent failure to comply or secure compliance with any other requirement imposed by or under this Act or any other enactment" (s 93(3)(c)).

Notice must be given to the governing body of the date at which the Secretary of State intends to cease maintaining the school (s 93(1)), stating the specific deficiencies (s 93(4)) and, if such is the case, that the deficiences are irredeemable and in consequence the Secretary of State will cease to maintain the school (s 93(5)). If the termination of support is not on grounds (i) - (iii) above, at least seven years' notice must be given by the Secretary of State (s 93(2)(a)) and prior consultation with various prescribed bodies must take place (s 93(2)(b)). If the Secretary of State feels that the deficiencies can be remedied, he may specify in the notice the measures which should be taken (within six months or longer) by the governing body, and can later extend the deadline if he feels that it is making progress (s 93(7) and (8)). The notice may, in fact, subsequently be withdrawn (s 93(8)(a)) or its terms varied (s 93(8)(b) and (c)).

The governors may themselves decide to publish proposals to discontinue a GM school, although the Secretary of State would not expect this to happen within ten years of the school acquiring its GM status (DES Circular 10/88, para 70). A governors' resolution to publish proposals relating to discontinuance must be confirmed at a subsequent meeting held not less than twenty-eight days after that at which the resolution was passed, otherwise it will be of no effect (s 92(2)(a)). After giving notice to the LEA as soon as may be practicable (s 92(2)(b) and (3)), the governors have six months in which to publish their proposals in the prescribed manner (s 92(2) and SI 1989 No 1469, *op cit*). Objections may be made to the Secretary of State within two months of such publication, by the same groups who have such right on a proposed significant change (see page 35): any ten or more local government electors, the governing body of any school affected by the proposals, and any LEA concerned (s 92(5)).

(c) Challenging closures

The statutory machinery governing closures is said to provide "little opportunity to the objector to present an effective case" (P Meredith, *Falling Rolls and the Reorganisation of Schools* (1984) JSWL 221) and to give the Secretary of State considerable power to exert his political will. In the face of falling rolls, and the financial pressures on LEAs, there has been rationalisation of provision which many parents and governors have been unable to resist. Legal challenges are difficult, and those that have been made have generally been on procedural grounds. For example, the failure to consult parents was one of the grounds on which Brent LEA's 1984 decision to close two schools was quashed in the High Court (*R v Brent LBC ex parte Gunning* (1985)) (see page 28). The effect of the ruling was merely a delay for the authority, although with local elections due in the near future the parents hoped for a more permanent victory (see *Education* 3 May 1985, page 390). There have been several successful challenges on the ground of failure to consult (as noted earlier at page 28). But councils are only required to act reasonably, and therefore the duty to consult is not absolute. In 1988 a group of parents failed in their attempt to have Gateshead LEA's planned reorganisation of its schools halted on this ground (see *The Times* 14 May 1988).

As pointed out earlier (see page 28), and as the *Gunning* case above illustrates, even in the absence of a statutory requirement to consult interested parties it has nevertheless been possible to argue that on public law grounds such consultation is necessary. Now, of course, there is a statutory requirement on LEAs to consult the governing body (on which parents are represented) before formulating their proposals to close a county school (ERA 1988 s 73(1)), although, as mentioned earlier, the main reason for this new requirement is to give the governors time to consider whether to apply for GM status.

Challenges on other procedural grounds have included one case where it was successfully argued that details of closure proposals, such as the date of closure, must be fixed by the education committee and not by its chairman alone (*R* v *Secretary of State for Education and Science ex parte Birmingham City Council* (1985)). A further case concerned a LEA's decision to proceed with a school closure without having considered a report on the matter. It merely acted on a bare recommendation for closure from the education committee, which was held not to be a "report", consideration of which was required by EA 1944 Sch 1 Part II para 7 before exercising certain functions in relation to education (*R* v *Kirklees MBC ex parte Molloy* (1988) – applied, but distinguished on the facts, in *Nichol* v *Gateshead MBC* (1989)).

Closures have also been challenged (without success) on the ground of denial of parental wishes (to which LEAs are required to have regard when exercising their powers and duties: EA 1944 s 76 and, in Scotland, Education (Scotland) Act 1980 s 28(1); see *Harvey* v *Strathclyde Regional Council* (1989)). (Section 76 is discussed further on page 153.)

10. Finance: local management of schools

(a) Introduction

The provisions of ERA 1988 dealing with local financial management of schools, referred to by the DES as local management of schools ("LMS"), represent the most spectacular reduction in LEA control since 1945. After the devolution of elements of control to governing bodies under the Education (No 2) Act 1986 (see Chapter 3), these bodies are now to acquire control of their own school budgets. Within the framework set by the approved formula for calculating a school's budget share, and apart from the retention by the LEA of a small percentage to cover central services, the governing body will have the entire budget delegated to it to spend as it thinks fit. Governing bodies, the argument goes, will be in a far better position to judge the real needs of the school than the LEA, and could respond to them more directly and efficiently. Spending decisions could be made more effectively by those who, because of their close involvement with the school, know what the chief priority is at any particular moment, for example maintenance of the buildings, more teacher hours, or new equipment. Decisions on such matters relating to schools covered by a delegation scheme could be implemented quickly, for they will no longer have to compete for the attention of the various tiers of the LEA bureaucracy.

LMS will not necessarily result in reduced overall cost. This point was made clear in the Coopers and Lybrand report, *Local Management of Schools* (1988), which is said to represent "not a statement of Government policy, but . . . valuable advice for LEAs and schools on the principles of local management and the practical steps necessary for its effective implementation" (DES Circular 7/88, *Education Reform Act: Local Management of Schools,* para 26). The report stressed that "LMS should not be seen as a means of cost reduction", but rather as a means of producing "a more effective and responsive school system".

The government emphasised that a key aim of LMS was to increase the education system's responsiveness to its "clients —parents, pupils, the local community and employers" (DES Circular 7/88, para 9). This in turn means greater accountability. Thus the governing bodies and head teachers who are making these decisions on expenditure must realise that, as Maclure puts it, "more power at the school level means more power to make mistakes and fail" (*Education Reformed* (1988), page 54). As we shall see, the Act provides protection for governors who act in good faith. In practice many decisions will be taken by, or at the behest of, the head teacher, to whom delegation of some of the governors' spending power may be made (ERA 1988 s 36(5)(b); DES Circular 7/88). (See Chapter 3 for discussion of delegation by governing bodies to head teachers.) In the past, most governing bodies have adopted what has been termed "the 'Woolwich' approach . . . where governors have automatically entrusted their reponsibilities to head teachers in whose hands the investment feels 'safe' " (Blanchard et al, *Managing Finance in Schools* (1989), page 95). In the future, however, governors will be required to play a more direct role and will have to meet more frequently (as a whole board or in sub-committees), although some may not wish to increase their level of involvement. There have already been reports of difficulties in recruiting the extra parent governors needed to fulfil the requirements of the E (No 2) A 1986 from September 1988. All governors, including those representing local commerce and industry, may lack the time, expertise and experience to perform their role in financial management. This lack of capacity has been described as one of the "most uncertain and worrying" aspects of the Education Reform Act changes (Blanchard, page 96).

A further major doubt concerns the amount of choice the governors will have when it comes to spending their budget allocation. Some will be left with little room to manoeuvre because of the way that schools' budget shares will be determined (see below). Moreover, some schools will be worse off than before. Schools will, in effect, be charged the *actual* cost of their teachers, while receiving an allowance in their budget based on *average* teacher costs across all the LEA's schools. The practice of averaging staff costs out in this way, thus ignoring the difference between schools in terms of proportion of experienced teachers (whose salaries are relatively expensive), and basing the allocation largely around pupil numbers at the school, creates inequities between schools. In a survey of over 1,500 schools by the National Association of Schoolmasters and Union of Women Teachers, 58 per cent of the schools would lose money, and 38 per cent would lose more than £25,000. In each of the five worst off authorities—Liverpool, Manchester, Derbyshire, Salford and Rochdale—schools lose a combined total of over £100,000 (*The Times*, 2 October 1989). Many LEAs, including some which are Conservative controlled, initially decided to ignore the government's guidelines on financial delegation schemes because they saw them as threatening some children's education. Teachers have expressed fears about redundancies. In fact, the government has built in certain safeguards to LMS, as we shall see. But some LEAs argue that they are inadequate.

Having considered some of the issues, we shall now examine the legal provisions. The aim here will be to explain the legal basis of financial delegation as comprehensively and clearly as possible, making reference to the sections of the Act and paragraphs of the circular—which readers might wish to examine for themselves at a later stage (if they have not done so already!). It should be borne in mind that whilst there is a uniform legal framework to LMS, there is bound to be variation between local schemes.

(b) The delegation scheme

By a date determined by the Secretary of State (fixed, under the power in ERA 1988 s 34(1), as 30 September 1989), each LEA in England and Wales was required to submit a financial delegation scheme for approval (s 33(1)). Only county and voluntary schools maintained by an authority have to be covered by a scheme (s 33(1)). In primary schools, the delegation scheme *must* apply if a school had two hundred or more pupils on a qualifying date in the previous financial year, or is forecast to have such a number on a qualifying date in the year to which the budget relates (s 39(2) and (3)). It *may* apply to smaller primary schools, if the scheme so provides. The Secretary of State has the power to amend s 39(3) to substitute a lower number than two hundred (s 41(1)(a)). All children at the school, including those aged under five years, whether in a reception or nursery class, are to be included in the calculation (see DES Circular 7/88, para 37); but note that financial delegation does not apply to nursery schools (nor, at present, to special schools—although there is a power, exercisable by regulation, to require delegation schemes for such schools (s 43)).

The scheme will not come into force until it has been approved by the Secretary of State or until such date as the Secretary of State, on giving approval for the scheme, specifies (s 34(5)). Once the scheme comes into force, delegation must take place within three years (s 40(1) and (2)). The actual date will be provided for in the scheme (s 40(2) and (3)), or by order of the Secretary of State (s 40(4)).

An approved scheme must be published on its coming into force and on any other prescribed occasions (s 42(1) and the Education (Publication of Schemes for Financing Schools) Regulations 1989). A statement of financial provision for schools must be published by a LEA before the start of each financial year; it must contain various detailed particulars (see s 42(4))(see below, page 54).

Such is the extent of the Secretary of State's powers that he can modify a scheme and/or attach such conditions to it as he considers desirable (s 34(5)). Moreover, if a LEA fails to submit a scheme, or, in the Secretary of State's opinion, unreasonably departs from his guidance on the preparation of schemes (which LEAs are required to take into account: s 34(2)), the Secretary of State can impose a scheme of his own (s 34(6)). Before doing so, the Secretary of State must consult the LEA and "such other persons as he thinks fit" (*ibid*). In such a situation, the scheme is to be treated as if made by the LEA (s 34(7)).

(c) A school's budget share

The scheme must provide for the annual determination of each school's "budget share" and for its delegation to the governing body as required or permitted under the scheme (s 33(2)). (The Secretary of State expects school budgets to be given as cash limits. Any in-year cost increases may be covered by virement from the LEA's school-specific reserve built into its general schools budget (defined below): DES Circular 7/88, para 130.)

A key element in the determination is the size of the LEA's *general schools budget* for the year in question:

> *General schools budget*—"the amount appropriated by the authority for meeting expenditure in that [financial] year in respect of all schools required to be covered in that year by any [delegation] scheme" (s 33(4)(a))—ie, direct costs such as salaries, repairs and maintenance, plus indirect costs such as school transport, central administration, and advisory services. Contingency provision at the start of the year for unpredictable costs arising out of an emergency (for example, gale damage) and which is not school-specific should not be included (DES Circular 7/88, para 56). School-specific contingency provision, to cover, for example, unpredictable changes in pupil numbers, *is* to be included (*ibid*, para 53).

From the general schools budget certain excepted items

must be deducted. The residue is known as the *aggregated schools budget*, representing the amount available for allocation to schools.

> *Aggregated schools budget*—"the part of the general schools budget of any . . . authority for any financial year which is available for allocation to individual schools under a [delegation] scheme . . . [being] the amount remaining after deducting from the amount of the general schools budget . . . excepted heads or items of expenditure . . . and . . . any other amounts which fall in accordance with the scheme to be deducted" (s 33(4)(b)).

The excepted heads or items of expenditure—which are to be left out of account in determining the LEA's aggregated schools budget for the year in question—comprise the *mandatory* and *discretionary* exceptions. The former are set out in s 38(4):

> *Mandatory exceptions—*
> (i) all expenditure of a capital nature;
> (ii) repayments on loans to cover capital expenditure;
> (iii) expenditure falling to be taken into account in determining central government grants of a prescribed description*;
> (iv) such other items as may be prescribed.*

*Regulations have been made defining the expenditure to be left out of account under these categories: the Education (Financial Delegation to Schools) (Mandatory Exceptions) Regulations 1989.

These mandatory exceptions under (iii) and (iv) comprise:

> (a) expenditure falling to be taken into account in determining central government grants of the following types:
> • Education Support Grants ("ESGs"), paid under Education (Grants and Awards) Act 1984 s 1;
> • LEA Training Grants paid under E(No 2)A 1986 s 50;
> • grants paid under Local Government Act 1966 s 11;
> • grants for the education of travellers and displaced persons, paid under ERA 1988 s 210;

- TVEI grants paid under Employment and Training Act 1973, as amended, s 2;
- Urban Programme grants paid under the Local Government Grants (Social Need) Act 1969 s 1;
- (LEAs in Wales only) Bilingual Education Grants paid under EA 1980 s 21;

(b) expenditure falling to be taken into account in determining specific grants from the EEC which support school activities.

The Secretary of State will "review and adjust as necessary the scope of items excepted by regulations. . . in the light of experience" (DES Circular 7/88, para 62). The Circular refers to other items to be excepted by regulations: central administration (including internal audit and legal services, but excluding EWOs), inspectors/advisers and home-to-school transport (para 60). But the above regulations make no mention of them. Nevertheless, LEAs would be expected to except costs on these items from the aggregated schools budget.

Discretionary exceptions are the items which the LEA wishes to except in addition to the mandatory exceptions:

Discretionary exceptions—"other amounts which fall in accordance with the scheme to be deducted in determining the authority's aggregated budget for [the year in question]" (s 33(4)(b)(ii)).

Because LMS is based on the principle of "maximum delegation", LEAs are advised that "provision should be delegated unless there is a clearly identified need for the LEA to retain control" (DES Circular 7/88, para 63). Thus the extent of any discretionary exceptions is expected to be limited (*ibid*). Indeed, initially (for the first three years) most of the categories of discretionary exception may not exceed, in aggregate, ten per cent of the general schools budget. LEAs will be expected to review the scope of excepted items within three years of their scheme's introduction and to reduce progressively the total cost of discretionary excepted items to seven per cent of the general schools budget (*ibid*, paras 96 and 97).

Perhaps the main category to be covered by the initial ten per cent limit is structural repairs and maintenance. This is likely to prove a difficult area in practice. The Circular (7/88, *op cit*) recommends that a typical "landlord-tenant" division should apply to responsibility for repairs. This means that the cost of day to day internal maintenance should be provided for in a school's delegated budget share. LEAs should be responsible for the structure and exterior of the buildings, maintenance of playgrounds, car parks and perimeter walls. It is felt desirable, however, to allow schools to carry out minor emergency repairs to items which would otherwise fall within the LEA's responsibility, such as a leaking roof or a protruding paving stone (*ibid*, para 68). Because of statutory and common law requirements concerning health and safety, however, schools may need advice from their LEAs. Schools may wish to consult the list of contractors vetted and approved by the LEA (see Blanchard et al, *Managing Finance in Schools*, pages 55–57). Maintenance work must, in any event, be put out to competitive tender. (The requirements concerning competitive tendering, and their interaction with LMS, are considered below.) In aided and special agreement schools, *all* the costs of maintenance met by the LEA are to be delegated to the governors, in the light of their "greater experience... in dealing with maintenance matters" (*ibid*, para 71). The Circular offers a possible division of responsibilities, in a detailed breakdown in Annex A—see Appendix 2.

The other categories falling within the ten per cent limit are:

- premises and equipment insurance (generally, a LEA will remain responsible);
- Education Act 1981: statemented pupils;
- educational psychologists;
- education welfare officers;
- peripatetic and advisory teachers;
- pupil support (uniforms, clothing, education maintenance allowances, etc);
- LEA initiatives (eg curriculum development);
- special staff costs (eg supply staff);
- school-specific contingencies;
- library and museum services;
- other approved items.

The categories *not* subject to the initial ten per cent limit are:

- school meals (this is an expensive area, and one in

which provision must meet health and nutritional standards, plus the requirements of the Social Security Act 1986 as regards free school meals; there could be no delegation until the expiry of any agreement entered into voluntarily by the LEA or under the competitive tendering requirements of the Local Government Act 1988. A LEA may bid to provide the meals service itself via its direct labour organisation);
- premature retirement compensation and dismissal costs;
- insurance for governors (LEAs to arrange for such cover under the terms of their schemes: see DES Circular 7/88, paras 86 and 183–187);
- transitional excepted items (especially contracted-out cleaning or grounds maintenance).

Competitive tendering: Certain activities must be put out for competitive tender by LEAs in accordance with the requirements of the Local Government, Planning and Land Act 1980 (construction and maintenance of buildings) and Local Government Act 1988 (cleaning of buildings, school catering, grounds maintenance and repair and maintenance of vehicles). Local authorities may bid to provide cleaning, meals services, etc, through their direct labour organisations. A timetable has been established for the switch to provision via competitive tendering under the 1988 Act. It is to be implemented in stages starting in 1989 and completed by 1993 (or 1994 in the case of grounds maintenance). This timetable overlaps with that for the introduction of LMS, where the intention is to enable governors to make their own arrangements for the provision of such services. As delegation comes into effect, contracts may already be in force, whether following on from competitive tendering or voluntary contracting out by the LEA, or the local authority may, at least, have published the specification for the particular activity for which tenders are to be invited (as required by s 7 Local Government Act 1988). DES guidance (in Circular 7/88, paras 192-195) on the chief implications of this overlap is as follows:

(i) If an activity has been contracted out voluntarily, the competitive tendering provisions will not apply: the governors will be bound by the contract until it comes up for renewal.

(ii) If the LEA has not yet published the specification for the particular activity to be put out to tender, the school with a delegated budget will be free to choose whether to make its own arrangements or have the LEA make arrangements for it. ("Probably the main consideration will be whether the school feels it can get an appropriate service at an equivalent or lower cost than the LEA": Blanchard et al, *Managing Finance in Schools* (1989), page 53.) If it decides to ask the LEA to make arrangements, it should be allowed to specify the standard of service which is required; the LEA should include that standard in its published specification unless, exceptionally, it considers that that would be unreasonable—in which case the school may make its own arrangements or adopt the LEA's specified standard.

(iii) Where the specification has been published, the governors will be bound by the arrangements which the LEA enters into; once LMS has come into effect in relation to the school, the school will continue to be governed by those arrangements until the contract has expired/come up for renewal (see (v) below).

(iv) It will be possible for a school itself to obtain services not covered by a published specification.

(v) Where any contract is due for renewal*, schools with delegated budgets may choose whether to continue with the LEA's arrangements or make their own. If the governors approach private contractors to carry out the work, the statutory provisions on competitive tendering do not apply.

*Minimum and maximum contract periods have been specified in relation to activities subject to competitive tendering:

	Years	
	Minimum	Maximum
Building cleaning	3	4
Grounds maintenance	3	4
School catering	4	5
Vehicle maintenance and repair	4	6

Note that similar requirements to those in (i)–(v) above operate in relation to contracts for the construction and maintenance of buildings (Part III Local Government, Planning and Land Act 1980).

Once the aggregated schools budget has been determined, the amount of a school's budget share will depend on the delegation scheme's allocation formula. This shall now be considered.

(d) The budget share formula

Provision in a delegation scheme must be made for the determination, in each financial year, of each school's budget share in accordance with "a formula laid down by the scheme for the purpose of dividing among all such schools the aggregated budget for that year of the local education authority concerned" (ERA 1988 s 38(1)). "Formula" is, for this purpose, defined as "methods, principles and rules of any description, however expressed" (s 38(2)). The formula need not be in algebraic form, "but it must apply a consistent set of criteria for distributing resources" (DES Circular 7/88, para 103).

The government expects that the formula should provide for "objective needs" rather than be based on historic costs (*ibid*, para 99). Through the opportunity afforded to take a fresh look at the way schools in an area are funded, a more "equitable" basis for allocation of resources is to operate. Nevertheless, there are innumerable variables which affect the amount needed to operate a particular school efficiently. In many cases, these include historic costs of sufficient magnitude to warrant allowance being made in the allocation formula for them. For example, some school buildings, because of the design or specification favoured at the time they were built, may be more expensive to heat or clean.

The government chose the numbers and ages of pupils at the school to be the key determinants of the resource allocation. The law states that the delegation scheme *must* take into account these indicators (s 38(3)(a)) and *may* take into account "any other factors affecting the needs of individual schools which are subject to variation from school to school" (s 38(3)(b)) (see below).

(i) Numbers and ages of pupils

The number of pupils in each school, weighted for differences in their ages, is to be the "central determinant" of the school's objective needs (DES Circular 7/88, para 104). The total amount allocated on this basis is to account *for at least 75 per cent of the aggregated schools budget*. The aim is said to be not only to help to ensure that schools' particular needs are met, but also to give schools a clear incentive to attract and retain pupils (*ibid*, para 105).

There is no prescribed method of working out the actual weightings. They might, however, be expected to take into account assumptions about teaching costs at various ages, given that teaching costs are the principal costs of providing education. Although no examples are given, a possible model is: up to age 7—weighting of 1.5; ages 7–10—weighting of 1.0; ages 11–16—weighting of 1.85; ages 16–18—weighting of 2.35. The Circular emphasises that although age-weightings may reflect teaching costs, governors will not be bound to deploy the resource allocation exactly in accordance with assumptions about staff costs. They will be free to make decisions about the teaching complement in the school and to vire between all expenditure heads in their delegated budgets (*ibid*, para 109).

The effect of basing the budget share largely around age-weighted pupil numbers was discussed earlier (see page 42). Because the allocation will reflect average teaching costs across the LEA's schools, some schools, whose costs are higher, might lose out. Particularly hard hit will be those schools carrying large numbers of experienced, and thus higher paid, teachers, and those with a lower than average staff-pupil ratio. Although adjustment may be possible, it will take some time. Moreover, small schools will attract fewer resources, enabling them to pay for fewer teachers (at a time when the statutory provision now demands a wider expertise) and less equipment. Consequently it is expected that formulae will make provision for the additional costs in small schools of making adequate curricular provision, either by providing for a minimum base cash allocation for any school regardless of its size, or by a higher weighting per pupil or group of pupils below a specific number (DES

Circular 7/88, paras 112 and 113). However, this additional support must, in common with support in respect of pupils with special educational needs, come from the remaining twenty-five per cent (or less) available under the formula.

(ii) Other factors affecting the needs of individual schools

As mentioned above, a school's requirements with regard to provision for pupils with special educational needs, or its need for what the Circular calls "curriculum protection" if the school is small, must be built into the remaining twenty-five per cent (or less) available under the formula. The Circular explains that both of these factors are to be included, although, in fact, only special educational needs provision is explicitly referred to in the relevant part of the 1988 Act (see s 38(3)(b)).

But there are other factors which cause the financial requirements to vary from one school to the next, and the Circular states that these too might be taken into account as "optional factors" (DES Circular 7/88, para 132). In fact, under the provisions of the Act, the factors listed as "optional" in the Circular, as well as special educational needs requirements, "may", rather than "must", be included.

One such factor relates to small schools. As stated above, they may be particularly hard hit by the effects of averaging teacher costs across a LEA's schools. If they have a high proportion of teachers on the higher scales, with protected salaries, there could be a wide difference between what the school is allowed in respect of staff salaries and actual staff costs. LEAs may make allowance for this problem in their budget formulae, but are expected to taper the degree of protection in such a way that such allowance is not made in budgets for schools with ten or more teaching staff (excluding the head teacher and deputy head) (*ibid*, para 113).

Further factors which might call for adjustment in budget allocations include the extent of social deprivation in the area, the location in which the premises are situated (which might make the school prone to vandalism), the type of premises (eg design—perhaps they have a flat roof: such roofs are prone to leak; or perhaps they are difficult to heat), the condition of the premises, and whether there are any special facilities such as swimming pools (see *ibid*, paras 116–121).

(e) Transitional arrangements

Inherited costs may make certain schools' particular requirements extraordinarily large. The scheme may provide for a period of phased adjustment where necessary. A transitional period of up to four years is to be allowed. After this period, variations in a school's total budget between years may be limited by LEAs (if their scheme so provides) to five per cent in constant prices (see *ibid*, paras 127 and 128). The government has stated that it will look sympathetically at transitional arrangements designed to ease the difficulties faced by schools with above average staff costs (DES Press Release 253/89, 3 August 1989).

(f) Conditions attached to delegation

Delegation of the school's budget share to the governing body may be subject to conditions under the scheme (ERA 1988 s 39(11)). These conditions "may in particular relate to" the following:

(i) the arrangements for management of expenditure from the delegated sum and transactions (and in particular for authorising such expenditure or transactions);
(ii) the keeping and audit of accounts and records relating to expenditure;
(iii) the provision to the LEA of information, in the form of copies of accounts and records, and other documentation and information as required (s 39(12)).

The Circular (7/88, *op cit*) contemplates that LEAs should carefully monitor financial management by individual schools, whilst allowing governing bodies a certain amount of freedom. For example, schools will be expected to purchase goods and services on a value-for-money basis, and LEAs should consider advising the governors on the best arrangements for ensuring that they receive value for money. At the same time, schools must be able to purchase from whichever source they think most appropriate taking into account not only price but also quality and convenience (para 137). Schools will need to open external bank accounts, but the LEA should regulate their use. Overdrafts should be forbidden by the LEA! (para 142).

(g) Publication of schemes and financial statements

Section 42 ERA 1988 provides for publication of schemes of financial delegation. Such publication is to be made in the prescribed manner (under the Education (Publication of Schemes for Financing Schools) Regulations 1989) on the coming into force of the scheme and on other occasions (s 42(1)), such as when a scheme is varied (see DES Circular 7/88, para 211).

LEAs are also required, *before the start of each financial year,* to prepare a statement of intended financial provision in respect of county and voluntary schools (s 42(3)). This statement must contain various particulars relating to the financial year in question, such as:

- the general schools budget;
- the aggregated budget;
- amounts deducted in arriving at the aggregated schools budget;
- the allocation formula used in the scheme;
- planned expenditure per pupil (i) arising from the division of the school's budget share, (ii) on matters excluded from the delegation scheme (eg welfare services);
- the amount of capital expenditure on the school (s 42(4) and (5)).

At the end of the financial year a statement giving information concerning total expenditure incurred on all schools covered by the scheme, and expenditure incurred, or treated as incurred, per school must be prepared (s 42(6)). The form of such statements and manner and time of their publication is prescribed in SI 1990 No 353 (s 41(7)). The LEA must furnish governing bodies with a copy of the above statements; for their part, governors must make such statements available for inspection (without charge) at the schools at all reasonable times (s 42(8) and (9)).

Note that a statement containing categories of information relating to expenditure, similar to those required by s 42, must also be prepared in respect of schools which are not covered by delegation schemes—either because they are special schools, or because the scheme has not yet come into force (see s 50, and the Education (Pre-Scheme Financial Statements) Regulations 1989 as amended by SI 1989 No 1288). Such schools will have limited control of their own budgets—over expenditure on books, equipment, stationery and other prescribed heads (s 49).

(h) Actual delegation

A sum equal to the school's budget share is to be "put at the disposal of" the governing body of the school at such times and in such manner as provided for in the delegation scheme (s 36(1)–(3)). The governors may, subject to any stipulations in the scheme, spend the school's budget share in such a way "as they think fit for the purposes of the school" (s 36(5)(a)). This appears, on the face of it, to be a far-reaching provision which concentrates much control in the hands of governors and gives them the responsibility of making hard choices about how the budget might best be allocated. In practice, governors will have to work in close harmony with senior staff at the school and, in particular, the head teacher who will be expected to make recommendations to the governors in addition to drawing up school development plans. The governors will be able to delegate to the head teacher powers of expenditure over any part of the delegated budget —to such extent as is permitted by the scheme (s 36(5)(b)).

In practice governors may have less actual freedom of choice than might first appear to be the case. It has been predicted that their scope to redirect spending could be, at least initially, "of the order of two or three per cent" (Maclure, *Education Re-formed* (1988), page 51).

(i) Governors' liability

Governors are protected by s 36(6) against personal liability in respect of losses incurred by doing anything in good faith in their disposition of the school budget. (Note that where the governors enter into a contract they do so on behalf of the LEA: see Circular 7/88, *op cit*, para 183.) Insurance cover in respect of any losses caused as a result of negligence by governors is expected to be arranged by the LEA (*ibid*, para 86) and is a discretionary exception deductable from the general schools budget in calculating the aggregated budget (above). Governors are advised to make sure that the LEA has made appropriate insurance arrangements (DES Circular 7/88, para 86). Governors' liability is discussed more fully in Chapters 3 (at pages 128–130) and 9 (page 247).

(j) Monitoring, evaluation, accountability

LEAs will have to monitor carefully the management of schools' delegated budgets, not only in view of LEAs' duties concerning implementation and provision of the National Curriculum and their wider duties under the 1944 Act, but also because of the need for provision to be effective and efficient. LEAs are required to incorporate into their schemes procedures for monitoring. In addition, schools are expected to develop their own school-based performance indicators, with advice and support from the LEA (DES Circular 7/88, *op cit*, para 152).

The Circular spells out how the government believes LEAs should approach the task of monitoring schemes effectively. LEAs will be expected to develop:

"(1) effective financial monitoring arrangements; (2) appropriate management information systems in schools and centrally; and (3) performance indicators for the financial and wider management functions of the governing bodies of schools with delegated budgets: these should be based on and take into account the indicators used by schools themselves" (DES Circular 7/88, *op cit*, para 153).

The Circular explains that the aim of effective monitoring is to identify potential problems so that they can be tackled before they become serious (*ibid*, para 154). In some cases LEAs may make use of various sanctions. They have a power (under s 37(1) and (2)) to *suspend financial delegation* on giving one month's notice to the governors (and a copy to the head teacher). The reason(s) for suspension should be specified in the notice. This power may be exercised if the governing body:

(a) has been guilty of a substantial or persistent failure to comply with any requirements applicable under the scheme; or
(b) is not managing the appropriation or expenditure of the sum put at its disposal for the purposes of the school in a satisfactory manner (s 37(1)).

What amounts to a failure to deal with the money in a "satisfactory manner" will be for the LEA to determine; disputes are clearly possible in view of the imprecision of the wording.

In certain cases the LEA will be able to suspend the right to a delegated budget before the date specified in the notice. It may do so if it appears necessary because of the "gross incompetence or mismanagement on the part of the governing body or other emergency" (s 37(3)). In such a case the LEA must immediately inform the Secretary of State of its action and the reason for it (*ibid*).

Any suspension must be *reviewed* before the beginning of every financial year that it remains in force (s 37(5)(a)) and the LEA's decision thereon communicated in writing to the governing body and head teacher (s 37(6)). The authority must give the governors and head teacher an opportunity to make representations before making its decision (s 37(5)(b); DES Circular 7/88, *op cit*, para 223). Suspensions should be revoked when the LEA considers it appropriate (s 37(5)(c)), such revocation to take effect at the start of the next financial year (s 37(7)). The governors have a right of *appeal* to the Secretary of State over the suspension or the continuation of it (s 37(8)). The Secretary of State may allow or reject the appeal (s 37(9)(a)), and must have regard, when making his decision, to "the gravity of the default on the part of the governing body and the likelihood of its continuance or recurrence" (s 37(9)(b)).

When delegation is suspended, the LEA's duty (in s 36(2)) to put a school's budget share at the disposal of the governors will not apply in relation to that particular school's governing body (s 37(4)). However, the school will still be funded at the level of its budget share—but the governors will not have power over the way in which this share is spent. Moreover, their powers concerning staffing (see ss 44–46, below) will also be suspended (DES Circular 7/88, *op cit*, para 223).

(k) Staffing

"The responsibilities governors will have in respect of staffing are an integral part of local management" (DES Circular 7/88, para 156).

Detailed provisions (ERA 1988 ss 44–46 and Sch 3) govern the appointment and dismissal of staff, teaching and non-teaching, at schools which have a delegated budget. These are discussed in the next Chapter.

(l) New schools

New schools (see ERA 1988 s48(2)) of a type to which a delegation scheme applies will be subject to LMS from the date their temporary governing body is constituted. A school which the LEA proposes to maintain, and which it did not before, is treated as a new school for this purpose. Generally speaking, new schools will be treated in the same way as other schools falling within the scope of a financial delegation scheme (ERA 1988 Sch 4). There may be modifications, for example to make allowance for the fact that significant teaching salary costs will not arise before opening, or to permit delegation to be phased in (DES Circular 7/88, *op cit*, para 44).

11. The education of travellers and displaced persons

ERA 1988 s 210 makes provision for the payment to LEAs of grants in respect of provision of education for travellers or displaced persons. Travellers are persons "of no fixed abode" and those who leave their main abodes to live elsewhere for much of the year (s 210(2)(a)). The Education (Grants) (Travellers and Displaced Persons) Regulations 1990 provide the scheme under which the grants are paid.

Chapter 2

Teachers and other staff

1. Introduction

The employment of teachers is closely regulated—by general employment law and by specific legislation. The latter includes E (No 2)A 1986, the Teachers' Pay and Conditions Act 1987, and ERA 1988; there are also various regulations. Among other things, the 1988 Act empowers the Secretary of State for Education and Science to "make such modifications in any enactment relating to employment and, in particular, in any enactment—

(a) conferring powers or imposing duties on employers;
(b) conferring rights on employees; or
(c) otherwise regulating the relations between employers and employees;

as he considers expedient in consequence of the operation of any of the provisions of this Act [relating to staffing following financial delegation]" (s 222).

An order has been made under s 222—the Education (Modification of Enactments Relating to Employment) Order 1989.

It is not really possible, in a work of this nature, to set out in detail major parts of general employment law. As employees, teachers and other school staff are covered by, for example, the provisions of the Employment Protection (Consolidation) Act 1978 concerning unfair dismissal and redundancy, and by the Sex Discrimination Act 1975 and Race Relations Act 1976. Trade union rights have been affected dramatically by the Employment Acts 1980–88. On these areas of general application, reference may be made to the specialist works on employment law—such as Wedderburn's *The Worker and the Law* (Penguin), Selwyn's *Law of Employment* (Butterworth), and Smith and Wood's *Industrial Law* (Butterworth)—although selective coverage appears below.

Provisions concerned specifically with the employment of teachers have increased in recent years, and much of the remainder of this chapter will be concerned with them. They fall into eight areas:

- (a) staffing levels in schools;
- (b) qualification for employment as a teacher;
- (c) appointment of staff;
- (d) discipline and dismissal of staff;
- (e) school teachers' pay and conditions;
- (f) pay and conditions of non-teaching staff;
- (g) the LEA training grants scheme;
- (h) appraisal of teachers.

Many of these areas are being affected by the introduction of schemes of financial delegation. The effect of the acquisition of grant-maintained status on teacher employment was considered above (see page 18).

2. Staffing levels in schools

The Education Act 1944 requires LEAs to ensure that there are for their areas schools which are "sufficient in number, character and equipment" for providing suitable education (s 8). As we saw earlier (page 4), LEAs have a duty under s 8, not only to make school buildings and equipment available, but also essential personnel—but where there are teacher shortages due to unavoidable recruitment difficulties the LEA will not be in breach of this "target" duty. In any event, ERA 1988 s 218(1)(d) empowers the Secretary of State to prescribe with regard to staffing in schools. The Education (Teachers) Regulations 1989 ("the Teachers Regs 1989") provide that:

> "At any school . . . there shall be employed a staff of teachers suitable and sufficient in numbers for the purpose of securing the provision of education appropriate to the

ages, abilities, aptitudes and needs of the pupils having regard to any arrangements for the utilisation of the services of teachers employed otherwise than at the school" (reg 6(1))."

The staff of teachers employed at the school must include a head teacher (reg 6(2)). Teachers at the school must be suitably qualified (see below) (reg 6(3)).

Section 34 E (No 2)A 1986, which applies only to schools which do not have a delegated budget, requires schools to have a "complement of teaching and non-teaching posts" (including part-time posts) determined by the LEA. In schools which have a delegated budget, it is for the governors to decide how many staff should work at the school (or how many the school can afford); advice from the head teacher will clearly be sought (DES Circular 7/88, para 158).

3. Qualification for employment as a teacher

(a) Introduction

As the National Curriculum is brought into effect, the biggest threat to its success appears to be the shortage of suitably qualified teachers, especially in certain subject areas, such as mathematics and modern languages (see *The Times*, 25 April 1990). Surveys have also highlighted teacher shortages in certain parts of the country, especially the South-East and inner London, where pay levels are lower than elsewhere, relative to living costs. Shortage of subject specialists has already prompted the government to pay bursaries and empower LEAs to offer incentive allowances (see below) to attract teachers qualified in these subjects to their schools (see *School Teachers' Pay and Conditions Document 1989*, para 7(5)(c)). As a response to the overall shortage of teachers, the government has made provision (via the Teachers Regs 1989) for the employment of "licensed teachers" and teachers from other European Community countries. Because the former involves recruiting as teachers persons without the normal entry requirements, the government has been accused of hypocrisy by advocating improved quality of educational provision whilst at the same time compromising on teacher qualification. But an education minister (Mrs Angela Rumbold) argued that:

> "Streamlining the routes to qualified teacher status will help schools and LEAs secure the teachers they need. It will allow mature, well-qualified people who want to turn to teaching in mid-career to do so without having to return to life as a full-time student. The new route will also make it easier for teachers from overseas to take up posts in our schools—their skills and expertise are welcome" (DES Press release 260/89, 17 August 1989).

These new provisions are the latest under which Secretaries of State have exercised their power to control teacher qualifications. (Until they were replaced by the Teachers Regs 1989, the Education (Teachers) Regulations 1982, made under EA 1980 s 27, laid down the requirements.) The Secretary of State also exercises control over teacher training; only initial teacher training courses which he has approved can offer teaching qualifications (see below).

(b) The Education (Teachers) Regulations 1989

These regulations apply to the employment of teachers in a school maintained by a LEA, a non-maintained special school or a grant-maintained school (reg 3(1)(a)). (Note that the regulations also deal with some aspects of teacher employment in further and higher education.) In addition to prescribing qualifications to teach, they:

(i) prescribe health and physical capacity standards necessary for employment, or continued employment, as a teacher or worker with children or young persons (regs 7–9); and

(ii) give the Secretary of State a power to bar a person in (i) from teaching, or to make his/her employment subject to certain conditions:
- on medical grounds;
- on the grounds of a person's misconduct (whether or not s/he has been convicted of a criminal offence in respect of it); or
- on educational grounds (teachers only). (See further regs 7 and 10).

So far as teaching in a school is concerned, a person may be:
  (i) qualified to teach;
  (ii) unqualified, but able to be employed (in some cases as a "licensed" teacher);
  (iii) unqualified and not able to be employed.

The general rule, laid down in reg 13 of the Teachers Regs 1989, is that "no person shall be employed as a teacher at a school unless he is a qualified teacher in accordance with Schedule 5". But there are certain exceptional categories, comprised in (ii) above (regs 15–18 and Schs 3 and 4).

Qualified to teach: A person cannot be a qualified teacher until s/he has received notification to that effect from the Secretary of State. (There is an exception to this in the case of a person who qualified before 31 August 1989 under the Education (Teachers) Regulations 1982 Sch 5.) The date from which the person is qualified to teach will be as specified in the notification (Teachers Regs 1989 Sch 5 para 1(1)). In an appropriate case, qualified teacher status may be conferred retrospectively: the date of qualification can be stated to commence one year before the date of notification (para 1(2)).

Where a licensed teacher is concerned, the date of qualification must be after the completion by him/her of a prescribed period of service (as stated in para 2(2)(c)—see below).

The normal route into teaching is via a Bachelor of Education (B Ed), Certificate in Education (Cert Ed), or Post-graduate Certificate in Education (PGCE) course. Provided such course is "approved" for the purposes of initial training of teachers (see the Teachers Regs 1989 Sch 5 para 5), and provided that the course may only be followed by those who have attained grade C standard in English and mathematics at GCSE level (or equivalent—see DES Circular 18/89 Appendix 1), a person will be qualified to teach (para 2(2)(a)). Detailed criteria for the approval of courses are laid down in Annex A to DES Circular 24/89, *Initial Teacher Training: Approval of Courses.* When deciding whether or not to grant approval for a course, the Secretary of State draws on the advice of the Council for Accreditation of Teacher Education (CATE).

Teachers whose qualification to teach was obtained in

Scotland or Northern Ireland or who are (i) registered as teachers in Scotland or (ii) recognised as teachers in schools in Northern Ireland by the DES (Northern Ireland Office), are qualified to teach in schools in England and Wales (Teachers Regs 1989 Sch 5 para 2(2)(b)).

In addition to making provision regarding licensed teachers (basically persons not qualified to teach under the above provisions but meeting other minimum requirements: see below), the Teachers Regs 1989 implement EC Council Directive 89/48 which requires Community member states to recognize each other's teaching qualifications where any such qualification is obtained after a minimum of three years' training (Sch 5 para 2(2)(d)).

A further category of teacher with qualified teacher status is a teacher of the mentally handicapped who possesses a prescribed diploma (or recognition), who at any time before 8 April 1982 served as a teacher in a special school, and who completed three years' satisfactory service in such a school before 1 September 1989 (Sch 5 para 2(2)(e)). In such a case, the LEA/governors (as appropriate) must have issued a recommendation in respect of such person to the Secretary of State.

Finally, there are those who made an application for qualified teacher status under prescribed categories laid down in the Teachers Regs 1982 and whose application was under consideration by the Secretary of State on 31 August 1989. They are qualified if the Secretary of State has since decided that they fall within one of the said categories (Sch 5 para 2(3)).

There are further requirements concerning teachers of pupils who are (i) *hearing impaired,* (ii) *visually impaired,* or (iii) *who suffer from both forms of disadvantage.* Unless he has an approved qualification for teaching hearing impaired or visually impaired children, a qualified teacher is qualified to give instruction to such children in a craft, trade or domestic subject only (regs 15 and 16). The same applies to a teacher of pupils with both forms of disadvantage (reg 17(1)). However, where the teacher has an approved qualification for the purposes of *either* (i) *or* (ii), s/he is qualified to teach pupils with *both* forms of disadvantage provided the employing authority is satisfied that no person with an approved qualification for teaching them is available (reg 17(2)).

Unqualified, but able to be employed: Certain teachers can be employed to teach at a school even though they are not qualified. In the majority of cases such employment as an unqualified teacher may only be temporary.

One such category refers to persons temporarily employed as teachers of the visually impaired, hearing impaired, or both, whilst not qualified for such teaching. Any such person may be employed for up to three years (in aggregate), with the proviso that their employing authority is satisfied that it is their intention to obtain an approved qualification for the teaching of such pupils (reg 18 – and see DES Circular 18/89, para 50).

Apart from these teachers of the visually/hearing impaired covered by reg 18, unqualified persons entitled to teach at a school fall within either Sch 3, which applies to teachers other than licensed teachers, or Sch 4, which deals with licensed teachers.

Schedule 3 applies to the following:

(i) existing unqualified teachers permitted by the Teachers Regs 1982 to work as teachers in nursery classes at nursery schools and employed there immediately before 1 September 1989—they can continue in their employment but cannot be further appointed after that date;

(ii) student teachers (persons accepted on to an approved initial training course but waiting to take up their place, and persons whose completion of their period of training has been delayed by up to one year: para 2(1)(a) and (b))—they can be employed for an aggregate period of up to two years (or longer if authorised by the Secretary of State), provided they are required "neither to take responsiblity for a class nor to teach a subject which is not also taught by a qualified teacher at the school" (para 2(2)(a) and (b));

(iii) persons employed to give instruction in any art or skill, or in any subject or group of subjects (including any form of vocational training) the teaching of

which requires special qualifications or experience; such a teacher may be employed "for such period as no suitable qualified teacher or licensed teacher is available for appointment or to give the instruction", provided that the LEA or governors (as appropriate) are satisfied as to his/her qualifications or experience (see para 3(1)(a));
(iv) teachers of the mentally handicapped, where a recommendation has been made by the LEA/governors to the Secretary of State (Sch 5 para 2(2)(e) (above)); such a person may be employed until 1 September 1990 (Sch 3 para 4).

The licensed teacher scheme (covered by Sch 4) came into operation on 1 September 1989. As indicated above (page 62), the scheme is intended to provide a more direct "route" into teaching for mature persons with appropriate experience and qualifications. It also enables certain teachers trained overseas to gain qualified teacher status after as little as one term's service.

Application for a licence may not be made by individuals, but by the "recommending body", defined in reg 3(2) as:

- the LEA, for maintained schools without delegated budgets;
- the governing body of a school with a delegated budget, provided the LEA consents (if it does not, it must inform the Secretary of State of its reasons: Sch 4 para 3(2));
- the governing body of a grant-maintained school and a non-maintained special school.

The application (on form P6(3)) is made to the Secretary of State, who is empowered to grant licences to teach to persons named in recommendations. A recommendation must contain such particulars as the Secretary of State may determine (Sch 4 para 4), some of which are prescribed by the regulations.

First there must be a statement by the recommending body that the proposed licensee:

(i) has grade C in GCSE mathematics and English (or equivalent: see above); and

(ii) has completed not less than two years full-time higher education in England and Wales or comparable full- or part-time education for an equivalent period here or anywhere in the world;
(iii) is aged at least twenty-six at the date at which his/her employment is to commence (unless trained outside the UK); and
(iv) is in its opinion a "suitable person to be a teacher" (Sch 4 para 5(1)).

Secondly, particulars of the training proposed to be given to the licensed teacher must be set out (para 5(2)). Not surprisingly, in view of the criticism of the licensed teacher scheme from teaching unions, to the effect that professional standards for teachers would be compromised, considerable emphasis is placed on training. Responsibility for ensuring that the licensee receives training rests with the recommending body and, in the case of schools with delegated budgets, with the LEA (para 7). The Circular (18/89) contains guidance on training and specifies the knowledge and competences which the licensee is expected to acquire (see paras 26–29 and Appendix 2 to the Circular). Particulars of the means for assessing, after his/her training and the completion of the licence period, the licensee's competence overall, are to be submitted with the licence application (*ibid*, para 26). The Circular advises that the LEA or governors (as appropriate) should make arrangements for such assessment (Circular 18/89 para 28). It is clear that the training institutions are expected to be used in one way or another in the training and assessment arrangements, although the expertise of the advisory service operated by LEAs is also expected to be harnessed (para 29).

Thirdly, there must be a statement of one of two types (Sch 4 para 5(3)):

(i) The first type of statement will refer to the fact that the teacher was trained on a three year (or more) course outside England and Wales, has served for at least one year as a teacher in an educational establishment in England and Wales or elsewhere and was not dismissed on any ground other than redundancy; the statement must also state that the teacher may be employed at more than one school during the period of licence. (Teachers falling within this category may be eligible for qualified teacher status after as short a period as one term as a licensee: see below.)

(ii) The alternative type of statement will simply detail prescribed particulars of the post in which the licensed teacher is to be employed.

The licence is to be granted for a period of two years in the first instance or, in the case of a part-time post or subsequent licence, for such period as may be specified in the licence (Sch 4 para 6(1)). In most cases the teacher would be expected to remain with the recommending school or, where the LEA makes the recommendation, a named school (Circular 18/89, *op cit*, para 34). In certain cases the licence may lapse if the teacher ceases to be so employed (Sch 4 para 6(2)); the Secretary of State may then have to be informed of the facts of the case by the recommending body (*ibid*, para 9).

If a licensed teacher is to attain qualified teacher status a recommendation must be made by the recommending body. If the recommending body is the governing body of a maintained school with a delegated budget, the LEA must give its consent (Sch 5 para 2(2)(c)). The recommendation is made to the Secretary of State. The recommendation should be accompanied by a statement that the licensed teacher has completed the necessary licence period in his/her case and meets any other requirements of the scheme (eg minimum age of twenty-six, completion of required minimum prior teaching experience). The minimum period of service as a licensed teacher is:

(i) in standard cases, two years (extendable by up to one year on application by LEA or governors who do not yet feel able to recommend qualified teacher status (Circular 18/89 para 32; Teachers Regs 1989 Sch 4 para 2(2)(c)(i)); or

(ii) one year, where the teacher is aged at least twenty-six and has at least two years' prior teaching experience in independent schools or in further or higher education or as an instructor or education officer in the armed forces and in whichever case was not dismissed for any reason other than redundancy (para 2(2)(c)(ii)); or

(iii) one term, in the case of an overseas-trained teacher who had three years' teacher training and at least one year's teaching experience in England or Wales or elsewhere (para 2(2)(c)(iii)).

The "articled teacher" scheme. Another scheme, to be run on a pilot basis from September 1990, is the "articled teacher" scheme. It will enable persons who are qualified for the PGCE to train in the classroom and receive payment for doing so—rather than spend a year as a student on a grant. At the time of writing, the plan is that the articled teacher's "remuneration" will be a bursary paid by the LEA, at a rate to be announced. This form of "on the job" training will be supervised by tutors from training institutions and selected members of the school teaching staff.

(c) Transitional arrangements concerning qualified teacher status

Various transitional arrangements are prescribed. Those which, at the time of going to press, remain relevant are as follows:

(i) Under Sch 1, persons who were, immediately before 1 September 1989, qualified to teach hearing impaired or visually impaired pupils, or both, will remain so qualified. If any such person was, on 31 August 1989, employed as an unqualified teacher of pupils with such disabilities (under regs 15–17 above), s/he may continue in such employment until 31 August 1994. However, the employers must be satisfied that it is his/her intention to become qualified (within three years, according to DES Circular 18/89, para 50, although the regulations do not say so).

(ii) Those persons seeking qualification before 1 November 1990 from the Secretary of State under the Education (Teachers) Regulations 1982 Sch 5 para 2(e) have a period of time in which to satisfy qualification requirements. Paragraph 2(e) has offered qualified teacher status to persons with, normally, ten years' experience as a teacher, whose qualifications are approved in their case by the Secretary of State and who have the GCSE (or a predecessor) in English and mathematics. The main aim of this particular transitional arrangement is to allow persons taking one or both of these GCSEs, in order to obtain qualified status via this route, to fulfil the necessary requirements (DES Circular 18/89, para 15).

(d) The probationary period

Newly qualified teachers working in LEA-maintained schools, non-maintained special schools and grant-maintained schools must serve a probationary period—with certain exceptions applicable to teachers with previous experience of teaching, teachers in City Technology Colleges and licensed teachers who have been granted qualified teacher status (see DES Circular 18/89, para 46). Decisions concerning probation, such as whether it is necessary and, if so, its duration, are to be made by the LEA ("relevant authority") or governing body of a non-maintained or grant-maintained school ("relevant body").

The probationary period is one year (or two years in the case of a part-time teacher) (Sch 6 para 3(1)), but can be extended (para 3(4)). Before extending the period of probation, the LEA (in the case of a maintained school) is required to consult the governing body and head teacher (E(No 2)A 1986 s 41(1)(b)). The relevant body or authority may determine a period of less than one year as the probationary period, having regard to the previous experience of the teacher and the particular circumstances of the case (Sch 6 para 3(3)). If, during the probationary period, the teacher is absent taking sick leave or maternity leave for an aggregate period in term time of more than six weeks, the probationary period is to be extended by the aggregate period of absence (para 3(5)).

While on probation, "the duties assigned to a probationary teacher, his supervision and the conditions under which he works shall be such as to facilitate a fair and effective assessment of his conduct and efficiency as a teacher" (para 3(2)).

If the relevant authority or body, after having regard to a probationary teacher's conduct and efficiency during the probation period, and having consulted the head teacher, considers that the probationary teacher is "not fitted and is unlikely to become fitted in the post he holds", it may determine that s/he has failed to complete his/her probation period successfully. Before making this determination, the relevant authority or body must give the teacher an opportunity to make representations to it (para 4(1)) and must consult with the head teacher and governing body (E(No 2)A 1986 s 41(1)(b)). As soon as practicable thereafter, and after giving an opportunity for the teacher to appeal against the determination (the relevant body or authority is to establish an appeals procedure: Circular 18/89 para 46), the relevant authority or body must dismiss the teacher from his post. If it is not proposed to employ him/her at another school, the teacher must be given one month's notice or one month's wages in lieu of notice and given an opportunity to resign (Sch 6 para 4(2)(a)). After being dismissed for failed probation, the teacher may not be reappointed to the post (para 4(2)(b)). If appointed to another post, s/he must serve a further period of probation.

(e) Transitional arrangements concerning probation

The following transitional arrangements apply under the Teachers Regs 1989:

(i) Approval of an abnormal probation period granted but not completed before 1 September 1989 shall remain in force until completion (Sch 1 para 8).
(ii) Probation decisions by the Secretary of State, to the effect that a person is or is not deemed suitable for further employment as a teacher, and the barring of a teacher from employment shall, if made under previous regulations, have continued effect (Sch 1 paras 9 and 2 respectively).

4. Appointment of staff

Once a financial delegation scheme is in operation the arrangements concerning appointment of staff will change. Until such time, appointments will continue to be governed by the procedures laid down in E(No 2)A 1986, which reflect the extended role of governing bodies under that Act. Both sets of arrangements are described below.

(a) Anti-discrimination provision

Whichever set of arrangements is in force, the provisions of the Sex Discrimination Act 1975 (and Equal Pay Act 1970 and regulations, as amended) and Race Relations Act 1976 (and Codes of Practice) are extremely relevant to appointments of all staff. The various types of outlawed discrimination, and the "justifiability" principle, are discussed in Chapter 5, but some of the legal provisions may conveniently be considered here. It may be noted that discrimination in the arrangements for the recruitment of staff, in the terms on which employment is offered, and in deciding whether to employ, is unlawful under the Sex Discrimination Act (s 6 and see Equal Opportunities Commission *Avoiding Sex Bias in Selection Testing* (1988)) and Race Relations Act 1976 (s 4). It may, however, be lawful to discriminate in certain situations—for example if either gender or race is a "genuine occupational qualification" for the post in question. In *Lambeth LBC* v *Commission for Racial Equality* (1990) advertisements for management posts in a housing benefit department, specifying that applicants from particular racial groups were required, was held to constitute a breach of the Race Relations Act because belonging to one of these groups was not a genuine occupational qualification. However, there may be situations where a teacher from an ethnic minority background, perhaps a speaker of a particular language, is needed, and discrimination in recruitment may not be unlawful. In the case of gender, the 1975 Act cites the need for the job to be done by a person of a particular sex "to preserve decency or privacy" or where "the holder of the job provides individuals with personal services promoting their welfare" (s 7(2)(b) and (e)). The latter exception also appears in the Race Relations Act 1976 and probably applies to teaching.

Employers may insist on various requirements, and some of these may be lawful. For example, to insist that a teacher has a good command of the English language would not amount to indirect racial discrimination, either because it is "justifiable" (*Raval* v *DHSS* (1985); and see Chapter 5) in the context of the employer's business (the provision of education) or because it is not the overriding requirement where selection is concerned (*Perera* v *The Home Office* (1980)). Moreover, an act of discrimination carried out in pursuance of regulations (for example, governing qualified teacher status) might be lawful (*Hampson* v *DES* (1990)). The onus is on the employer to show that the condition or requirement is justifiable (*Mandla* v *Dowell Lee* (1983)—discussed in Chapter 5). But the burden of proving discrimination rests with the complainant (see *Barking and Dagenham LBC* v *Camara*(1988)), and may present him/her with great difficulties because, taking as an example race discrimination,

> "there is normally not available to him any evidence of overtly discriminatory words or actions used by the respondent. All that the applicant can do is to point to certain facts which, if unexplained, are consistent with his having been treated less favourably than others on racial [or sex] grounds" (*Chattopadhay* v *Headmaster of Holloway School* (1981) *per* Browne-Wilkinson, President EAT).

To be unlawful as indirect discrimination, the requirement or condition must affect one sex or racial (etc) group more than another. In *Price* v *Civil Service Commission (No 2)* (1978) a maximum recruitment age limit of twenty-eight was held to be unlawful sex discrimination because in practice many women spend a period out of work during their twenties in order to bring up children whereas far fewer men do.

Complaint may be made to an industrial tribunal (Sex Discrimination Act 1975 s 63, Race Relations Act 1976 s 54) which may award compensation if a case is made out. The tribunal may also make a recommendation that action be taken to stop a discriminatory practice in order to prevent further harm to the applicant.

(b) Appointments to schools without delegated budgets

Appointments procedures for *county, controlled, special agreement and maintained special schools* are laid down in ss 36–39 of E(No 2)A 1986. They apply only to posts within the school's "complement", as determined by the LEA under s 34. The complement is to include all full-time teaching posts, all part-time teaching posts specific to the school, and other non-teaching staff at the school apart from persons employed by the LEA solely in connection with the provision of meals and/or the supervision of pupils at midday (s 34(2) and (3)). The LEA has a duty to consult the governing body and head teacher before appointing a person to work whole-time at the school but not as a member of its complement or meals or supervision staff (s 35(2)).

So far as the appointment of head teachers and deputy head teachers is concerned, a selection panel is to be convened (s 36). The panel is to comprise equal numbers of LEA and governor members, being not less than three from each category. The LEA and governors may replace one or more of their appointed members at any time. Regulation 29(1) of the Education (School Government) Regulations 1989 states that the panel must make its decision by majority (no casting vote). The panel may decide who is to attend the meeting (reg 29(3)).

Specific rules concerning the appointment of *head teachers* and, by virtue of s 39(1)(a), *deputy head teachers*, are contained in s 37. If a post is vacant it must be advertised nationally. (In the meantime the LEA must appoint an acting head teacher, after consulting with the governing body, but there is no duty to appoint an acting deputy head teacher: s 39(3).) Suitable applicants are to be interviewed. If the panel is unable to agree on the applicants it wishes to interview, up to two candidates may be selected by the governor and LEA factions respectively. An appointment may be made only if the selection panel has recommended the candidate concerned. If the panel feels unable to recommend an appointment, it may re-interview such of the candidates as it wishes, or may require the LEA to re-advertise the post. These repeat steps would occur if the authority declines to appoint the person recommended by the panel (as it has the power to do).

The chief education officer or his/her nominee has the right to attend all proceedings of the panel, including interviews, for the purpose of giving advice to its members. In the case of interviews for deputy headships, the head teacher is also entitled to be present (whether as a member of the panel or not) and, if not a member of the panel, may give advice to panel members (s 39(2)(a)). Whether or not the head teacher attends selection panel proceedings, s/he is entitled to be consulted before the panel offers a recommendation to the LEA concerning an appointment of a deputy head teacher (s 39(2)(b)).

Appointments to *other posts* forming part of the complement of the school are not subject to the selection panel procedure. Where there is a vacancy in an existing post, the LEA must decide whether or not it should be retained (s 38(1)(a)—this applies also to vacancies at deputy head level, by virtue of s 39(1)(b)). If the post is to be filled, the LEA must advertise the vacancy, unless the intention is that the post should be filled by an employee who is currently in post with the authority (s 38(1)(b) and (c)). The procedure for making appointments (other than to the post of head or deputy head teacher or to a temporary appointment pending either the return to work of a member of staff or formal selection in accordance with the articles) is laid down in s 38(3). The LEA must advertise the post in such a way as will bring it to the attention of persons qualified to fill it. The governing body must interview any suitable candidates and recommend an appointment (if it can agree and if it considers a candidate suitable—if it cannot agree, or does not wish to appoint, it may re-interview or ask the LEA to re-advertise the post, which normally the authority must do: see s 38(3)(e)). The LEA cannot appoint a person to a post which it has advertised in accordance with the requirements of s 38(3) unless the appointment has been recommended by the governors, or the person appointed is already one of its employees (s 38(5)). But the authority may decline to appoint a person recommended by the governors.

If the intention is to fill a vacancy from among persons already employed by the authority (or appointed and waiting to take up a post), the post does not have to be advertised (s 38(1)(c)—above). In such a situation, the governing body may determine a specification for the post, in consultation with the head teacher, and must send a copy to the LEA (s 38(4)(b) and (c)). The LEA must consult with the governing body and the head teacher over the appointment which it makes. (Consultation with the governors is not required where the appointment is required urgently and the chairperson or vice-chairperson cannot be contacted: Education (School Government) Regulations 1989 reg 31.) If it is an appointment with which the governing body disagrees, the LEA must report that fact to the next meeting of its appropriate education committee (s 38(4)(c)).

Delegation of appointments of staff under s 38 (ie not head teachers, deputy head teachers and certain temporary appointments) may be made to (i) one or more governors, (ii) the head teacher, or (iii) a combination of (i) and (ii) (s 38(6)).

The appointment of *clerks to governing bodies* of county, controlled, special agreement and maintained special schools is also regulated (s 40).

In *voluntary aided* schools, teachers are employed by the governing body, although, subject to agreement between the LEA and governors, the articles of government may provide that the LEA may prohibit the appointment, without its consent, of staff to give secular instruction at the school (EA 1944 s 24(2)).

Power over the appointment of persons to give religious instruction at controlled schools (reserve teachers) and voluntary schools remains substantially in the hands of governing bodies (EA 1944 ss 27 and 28; E(No 2)A 1986 s 35(1)(g)).

Note that the requirements of the Education (School Government) Regulations 1989, concerning governor withdrawal from a meeting where matters in which s/he (or her/his spouse) has a pecuniary interest, apply also to meetings concerned with appointment of staff to all maintained schools. (See, further, Chapter 3.)

(c) Appointments to schools with delegated budgets

Schools other than aided schools: The provisions of the 1986 Act concerned with a "complement" of staff and staff appointments (and suspensions and dismissals—see below) in county, controlled or special agreement schools do not apply where the school has a delegated budget (ERA 1988 s 44(2)). Within five years of the beginning of the financial year in which a school first has a delegated budget, the articles of government must be amended to include a statement that these 1986 Act provisions do not apply; and to the effect that s 44 of and Sch 3 to ERA 1988 govern staffing matters (ERA 1988 s 44(4)). These provisions of the 1988 Act concerned with staffing will become of increasing importance as financial delegation (or LMS) is implemented. (As noted above (page 43) maintained special schools are not covered by the financial delegation provisions of ERA 1988, including those relating to staffing, although they may become subject to financial delegation schemes in the future, if the Secretary of State makes provision under s 43.)

Appointment of staff is to be in accordance with Sch 3, which places appointments firmly in the hands of governing bodies, with increased powers and duties, although the required procedures do not differ markedly from those contained in the 1986 Act.

Where *headships* are concerned, the governing body must notify the LEA of any vacancy or prospective vacancy before it can proceed to select a candidate. While the vacancy remains open, the governing body is to recommend a person for appointment as acting head teacher, and the LEA must appoint him/her unless s/he is not qualified (on academic, professional, physical capacity, etc, grounds: para 1(6)) (para 1(4))—in which case the governors must choose another acting head (para 1(12)). (Unlike the situation under the 1986 Act, the governors also have the power to appoint acting *deputy head* teachers (para 1(5)).) The governors (not the LEA) must ensure that any vacant headship or deputy headship is advertised nationally (para 1(7)). Candidates whom the governors consider worthy of consideration for the post must be interviewed by a selection panel consisting of at least three governors (para 1(8) and (9)). If the selection panel chooses a suitable candidate, it must recommend that person to the governing body. If the governing body approves the recommendation, it must recommend the applicant for appointment by the LEA (para 1(9)). If, on the other hand, the panel or governing body does not wish to recommend a candidate, the governors may re-advertise the vacancy and/or re-interview the candidates (para 1(10)). The LEA has no power to veto a recommended appointment to a headship or deputy headship other than on qualification grounds (as defined in para 1(6) above) (para 1(11)). Note that the

LEA's chief education officer (or his/her nominee: para 11(3)) and, in the case of deputy head appointments, the head teacher, may attend all proceedings of the governing body or selection panel in order to give advice (para 3(1) and (4)). The chief education officer or his/her nominee (or head teacher where a deputy headship is concerned) is under a duty to offer such advice as s/he considers appropriate in relation to appointments of head and deputy head teachers, including appointments to act in such capacity (para 3(2)). If such advice is offered, the selection panel or governors must give consideration to it (para 3(3)).

Appointment of *other teachers* is governed by Sch 3 para 2. The governors have virtually total control. Note that they may delegate any of their functions in the selection process to (i) one or more governors, (ii) the head teacher or (iii) a combination of (i) and (ii). The first stage in the selection process is the drawing up by the governors of a specification for the post, in consultation with the head teacher, following which a copy is sent to the LEA (para 2(4)). The authority is entitled to nominate for consideration a person already employed by it and, with the permission of the governors, a person employed by the governing body of an aided school maintained by the LEA (para 2(5)). The governors are required to advertise the post unless they decide to recommend a person already employed at the school or a person nominated by the LEA (under para 2(5) above) (para 2(6)). The governors are not required to advertise the post nationally, but must advertise it in a manner likely to bring it to the attention of persons who are qualified for it (para 2(7)). Candidates, including those put forward by the LEA (as above), are to be interviewed (para 1(8)(a)). If a candidate is selected, the LEA must appoint him/her unless s/he lacks a necessary qualification (as above) (para 1(10))—in which case the governors must repeat any of the steps in the above selection process which they deem necessary in the circumstances (para 1(11)). Note that as in the case of senior appointments, the chief education officer (or his/her nominee) and head teacher may attend various proceedings in the selection process to give advice—which advice must be taken into consideration by the relevant person(s) (para 3, *op cit*).

There is a simple procedure for the appointment of *temporary staff*. If the appointment is for a period not exceeding (or not likely to exceed) four months the LEA must appoint the person recommended by the governors (or their delegate—see below) unless s/he does not meet any applicable staff qualification requirements (as defined earlier) (para 2(2) and (3)).

Provision is also made in respect of the appointment of *non-teaching staff* (para 4). The governors are able to select staff for non-teaching posts, and normally the LEA will be required to appoint them (para 4(4)). The governors must, in recommending an appointment (in writing), state the duties to be performed (including the hours, where the appointment is part-time), the grade considered appropriate, and the remuneration (where the LEA has discretion over pay: see para 4(5)) (para 4(2)). The governors must consult the head teacher (and, if the post involves more than sixteen hours' work per week at the school, the chief education officer) before selecting (para 4(3)).

The governors may select a person for appointment as their *clerk*, after consultation with the LEA. The LEA must appoint the person recommended (para 5). But the governors have no control over the appointment of a school's *meals staff* where no allowance is made for preparation of meals in the school's budget share (para 10).

Voluntary aided schools: The above procedures, laid down in Sch 3, do not apply to voluntary aided schools. Instead, provisions laid down in ERA 1988 s 45 apply, superseding those arrangements contained in the school's articles under EA 1944 s 24(2). The articles must be amended to contain a statement to that effect within five years of the start of financial delegation at the school (s 45(11)). The governors have full powers over appointment of staff. The chief education officer may give advice on staff appointments (as under Sch 3 above) if either a voluntary agreement (in writing: s 45(7)) has been struck by the governors with the LEA concerning advisory rights or if the Secretary of State orders that the officer should enjoy such rights (s 45(4) and (6)). Such advice may, *inter alia*, be in respect of the appointment of head teachers and deputy head teachers alone, or of all teachers at the school (s 45(5)).

Community schools: The financial delegation staffing rules in ss 44 and 45 and Sch 3 (all of which were outlined above) may apply to persons employed to work at any "community schools" which are maintained schools of the type to which financial delegation may apply (s 47(1)). A "community school" is one where (a) non-school activities are carried on on the school premises, and (b) all such non-school activities are carried on under the managing control of the school's governing body (s 47(2)). A delegation scheme may, for the purposes of these staffing rules, treat positions involving work solely or partly for the purposes of non-school activities carried out on the school premises as though such activities were school activities (s 47(3)), thus enabling the staffing provisions to apply.

5. Discipline and dismissal of staff

As is the case with appointments, different arrangements concerning discipline and dismissal of staff apply to schools once they have delegated budgets. The shift towards even greater control by governing bodies over appointments (see above) has occurred with equal intensity in relation to discipline and dismissal. The most remarkable of the changes is the power of governing bodies of county, controlled or special agreement schools to require LEAs to dismiss individual members of staff. This has removed a cause of conflict between LEAs and governors, which was highlighted in the *Honeyford* and *McGoldrick* cases in 1986 (discussed below, see page 130).

Note that the Sex Discrimination Act 1975 and Race Relations Act 1976, discussed above in relation to appointment of staff, outlaw discrimination when dismissing employees or subjecting them to "some other detriment". The scope of this is somewhat limited, as *De Souza* v *Automobile Association* (1986) illustrates. Here an employee referred to a black colleague in a racially insulting manner. Despite the

Teachers and other staff

obvious offence caused to the woman concerned, the Employment Appeal Tribunal held that the words "or other detriment" had to be taken to refer to a detriment of a type similar to dismissal. In the tribunal's opinion, the insult was not of this category. It is clear, however, that sexual (or racial) harassment can amount to "other detriment" (*Porcelli* v *Strathclyde Council* (1985); *Snowball* v *Gardner Merchant Ltd* (1987)). The role of industrial tribunals, to whom complaints may be directed, was discussed earlier in relation to appointments (see page 73). For the purposes of relevant parts of the Sex Discrimination Act 1975 and Race Relations Act 1976, the governing body is the employer following financial delegation (Education (Modification of Enactments Relating to Employment) Order 1989, arts 2(2) and 3(1)).

(a) Schools without delegated budgets

County, controlled, and special agreement schools are required to incorporate the provisions of s 41 E(No 2)A 1986 into their articles of government (see DES Circular 7/87 Annexes 5–7 for *Model Articles*). The section applies to staff employed in a post which forms part of the "complement" of the school (as defined in s 34—see page 73) and to staff employed to work solely at the school in any other post, apart from one involving only the provision of meals or midday supervision of pupils (s 41(3)).

The power of dismissal rests with the LEA as employer. But under the section, the LEA must consult the head teacher (except where s/he is the person concerned) and governors before dismissing a member of staff (other than a reserve teacher at a controlled or special agreement school—who can be dismissed by the foundation governors (EA 1944 s 27(5) and 28(4))). Such consultation is also required where the LEA requires a person to cease to work at the school or allows a person to qualify for premature retirement compensation by taking early retirement (E(No 2)A 1986 s 41(1)(a)).

The governing body is entitled to recommend that a person should cease to work at a school. In such a case the LEA must consider the governors' recommendation (s 41(1)(c)). There is also a power, resting with the governors and the head teacher, to suspend (without loss of pay) a teacher or other member of staff employed to work at the school (s 41(1)(d) and (2)). The head teacher or governors (as the case may be) must be notified by the party suspending the member of staff, and so must the LEA (s 41(1)(e)).

Disciplinary and grievance procedures are generally drawn up by the LEA in consultation with trade unions.

(b) Schools with delegated budgets

Suspension and dismissal of staff working at *county, controlled* and *special agreement schools* with delegated budgets are governed by ERA 1988 Sch 3 (ERA s 44(3)). The requirement to amend the articles within five years of the start of financial delegation, to incorporate the Sch 3 provisions (above), applies also to such matters (s 44(4)). The only earlier provisions which remain operative are those giving foundation governors of controlled or special agreement schools the right (under EA 1944 ss 27(5) and 28(4)) to insist on the dismissal of unsatisfactory reserve teachers (s 44(5)).

So far as discipline is concerned, the position is that:

> "The regulation of conduct and discipline in relation to the staff . . . and any procedures for affording to members of the staff opportunities for seeking redress of any grievances relating to their employment, shall be under the control of the governing body" (ERA 1988 Sch 3 para 6(1)).

The governing body is required to establish disciplinary rules and procedures and grievance procedures and take steps to make them known to staff at the school (para 6(2)). The Circular warns that this is "a sensitive area of industrial relations" and advises governing bodies to take account of existing *good* practice by LEAs (7/88 para 165). If the governing body is not empowered by the Schedule to take the particular measures which it considers are necessary in the particular case, it may request the LEA to exercise its powers, and the LEA must comply (para 6(3)). The governors and head teacher will continue to enjoy the power to suspend a member of staff (without loss of pay) (para 7(1)), as previously enjoyed under the 1986 Act. As before, they must inform each other of any decision to suspend (para 7(2)). In schools without delegated budgets, the governors or head teacher must end the suspension of a member of staff when required to do so by the LEA (E(No 2)A 1986 s 41(1)(e)); but in schools with delegated budgets a suspension may be ended only by the governing body (ERA 1988 Sch 3 para 7(3)). (The governors must immediately inform the head teacher and LEA of their decision (*ibid*).)

The power to order the dismissal of a member of staff (or the clerk to the governing body) rests almost exclusively with the governing body, although the LEA must be informed of its decision (paras 8(1) and (6) and 9). A person employed to work solely at the school concerned must be given an opportunity to resign; if s/he does not do so, then within fourteen days of being notified of the governors' decision the LEA must terminate his/her contract of employment—if entitled by law to do so (para 8(2)). If the person concerned is not employed to work solely at the school, the LEA must take him/her away from the school in question, whereupon the cost of his/her salary shall cease to be included in the school's budget share (para 8(3), (4) and (5)). A person threatened with dismissal must be given an opportunity to make representations (orally, if s/he wishes) and to appeal against the decision; the governors are required to make appropriate arrangements (para 8(7) and (8)). The chief education officer (or his/her nominee) and, unless it is s/he who is threatened with dismissal, the head teacher, are entitled to attend in an advisory capacity any meeting or hearing at any stage of the dismissal process under paragraph 8 (para 8(9)).

Note that the LEA may dismiss only on the grounds of failure by the teacher to satisfy prescribed standards of health, physical capacity, qualifications etc (para 9(2)).

In *aided* schools with delegated budgets, the power to suspend or dismiss rests with the governing body (ERA 1988 s 45(3)). If they decide to dismiss a member of staff, the governors must notify the LEA of their decision in writing (s 45(9)). If the governors agree with the LEA that the chief education officer shall enjoy advisory rights, or if the Secretary of State requires such rights to be conferred, the chief education officer may attend any meeting and give advice on the suspension or dismissal of a teacher. Advisory rights may be limited to dismissals of certain grades of personnel (eg head and deputy head teachers) (s 45(4)–(8)). Where the member of staff who is to be suspended or dismissed is employed by the LEA, the provisions of ERA 1988 Sch 3 paras 8 and 9, outlined above, apply (s 45(10)). Within five years of the school receiving a delegated budget, the articles of government must be amended to include a statement that the above provisions are applicable while the school has such a budget (s 45(11)).

(c) Period of notice to terminate employment

The statutory minimum period of notice, laid down in the Employment Protection (Consolidation) Act 1978 ("EPCA 1978") s 49, is one week for a person with one month to two years' service, plus one further week for each further completed year of service up to twelve years. Twelve weeks is therefore the maximum notice that need be given. Where teachers are concerned, the usual requirement is for two months' or one half term's notice—or longer if the appointment is to end at the end of August.

(d) Unfair dismissal and redundancy

When exercising the power of dismissal, governors and LEAs should bear in mind the provisions of EPCA 1978 concerning unfair dismissal. This is distinguishable from "wrongful dismissal", which refers to summary dismissal without notice in breach of the employment contract—for which damages may be obtained at common law. (The employee is entitled to a written statement of his/her terms and conditions of employment if s/he requests one within thirteen weeks of commencing employment with the employer (EPCA 1978 s 1). The written "contract of employment" may refer to terms contained in other documents, such as the letter offering the post. The teacher's responsibilities will not need to be spelt out because they are prescribed under the Teacher's Pay and Conditions Document—see below.)

Dismissal occurs where an employer terminates an employee's contract of employment, or fails to renew a fixed term contract, or where an employee resigns because of the employer's conduct which amounts to a repudiation of the contract of employment. This last type of dismissal is known as "constructive dismissal".

Unfair dismissal is a complex area and warrants considerably more space than this book can provide. Moreover, oversimplification could be potentially misleading. Consequently it is desirable to limit discussion to a few basic principles which may assist in identifying possible cases of unfair dismissal.

An important point to note here is that for the purposes of unfair dismissal and by virtue of the Education (Modification of Enactments Relating to Employment) Order 1989, the employer is, following financial delegation, always the governing body (art 4(b)). But any award made by an industrial tribunal against an "employer" is treated as made against the LEA, not the governors. In other words, the position seems to be that if the governors unfairly sack an employee, the LEA must foot the bill! However, in the arrangements concerning financial delegation spelt out in DES Circular 7/88, LEAs are advised that they could withhold from a school's budget share the cost of any dismissal which the LEA considered was "likely to be found unfair before an Industrial Tribunal" (para 167).

It should be noted that rights in respect of redundancy and unfair dismissal apply only to staff with at least two years' continuous service with the LEA or governors or with them and other LEAs or governors (EPCA 1978 Sch 13 para 18A —if a school becomes grant maintained, continuity is preserved: ERA 1988 s 75(6) and (7)). Breaks between successive fixed term *temporary contracts*, such as are used quite often by LEAs, could be construed as temporary cessations of work which would not break continuity of employment (*Ford* v *Warwickshire County Council* (1983)). A period of maternity leave (see below) will not break continuity of employment.

Moreover, if the employee is to qualify for statutory protection and redundancy pay, the employee must have been employed for at least sixteen hours a week, or for at least eight hours if the employment has continued for five years or more. An employee cannot, for this purpose, add together the hours worked under separate employment contracts with the same employer if they truly are separate (*Surrey County Council* v *Lewis* (1987)—a teacher of photography was employed by the LEA on a series of part-time and temporary contracts over a fourteen year period. She taught on three courses and had a separate contract for each. In 1983 she was not offered contracts and claimed to have been dismissed and entitled to redundancy pay or compensation for unfair dismissal. Her aggregated hours per week exceeded eight, but her hours under the individual contracts were less than six in each case. The House of Lords found that as the contracts were entirely separate from and independent of each other, and thus did not form part of a composite whole, she was not working under *a contract* for the requisite hours per week to qualify under the Act. However, the court left the door open to an industrial tribunal to find, "if the facts fitted", that "even though there were separate contracts, there was also . . . an [implied] 'umbrella contract' of employment under which the minimum hours requirements were satisfied" (*per* Lord Ackner at 653).).

For dismissal not to be classifiable as unfair, the employer must show that it was for one or more of the reasons set out in EPCA 1978 s 57:

(i) The employee's capabilities or qualification for the post for which s/he is employed. "Capability" here refers to skill, aptitude, health or other physical or mental quality. The question of whether a teacher with HIV/AIDS could be fairly dismissed on health grounds remains to be resolved. Lying about one's qualifications to the employer could amount to "some other substantial reason" which justifies dismissal (see (v) below).

(ii) The employee's conduct, in work (eg persistent and unjustified lateness or absenteeism, assault of pupils, sexual harassment of member of staff) or outside—if capable of prejudicing the employer's business (eg (a) *Gardiner* v *Newport County Borough Council* (1974)—art college teacher's gross indecency with another man in a public convenience so regarded; see also *Wiseman* v *Salford CC* (1981); (b) *Tabor* v *Mid-Glamorgan CC* (1982)—teacher of teenagers allowed others to grow cannabis in his garden and was convicted of possession of the drug. Even though he did not use cannabis, his dismissal was regarded as fair (cf

Norfolk County Council v *Bernard* (1979)); (c) *Vogler* v *Hertfordshire County Council* (1975)—teacher had sexual intercourse with sixteen year old pupil. His dismissal was fair).

(iii) The employee is redundant. Redundancy occurs where a dismissal is attributable wholly or mainly to either one of two factors:

(a) that the employer has "ceased or intends to cease, carrying on the business for which the employee was employed by him, or. . . to carry on that business in the place where the employee was so employed" (s 81(2)(a)); or
(b) "that the requirements of that business for employees to carry out work of a particular kind in the place where he was so employed, have ceased or diminished, or are expected to cease or diminish" (s 81(2)(b)).

If the employee unreasonably refuses an offer of suitable alternative work from the employer, s/he will not be redundant and so will qualify for no redundancy payment regardless of length of service (eg *Taylor* v *Kent County Council* (1969)). No redundancy payment is required where the employee is a man aged sixty-five or over or a woman aged sixty or over (s 82).

A case which illustrates some of these issues is *Murphy* v *Epsom College* (1985). The college, which already employed one plumber to help run the boiler and carry out plumbing work, employed a second (M). The boilers were modified but caused a good deal of trouble, and eventually the college decided to hire a heating engineer and retain only one of its two plumbers. M was dismissed. He claimed that his dismissal was unfair. The employers argued successfully that he was redundant, because of a change in the requirements of the business for work of M's kind. A heating engineer was needed for the new system and could assist with the plumbing too.

Consultation and notice (in some cases to the Secretary of State) concerning proposed redundancies are required under both statute and national agreement.

(iv) The employee could not continue to be employed without the employer breaking the law (eg the employee is employed as a driver but has been disqualified from driving).

(v) There is some other substantial reason justifying an employee's dismissal. For example, in *Saunders v Scottish National Camps* (1980) the Employment Appeal Tribunal held as fair a dismissal on this ground where the employee had been dismissed from his job as a maintenance handyman in a children's camp when it was discovered he was homosexual—even though he was not a danger to children nor worked in close proximity to them. Note that dismissal of a member of staff appointed to cover an employee's temporary absence due to pregnancy or "medical suspension" falls within dismissal for the purposes of "some other substantial reason" (EPCA 1978 s 61).

If the employer can prove that one of (i)–(v) above applies, the dismissal will be fair provided that s/he acted reasonably in the circumstances (having regard to the size of the employer's business and its administrative resources) in treating the reason as sufficient to warrant dismissal (EPCA 1978 s 57(3)). The question of whether or not the employer did act reasonably is to be determined "in accordance with equity and the substantial merits of the case" (*ibid*).

If a tribunal finds that dismissal was unfair, it may award compensation and/or (although rarely ordered) re-engagement or re-instatement. Compensation may consist of a "basic award" (s 73), which is calculated in exactly the same way as statutory redundancy pay and takes into account the employee's age, length of service and rate of pay on dismissal (subject to a statutory maximum, currently £172). There may also be a "compensatory award" (s 74) of an amount up to a prescribed maximum, currently £8,925. (Extremely generous compensation (under a special award) can be awarded if the employee is dismissed for belonging to, or refusing to join, a trades union.) Both compensatory and basic awards can be reduced on the grounds of the employee's conduct.

An order for compensation for unfair dismissal is against the LEA (see page 85). Similarly, the LEA must pay redundancy payments where they are due. (Employers can no longer, except where firms with fewer than ten employees are concerned, claim a rebate from the government: Wages Act 1986 s 28.)

(e) Pregnancy/maternity

An employee may not lawfully be dismissed on the grounds of pregnancy unless her pregnancy means that she would not be capable of carrying out her duties adequately or, even if she could, her employment would be in breach of another statutory provision (eg prohibiting expectant mothers from working with radioactive substances) (EPCA s 60). Before the employer can dismiss on this basis, however, the employee must have been offered any suitable alternative work which is available and must have unreasonably turned it down.

The employee can take her statutory maternity leave without fear of being dismissed (otherwise than unfairly) for being absent from work due to pregnancy or caring for her baby. Under the statutory maternity leave provisions (see EPCA 1978 ss 33, 45–48 and Sch 2), the employee may be absent for a period of up to twenty-nine weeks after the birth (and a further four weeks on certain grounds, eg illness—s 47) and eleven weeks before the expected week of confinement (or less if she so elects—see *ILEA* v *Nash* (1979)), and has a right to return to work, although not necessarily to the same post, thereafter. The employee must, however, give three weeks' written notice of her return. The employer may postpone her return for up to four weeks if s/he gives her reasons. The employment made available on the employee's return need not be in the same post. If the job is no longer available, the employer is (unless he employs five or fewer employees) required to offer a suitable alternative, and if this is turned down dismissal would not be unfair (s 56A). On her return, the employee must be offered work of a similar nature which she is capable of doing and which is in the same place (see s 153(1)). (Note that in some circumstances a refusal to allow a full-time employee who has been on maternity leave to return on a part-time basis could amount to unlawful indirect sex discrimination: *Home Office* v *Holmes* (1984); cf *Kidd* v *DRG (UK) Ltd* (1985).)

An employee qualifies for the right to return only if no more than eleven weeks before the expected week of confinement, she has been continuously employed (see above) for at least two years and gives notice (at least twenty-one days, unless impracticable) to her employer that she will be absent due to pregnancy and wishes to return. Note that the employee may be required by her employer to confirm that it is her intention to return to work at the end of her leave. Seven weeks after the birth, the employer may demand an answer to this question from the employee, who has two weeks in which to reply (s 33(3A)).

(Note: section 35 used to give an employee who qualified for the right to return the right to *maternity pay*, whether or not she intended to return. It was paid for six weeks at the rate of ninety per cent of a week's earnings minus state maternity allowance. Payment fell due from the beginning of the eleventh week before the expected week of confinement or later if the start of leave was delayed by the employee. Now the employee must claim statutory maternity pay under the Social Security Act 1986 (Part V and Sch 4). For the first six weeks this is paid at the higher rate of nine-tenths of the woman's normal weekly earnings (s 48(2)), broadly the same amount as would have been available under the previous system.)

These rights are additional to any maternity rights available to the employee under the terms of her contract of employment. If there is any overlap or conflict between the rights under the contract and those in the statute, the employee may choose whichever she considers are the more favourable (EPCA 1978 s 48; see *Bovey* v *Board of Governors of the Hospital for Sick Children* (1978)).

6. School teachers' pay and conditions

The system of free collective bargaining through which teachers' pay and conditions in state schools were determined before 1987 was replaced in that year. Parliament replaced the Remuneration of Teachers Acts and the Burnham Committee forum for the negotiation of pay and conditions with a system through which the Secretary of State can impose a pay award on teachers. Under the Teachers' Pay and Conditions Act 1987 the Secretary of State gives legal effect to teachers' pay and conditions by Order (s 3). Although the Secretary of State receives advice from an Interim Advisory Committee of between five and nine persons with knowledge of or experience in education,

Teachers and other staff

and despite a statutory consultation process in which LEAs, teacher unions, governors' organisations and others may make representations, at the end of the day the Secretary of State may determine these matters as he thinks fit.

The method of calculating pay, the rates and scales of remuneration and the conditions of employment (including professional duties of head teachers, deputy head teachers and others) are, at the time of going to press, set out in the *Teachers' Pay and Conditions Document 1989,* which is given legal effect by the Education (School Teachers' Pay and Conditions) Order 1989 (as amended by SI 1989 No 1453). The 1989 Document will be replaced by the 1990 Document with effect from 1 April 1990 (see below). The 1989 Document applies to all schools maintained by LEAs and grant maintained schools (para 1(1) and ERA 1988 Sch 12 para 38). The 1990 Document was not available at the time of going to press, but the government accepted the Interim Advisory Committee's recommendations (*Third Report of the Interim Advisory Committee on Teachers' Pay and Conditions,* Cm 973, January 1990) in full. Paragraph and Appendix references below refer to the 1989 Document. Changes applicable from 1 April 1990, or 1 January 1991, are noted in appropriate places.

(a) Pay

"The relevant body": Although there are prescribed scales of remuneration, various matters, such as the distribution of incentive allowances and the determination of certain duties, fall to be decided by the "relevant body", which is: in the case of a school without a delegated budget, the maintaining authority; in the case of a grant-maintained school or a school with a delegated budget, the governors (para 1(1)).

Unit total and group: The determination of head teachers' and deputy head teachers' pay is by reference to the size of the school (or its "group"), as under previous arrangements. In schools other than special schools, unit totals (para 3) are calculated with reference to the numbers and ages of pupils at the school (Appendix I Part A (ordinary schools) and Part B (special schools)). For example, each pupil aged under fourteen counts as two units and each pupil aged fifteen counts as five units. (Pupils with special educational needs can count as more—see Appendix I para 3(3).) The grouping of the school is determined by reference to the unit total (Appendix I paras 2, 3 and Annex A) or, where the unit total is expected to rise, possibly the expected total (Appendix I para 3(5)). In special schools the group (designations start at group 3(S) and rise to 10(S)) is determined, *inter alia*, with reference to the number of children shown on Form 7M or Welsh Office Form STATS 1 and the number of staff (Annex B).

In schools other than special schools there are presently fourteen groups. From 1 January 1991 there will be a single forty-nine point pay spine for heads *and* deputy heads, and just six school groups.

Head teachers: The 1989 Document sets out a fourteen point scale for head teachers' pay, ranging from £17,370–£34,179, or £19,050–£29,136 in the case of special schools (para 4(1)). From 1 April 1990 the range will be £18,588–£36,573 (and £20,385–£31,176 in the case of special schools). The relevant body can determine a higher rate than that dictated according to the appropriate grouping, if it considers that "the salary payable . . . is not adequate having regard to [the head's] duties and responsibilities or the circumstances of the school" (para 4(2)). (As noted above, from 1 April 1990 there will be a forty-nine point pay spine applying to heads *and* deputy heads.) Head teachers' salaries are protected against reduction if the schools at which they are employed become assigned to a lower group (Appendix I paras 4(1) and 7(1)).

Deputy head teachers: The grouping of the school will also determine the number of persons who may be *paid* as deputy head teachers at the school (Appendix I paras 4(2) and 7(2), Annex A and Annex B Table 1).

Deputy head teachers' salaries are similarly protected against reductions (Appendix I paras 4(3) and 7(3)). The relevant body may award a salary in excess of that determined by the pay scale (in para 5(1)) in the same situation as for head teachers (para 5(2)).

Other qualified teachers: The pre-1987 "scales" were replaced by a single scale (the "main scale") with eleven points under which the salary in 1989–90 ranged from £8,394–£14,694 (para 6(1)). (From 1 April 1990, this scale is to be known as the "standard national scale" and it will range from exactly £9,000–£15,723. From 1 January 1991 the range will be £9,000–£16,000, although local scales may be set, with a maximum of £18,000.) A qualified teacher is generally to enter the main scale at point 2 if s/he is a graduate and point 1 if s/he is not. A "good honours graduate" is entitled to start on point 4. A graduate for this purpose is a graduate of a UK or Eire university with a third class honours degree or a degree which was not awarded with honours, or an equivalent qualification (Appendix II para 1(7)). A good honours graduate is one holding a first or second class degree or a higher degree, or the equivalent of one of these (*ibid*). Provision is made for placing an entrant who is aged twenty-three or over on a higher incremental point, at the discretion of the relevant body (Appendix II para 1(2)), and for determining the salary of a teacher taking up a new appointment or re-entering teaching after a break in service (*ibid*, para 1(3)).

The relevant body also has the power to award a qualifying teacher who is taking up employment in a school in an "urban area" up to two extra increments if it considers it appropriate, having regard to various economic, social and environmental factors relating to the school (*ibid*, para 1(4)). Regard should be had to:

- (i) the difficulties of recruiting and retaining teachers to serve in the school;
- (ii) the social and economic status of the parents of children in the school;
- (iii) the absence of amenities in the homes of children attending the school;
- (iv) the proportion of children in the school belonging to families receiving income support (this can be determined with reference to the numbers of children entitled to free school meals);
- (v) the proportion of children in the school who were born outside the UK, Eire, Australia, Canada, New Zealand, or the USA, or whose head of household was born outside those countries.

A deputy head or head teacher who takes up a new full-time post on the main scale is entitled to be paid on point 11, the top of the scale (*ibid*, para 1(5)).

In most cases a teacher can expect to receive an increment from 1 September for each completed year's continuous full-time service (Appendix II para 4(1)) or its part-time equivalent (*ibid*, para 4(3)). Those teachers completing, before 1 September, six months' full-time (or equivalent) service after their appointment are entitled to an increment from that date (*ibid*, para 4(2)). A teacher who has been absent under the right to return maternity provisions of the EPCA 1978 (see above, page 89) is entitled to have the period of absence treated as teaching service for incremental purposes (*ibid*, para 4(5)). The relevant body may withhold an increment from a teacher "if they are of the opinion that [his/her] service in the year preceding 1 September is unsatisfactory and they have so notified him in writing" (*ibid*, para 4(6)). The increment that has been withheld can be paid to the teacher concerned at a later date in addition to any further increment due at that time (*ibid*).

From 1 April 1990 the relevant body will be entitled to pay additional amounts to teachers, on top of increments. Depending on which scale point a teacher is on, s/he could be paid an extra £250 or £500 (points 1–4), £250, £500 or £750 (points 5–8), or any multiple of £250 up to £1, 000 (points 9 or 10). The Interim Advisory Committee urges that individual salary enhancement is reviewed each September.

There are various additional allowances for certain teachers:

    (i) teachers of visually or hearing impaired pupils;
    (ii) teachers who were in receipt of social priority school allowances—paid under *Teachers' Pay and Conditions Document 1988* para 17, but not paid to those taking up employment after 31 July 1988—and who are still working at the same school;
    (iii) those teaching in the London area; and
    (iv) those who are acting deputy or head teachers (1989 Document Part V).

Teachers in London are entitled to the following *London weighting allowances* (applicable from 1 July 1989):

Inner London	£1, 500
Outer London	£ 984
Fringe	£ 384

In addition, from 1 April 1990 there is a London supplement of £750 payable to teachers in the Inner London weighting area, at the discretion of LEAs and governing bodies. This new payment is a response to the shortage of teachers in London. The allowance may be paid to around half the teachers in Inner London (see *Times Educational Supplement,* 9 February 1990, page A10).

For most teachers the allowances which will be particularly prized, because in many cases they represent career progression, will be the *incentive allowances*. (From 1 September 1990 there will, nationally, be 14, 400 additional incentive allowances available for allocation.) There are five rates of allowance (A–E):

	1989–90	1.4.90	1.1.91
A	£ 858	£ 925	£ 925
B	£1,284	£1,389	£1,500
C	£2,568	£2,775	£3,000
D	£3,426	£3,702	£4,000
E	£4,710	£5,088	£5,500

These allowances reflect responsibility attached to a particular teacher's role within a school. But they also have a broader purpose—in enabling those with special skills (eg for teaching pupils with special educational needs) or outstanding ability as a classroom teacher to be appropriately rewarded. They may also be used to attract those with specialisms which are in short supply or where the post is difficult to fill. Apart from teachers in special schools or teachers of pupils in special needs classes in ordinary schools, who in both cases must be awarded not less than allowance B (para 7(3)), the relevant body is free to allocate incentive allowances as it thinks fit (para 7(2)). However, they are subject to the constraints imposed by Appendix I paras 5 and 8 and Annexes A and B as to the minimum and maximum percentages of teachers at the particular school who may be awarded an allowance at each of the five rates and as to the consequent total number of teachers who may be awarded incentive allowances at the school. These percentages were increased in 1989. Taking a group 7 school (non-special) as an example, the school is entitled to give incentive allowances to between 50 and 60 per cent of its teachers. Between 8 and 20 per cent of all teachers at the school should receive allowance B.

Head and deputy head teacher(s) are not entitled to incentive allowances (para 7(6)) but are counted as though in receipt of them for the purposes of calculating the percentage limits above (Appendix I para 5(2)).

In some circumstances a higher or lower proportion of teachers at a school may be awarded incentive allowances (apart from allowance A). (In special schools, only the individual limits for allowances C, D and E may be exceeded.) The relevant body must be of the opinion that "the staffing and organisational needs of the school cannot be met by the payment of allowances within the prescribed limits . . ." (*ibid*, paras 5(5) and 8(4)). Where schools which are not special schools are concerned, the relevant body, in forming this opinion, should have regard to whether the school is a secondary school in a group below group 9 or a sixth form college. It should also have regard to those factors justifying additional increments to teachers in schools in urban areas (see (i)–(v) above) (*ibid*). In some groups of school no allowances at certain rates above B are required (eg a group 7 school is not required to give any D or E allowances) but they may be paid in exceptional prescribed circumstances (Appendix I para 5(6)).

If the school's entitlement to incentive allowances declines because of a reduction in its teaching establishment and, as a result, it has more teachers on allowances (or particular allowances) than its limit, all allowances actually in payment shall continue to be paid to those concerned—until they leave the school (or are promoted to deputy head or head teacher) (*ibid*, para 5(7)). This provision is additional to that safeguarding teachers' salaries where schools close or are reorganised (see para 21).

The salaries of teachers not attached to a particular school are to be determined in accordance with any of the provisions of the Document that the LEA considers appropriate (para 20).

Unqualified teachers: In some cases unqualified teachers are entitled to the same remuneration as if they were qualified teachers: for example, if they are head or deputy head teachers or if they hold certain prescribed diplomas relating to the teaching of the mentally handicapped (see paras 12–14).

When s/he is notified that s/he has qualified, an unqualified teacher who is in post may be entitled to a lump sum based on the difference between his/her actual salary and what it would have been as a qualified teacher, over not more than the previous twelve months (see para 15).

Depending on the particular provision under which their employment is authorised, unqualified teachers are entitled to be paid on one of five scales U1–U5. Only U5 has incremental points (1–10). The entry point is determined in accordance with what the relevant body considers appropriate having regard to the teacher's qualifications and experience, but the salary may not exceed that which would be paid to a qualified teacher of the same age and with equivalent academic qualifications (Appendix II para 2). No provision is made for incentive allowances, but there are allowances of prescribed amounts for teachers in special schools, those engaged wholly or mainly in charge of hearing or visually impaired pupils in ordinary schools (para 9(1)), and, at the discretion of the relevant body, those mainly responsible for teaching pupils with special educational needs in ordinary schools (para 9(2)). There is also a discretion to pay certain unqualified teachers (those on scales U3–U5) such additional allowances as the relevant body regards appropriate "where they consider that [the teacher's] salary is not adequate having regard to his responsibilities or to any qualifications or experience relevant to his specialised form of teaching" (para 11).

The Teachers' Pay and Conditions Document was amended (SI 1989 No 1453) to take account of the licensed teacher scheme (see pages 66–69).

Supply teachers: From 1 January 1991 supply teachers are to receive remuneration at a rate which is equivalent to that which a full-time or regular member of staff would receive. The Interim Advisory Committee expressed concern about the reductions by some LEAs in the rates of pay for supply staff in 1989.

(b) Conditions

The precise scope of teachers' professional duties was always unclear. Some aspects, such as lunch-time supervision, were highly contentious. One work written before the Teachers' Pay and Conditions Act 1987 notes that "In over a century of public education, there has been no agreement between LEAs and their teacher employees on what teachers are required to do in order to earn their salaries" (D Nice (ed), *Education and the law* (1986), page 136). Often teachers argued that certain activities, such as those taking place outside school hours, were voluntary, while their employers argued that they were contractual. Now these duties are spelt out in detail in the Teachers' Pay and Conditions Document. While there may still be argument over matters of interpretation, the scope of teachers' duties and the extent of their (paid) working time are generally clear. In some cases, the precise duties to be performed by main standard scale and deputy head teachers will depend in part on the particular duties from time to time assigned to them by the head teacher (para 34(1)).

The 1989 Document sets out the conditions (likely to be virtually the same in the 1990 Document) as follows (reference via paras 25 and 26):

- Conditions of employment of head teachers (Part VIII);
- Conditions of employment of deputy head teachers (Parts IX and X (paras 33–35 only));
- Conditions of employment of other school teachers (Part X).

These conditions are set out in full in Appendix 3.

Various matters, such as a teacher's timetable, class contact time, entitlement to travel expenses and sick leave arrangements, will continue to be determined locally—either by LEA-wide or school-based negotiation. While "consultation" has largely superseded "negotiation" over teachers' conditions (which produced the *Burgundy Book* spelling out teachers' conditions of service), there is still scope for national agreement.

7. Pay and conditions of non-teaching staff

Pay and conditions for non-teaching staff employed by local authorities are almost entirely determined via collective bargaining and national agreement between employers and unions. Local authority services tend to be heavily unionised —the major unions being the National Association of Local Government Officers (representing administrative and clerical staff such as school secretaries but also education welfare officers and social workers), the National Union of Public Employees and the General, Municipal and Boilermakers' Union (which represent school caretakers, delivery drivers, school meals staff and others). Reference should be made to the various "books", such as the Purple Book governing town hall workers' pay and conditions. Local agreement, on various matters such as manning levels, overtime, supervision and other work arrangements also plays a role.

But local financial management and grant-maintained status may produce changes in the way that new non-school staff are employed.

(a) Local financial management

So far as pay and conditions are concerned, the position of administrative, professional, technical and clerical (APTC) staff and manual workers following financial delegation is explained in DES Circular 7/88 para 163 as follows:

> "Pay and conditions of non-teaching staff will continue to be on a non-statutory basis. For new non-teaching staff, the governing body will be able to specify the duties to be performed and the appropriate grade within the scale of grades currently applicable to employment with the LEA. In most cases these grades will be those resulting from. . . national agreements. . . It will be for the governing body to select the grade that it considers appropriate for the post. The governing body will also be able to exercise any discretion over remuneration which the LEA has in making the appointment. An example would be the point of entry to a scale for APTC staff. Other conditions of service will be for the LEA and will usually be those which are defined in the relevant collective agreement. . ."

So far as appointments are concerned, the LEA will make the appointment but selection will be made by the governing body. When making the appointment the LEA will have to take account of national and local collective agreements, except where they conflict with the legal powers enjoyed by the governors. For example, governors are responsible for disciplinary procedures (ERA 1988 Sch 3 para 6). (See further DES Circular 7/88, para 164).

(b) Non-teaching staff at grant-maintained schools

When a school becomes grant-maintained, all employed to work wholly at the school are transferred to the employ of the governing body. In some cases staff who work only partly at the school will also be transferred (DES Circular 10/88, para 49). Transfer of staff on acquisition of GM status was discussed above (see page 18). The governors will have the rights, powers, duties and liabilities of the former employer. It would appear, therefore, that existing arrangements under national or collective bargaining agreements will have to continue in relation to transferred staff. So far as new non-teaching staff are concerned, "pay and conditions. . . will be agreed between those staff and the governing body" (*ibid*, para 52). Any differentials in the pay and conditions of transferred as against new staff would undoubtedly be a cause of friction, and governors would be well advised to continue with existing arrangements for so long as they feel able, and to conduct careful negotiations with all non-teaching staff if they seek changes.

8. Local education authority training grants and education support grant schemes

The government recognises that a considerable amount of in-service training is necessary if schools are going to be able to cope with the challenges imposed by the National Curriculum, local financial managment and other changes designed, as the government puts it, to improve the quality of education.

(a) The LEA training grants scheme

The LEA training grants scheme is the major scheme for funding the in-service training of teachers and other personnel. The scheme, which in its present form is designed to promote more systematic and purposeful planning of in-service training, enables the Secretary of State to determine to a considerable extent the disposition of training resources.

Through the scheme, central government resources are directed into training to meet national and local priorities, for which separate total sums are allocated (£122.3m and £92.4m respectively, in 1990–91). LEAs do not receive the total amount of expenditure on training. In 1990–91 they are to receive 65 per cent of eligible expenditure on training to meet national priorities and 50 per cent in respect of local priorities. LEAs may, subject to certain exceptions where the Secretary of State's permission is required, vire expenditure between the various national priority areas. They may also support their expenditure on national priorities from their grant for local priorities—but not vice versa (see DES Circular 20/89, para 13).

The scheme covers: training or further training of unqualified or qualified teachers as teachers or as youth and community workers, educational psychologists, LEA inspectors or education advisers; training or further training of youth and community workers, educational psychologists, LEA inspectors and education officers (the Education (Training Grants) Regulations 1987 (as amended by the Education (Training Grants) (Amendment) Regulations 1988 and 1989), reg 4). The training of "articled teachers" is now covered by reg 4.

The national priority areas for 1990–91 and the amount of expenditure which the grant will support in each LEA are set out in DES Circular 20/89, Annex B. The most support is allocated to "Basic curriculum and collective worship"—nearly half the overall total. Already teachers, pupils and parents have become familiar with the setting aside of non-contact days ("Baker days") for staff training covering preparation for the National Curriculum, records of achievement, and other aspects of the "new" curriculum. LEAs are expected to set aside two or three training days in the spring term of 1991 for assessing and recording achievements of pupils under the National Curriculum (DES Circular 20/89, Annex A). Other major areas include "Management", "Appraisal" (of school teachers), "Primary Maths", "Primary Science" and "New Technologies".

(b) The education support grants scheme

Under the education support grants scheme the Secretary of State provides an annual grant to LEAs to meet part of the cost of certain (prescribed) heads of expenditure (Education (Grants and Awards) Act 1984; Education (Grants and Awards) Regulations 1984, as amended). Up to 70 per cent of the cost of expenditure has been met under the scheme (generally 60 per cent from 1 April 1990), but only 50 per cent is available in certain cases (SIs 1988 No 2037 and 1989 No 2446). Under the 1989–90 education support grant allocation, the government made available, *inter alia*, £4.9m for governor training and £25m in respect of local financial management—to cover the introduction of management information systems into schools, the establishment of central LEA teams for LMS preparation and implementation, and training of school administrative staff. (For commentary on the role of the 1984 Act, see D Nice (ed) *Education and the law* (1986), pages 54–56.)

9. Appraisal schemes

Statutory machinery exists for the regular appraisal of the performance of teachers in the discharge of their duties (E(No 2)A 1986 s 49(1)). Appraisal wouldbe carried out by LEAs or other prescribed persons (*ibid*). Under regulations which would be made by the Secretary of State, governors could be obliged to ensure that appraisal arrangements are complied with and that LEAs receive proper assistance (s 49(3)). Provision may also be made for teachers to be informed of the results of an appraisal and to be given an opportunity to make representations. Appraisal regulations may apply to teachers at any maintained school (including one which is grant-maintained) and any non-maintained special school; they may also apply to unattached teachers employed by a LEA (*ibid*, and ERA 1988 Sch 12 para 36). Section 49 came into force on 7 January 1987; but no regulations have yet been made.

Chapter 3

School government

1. Introduction

School governing bodies have had their role changed dramatically under the education legislation of the 1980s. Under the Acts of 1980, 1986 and 1988, LEAs' powers and responsibilities with regard to the running of schools have been restricted. In many areas over which the LEA has traditionally, in the majority of schools, been autonomous, such as staff appointments, the school day, use of school premises, exclusion of pupils and, most significantly, expenditure, governing bodies have gained considerable sovereignty.

Of course, the LEAs continue to have an important if diminished role, but increasingly this will be played in partnership with governing bodies. Before education committees can make certain determinations or adopt policies of various types, they must consult governing bodies. Numerous examples appear in the various chapters of this book: they include a decision to order the re-instatement of a pupil excluded for a fixed period (E(No 2)A 1986 s 24(d)), appointment of a serving employee to a post at a school (*ibid* s 38(4)), the establishment of complaints procedures (ERA 1988 s 23(1)), and the preparation of a scheme of financial delegation (*ibid* s 34(4)).

By taking much of the decision-making away from LEAs, the government hoped, amongst other things, to reduce the influence of local party politics (especially those of the left) in education. But this object could not have been achieved had local councillors retained their full power on school governing bodies. So the government sought to dilute the influence of local authority governors by (i) a requirement that all school governing bodies should have parent governors (EA 1980 s 2(5)), (ii) a limitation in the number of schools at which a person could serve as a governor (currently four —Education (School Government) Regulations 1989 reg 5), and (iii) placing LEA members firmly in the minority on governing bodies (E(No 2)A 1986 ss 3 and 4).

With their role to be expanded considerably (the E(No 2)A 1986 (s 16(1)) states that the conduct of a school is to be "under the direction of the governing body"), it was clearly important for governing bodies to become more accountable. This was achieved through, *inter alia*, election of parent governors, a requirement that governors publish various matters (such as their policy on the secular curriculum), and through the establishment of a system of reporting and meetings—all of which aimed to provide a bridge between the school and the local community (especially parents).

The numerous functions of governing bodies, and their powers and duties, are discussed throughout this book and there is little point in trying to list them here. A summary can be found below, in the section dealing with delegation of functions (see page 124).

2. Instrument and articles of government

Every county, voluntary and maintained special school, is required by the E(No 2)A 1986 to have:

> "(a) an instrument providing for the constitution of a governing body of the school (to be known as the *instrument of government*); and
> (b) an instrument in accordance with which the school is to be conducted (to be known as the *articles of government*)" (E(No 2)A 1986 s 1(1)).

The *instrument of government* is to contain such matters as the size and composition of governing bodies and the procedures for electing members and filling vacancies (E(No 2)A 1986 s 1(3), referring to Part II of the Act). In grant-maintained schools, the instrument of government is to have a broader function. For example, it is to make provision for meetings and proceedings of governing bodies (ERA 1988 s 55(3)). In county, voluntary and maintained special schools, such provision is to be by way of regulations made by the Secretary of State (E(No 2)A 1986 s 8(6)). (See the Education (School Government) Regulations 1989, below.)

The *articles of government* are to be concerned with, amongst other things, the way that a school is to be conducted and the allocation of functions between governors, head teacher and LEA (and Secretary of State, where GM schools are concerned) (E(No 2)A 1986 s 1(4), and ERA 1988 s 58 (GM schools)). Also covered by the articles are responsibilities in relation to admissions, discipline, reports and meetings, and certain other matters.

The instrument and articles of government are to be made or altered by order of the LEA (s 1(2)) in accordance with the prescribed procedure (in s 2). (Note: this procedure will not be required to give effect to alterations consequent on financial delegation (see below).) Grant-maintained schools are also required to have instruments and articles of government made by order of the Secretary of State (ERA 1988 ss 53(1) and (2) and 58(1) and (2)).

The instrument and articles of government form part of the legal framework within which the school operates, and must contain no provision which is inconsistent with any enactment (E(No 2)A 1986 s 1(5)(a)). For example, the model articles of government for county schools made in pursuance of E(No 2)A 1986 (s 1(1)(b)), and set out in DES Circular 7/87, Annex 5, were required to contain various matters, including the statutory rules relating to the appointment and dismissal of staff (ss 36–41). But within five years of the start of financial delegation (see Chapter 1) the articles must be amended to show that during financial delegation the paragraphs dealing with staff appointments and dismissal are superseded by those contained in ERA 1988 s 44 and Sch 3 (ERA 1988 s 44(4)). Moreover, during financial delegation, any provisions of the articles which are inconsistent with those of a delegation scheme shall be of no effect (*ibid*, s 51(3)) and the articles must, within five years, be amended accordingly (s 51(4) and (5)).

Some schools also operate under a trust deed. The articles

and instrument of government must comply with any trust deed relating to the school (E(No 2)A 1986 s 1(5)(b); ERA 1988 ss 53(3) and 58(3) (GM schools)). Where there is an inconsistency between statutory requirements concerning instruments and articles and the terms of a trust deed, the Secretary of State may make modifications to the deed (E(No 2)A 1986 s 2(7)).

New instruments and articles had to be made to give effect to the important changes to the composition and functions of governing bodies which were introduced under E(No 2)A 1986. The new system has applied in county and maintained special schools since 1 September 1988 and in voluntary schools since 1 September 1989.

3. Composition of governing bodies

The Education Act 1980, in implementing a recommendation of the Taylor Committee (*A New Partnership for our Schools* (1977)) for greater parental representation on school governing bodies, required all schools to have parent governors, elected by secret ballot. A government Green Paper in 1984 proposed a parental majority on governing bodies (*Parental Influence at School*, Cmnd 9242, May 1984). The response to this was unfavourable, and the government opted instead for parity between parent and LEA representation (White Paper *Better Schools,* Cmnd 9469 March 1985).

The composition of a governing body is to be in accordance with E(No 2)A 1986 s 3 (county, controlled or maintained special schools) or s 4 (aided and special agreement schools) and should be stated, in relation to each school, in its instrument of government. Adjustment in the number of governors in any one or more categories may be necessary if there is an excess of governors in any such category (s 14). (Note: No one may at any time hold more than one governorship of the same county, voluntary or special agreement school: s 15(10).)

The rules governing eligibility are discussed below. It may be noted here that there is no requirement for pupil representation on school governing bodies. It is possible that a pupil could be co-opted; but s/he would have to be at least eighteen years old, for that is the minimum age at which a person may be appointed or elected a governor (s 15(14)).

(a) Grant-maintained schools

When it is proposed that a school is to become grant-maintained, an "initial governing body" must be assembled, whose role will be "to prepare it for the transition to its new status and to conduct it from the date of incorporation" (DES Circular 10/88, para 23). The composition of the "initial governing body" and its successors will basically be the same, but the initial body may contain elected parent or teacher governors who were on the governing body before the school decided to become GM, whose term of office had not expired, and who were willing to continue as governors. Where there are too many governors in these categories who are willing to continue, the matter may be decided by the drawing of lots (ERA 1988 s 66(3)). Where there are fewer than required, elections will be necessary (s 66(5)).

(b) Grouping

Subject in most cases to approval from the Secretary of State (E(No 2)A 1986 s 10), a LEA may resolve that two or more schools (excluding GM schools) be grouped for the purpose of school government (*ibid* s 9(1)). If schools are grouped, they are treated as one school (s 9(2)) as:

   (i) an aided or special agreement school if one or more of the schools is of one of these types; or
   (ii) a controlled school if one of them is of that type and none of the others are aided or special agreement; or
   (iii) a maintained special school if all of the schools are of this type and the others are all county schools; or
   (iv) in any other case, a county school (s 9(3)).

Where certain changes or alterations are proposed to any school in the group, the LEA must review the need for the grouping and, if it decides to continue with it, it must refer the matter to the Secretary of State (provided his consent to the grouping was required in the first place under s 10) (s 9(4) and (5)). A grouping may be ended by the Secretary

Composition of school governing bodies—county, controlled and maintained special schools (Education (No 2) Act 1986)

	Size of school (no of pupils)			
	Below 100	100–299	300–599	600 or more
Parents[a]	2	3	4	5
LEA[b]	2	3	4	5
Head teacher[c]	1	1	1	1
Teachers[d]	1	1	2	2
Co-opted[e]	3	4	5	6
[or, in controlled sch., foundation/co-opted[e]]	[2/1]	[3/1]	[4/1]	[4/2]
TOTAL	9	12	16	19

Notes

[a] Parent governors are to elected in accordance with arrangements laid down in s 15. LEAs must arrange for elections. Where an insufficient number of parents stand for election (or where at least 50 per cent of a schools' pupils are boarders and election would, in the opinion of the LEA, be impracticable), the governors are to *appoint* parents to the vacancies (s 5(1), (2) and (4)).

[b] These governors are appointed by the LEA. Some LEAs, eg Manchester, Barnet and Wandsworth, have apparently used their discretion over nomination of governors to remove opposition councillors from, or to refuse to appoint them to, school governing bodies. A private member's bill, aimed at ensuring that all political parties with elected councillors on a particular council are represented in LEA governor nominations, was presented in the Commons by Labour's Jack Straw in February 1990 but, at the time of going to press, appeared not to have government support (*The Times*, 8 February 1990).

[c] The head teacher can elect not to be a governor (ss 3(2)(d), (3)(d) and (5)(d)). If s/he chooses to be a governor, s/he is to be treated as an *ex-officio* governor (s 3(7)). Even if not a governor, s/he generally has a right to attend governors' meetings (Education (School Government) Regulations 1989 reg 11—below). Note that where a school has more than one head teacher, each of them may be a governor (s 15(1)).

[d] Teacher governors are elected by teachers from their own number (see s 15).

[e] It is the duty of the governors, when looking to co-opt any person to be a member of the governing body (otherwise than as a foundation governor), to ensure that the local business community is represented on the governing body (if it is not already) (s 6). In maintained special schools with less than 100 registered pupils, a co-opted governor may be appointed
by one voluntary organisation or two or more jointly (s 7). Two may be appointed if the school has 100 or more pupils. (On co-opting, see further DES Circular 7/87, paras 5.3.9–5.3.12.)

Composition of school governing bodies—aided and special agreement schools (Education (No 2) Act 1986)

	Size of school (no of pupils)	
	Below 300	300 or more
	at least . . .	
Parents[a]	1	1
LEA appointee	1	1
Teachers[b]	1	2
	plus . . .	
Head teacher[c]	1	1
Foundation governors[d]	6[e]	7[e]
TOTAL[e]	10 (plus)	12 (plus)

Notes

[a] To be elected in accordance with the arrangements laid down in s 15. Governing bodies are responsible for arranging the elections.

[b] Teacher governors to be elected from their own number (see 15).

[c] The head teacher may choose not to be a governor (s 4(2)(g)) but, whether or not s/he is one, will be counted as a governor for the purpose of calculating the number of foundation governors (s 4(4)) (see d below). Where the head teacher is a governor s/he is to be treated as an *ex-officio* governor (s 4(6)). If the school has more than one head teacher, each may be a governor (s 15(1)).

[d] At least one of the foundation governors is to be, at the time of his/her appointment, a parent of a pupil at the school (s 4(3)(b)).

[e] This is not a prescribed figure. The law states that the instrument of government shall provide for such number of foundation governors as will lead to their outnumbering the other governors (plus a head teacher non-governor) by two, or three if the total number of governors is nineteen or more (s 3(3)(a)).

Composition of school governing bodies—grant-maintained schools (Education Reform Act 1988)

Parents	5
Teachers[a]	1 or 2
Head teacher[b]	1
First[c] or foundation[d] governors	8 or 9[e]
TOTAL[f]	15 or 17

Notes

[a] To be eligible, the governor must be a teacher at the school in question (s 53(8)).

[b] The head teacher serves in an *ex-officio* capacity (s 53(4)(c)), but does not have the option of choosing not to be a governor.

[c] A school which was a county school when deciding to become grant-maintained has "first" governors (s 53(4)(d)(i)). The Secretary of State may make provision for the appointment of first governors if the governing body is unable or unwilling to fill vacancies (s 53(7)). At least two of the first governors must be parents of pupils at the school (ss 53(5)(b) and 64(3)). First governors must include in their number persons who are members of the local business community (ss 53(10) and 64(4)). A person who is an employee of the school may not be a first governor (s 56(8)).

[d] A school which was a voluntary school immediately before it became grant-maintained is to have foundation rather than first governors (s 53(4)(d)(ii)). Sections 53(5)(b) and 64(3) (see c above) apply also to foundation governors.

[e] The first or foundation governors must outnumber the other governors (ss 53(5)(a) and 64(2)).

[f] The Secretary of State may appoint up to two additional governors "if it appears to him that the governing body of the school are not adequately carrying out their responsibilities with respect to the conduct or management of the school" (s 53(6)(a)). Additional first/foundation governors, equal in number to those additional governors appointed by the Secretary of State, may be appointed (s 53(6)(b))

of State (s 9(6)). The LEA also has a power to end the grouping: simply by resolution if it does not include a voluntary school (s 9(7)(a)); or, in any other case:

(i) by resolution and with the governors' agreement; or
(ii) after expiry of one year's notice given by the LEA or governors (s 9(7)(b)).

Provision is made for the procedure for making the instrument of government and election of parent and teacher governors in grouped schools (Sch 1).

4. Elections

In the categories "teacher governor" (which excludes the head teacher) and "parent governor", election to the governing body is required. The next wholesale round of elections will take place in 1992 and 1993 when initial four year terms of office expire. It may be noted here that in certain situations parent governors can be *appointed* to office by the other members of the governing body (s 5(1)–(3); see, in relation to GM schools, ERA 1988 s 54). For example, in county, controlled or maintained special schools not established in a hospital, direct appointment may take place if, *inter alia*, the number of parents standing for election is fewer than the number of vacancies. When making such appointments, the governors who are not parent governors may appoint a parent of *any* child of compulsory school age, including, if necessary, a parent whose child attends another school (E(No 2)A 1986 s 5(4)(a)). But they may not appoint:

(i) an elected member of the LEA; or
(ii) an employee of the LEA or governors of an aided school; or
(iii) a co-opted member of any committee of the LEA (s 5(4)(b)).

Responsibility for arranging elections rests, as noted earlier, with LEAs in the case of county, controlled and maintained special schools, and with the governing body in the case of other maintained schools (s 15(2)(b)) and GM schools. Certain aspects of the conduct of the elections may be delegated to the head teacher, although the LEA/governors retain overall responsibility. The LEA/governors are also responsible for determining whether a person is a parent of a registered pupil or a teacher at the school for the purpose of eligibility for candidature at an election to the governing body (s 15(2)(a)).

Election must be by secret ballot (s 15(4)). In the case of election of parent governors, an opportunity to vote by post or return a ballot paper via a registered pupil at the school must be given (s 15(5)). Proper notice of the election must be given. The governors' annual report should contain information about forthcoming elections (s 30(2)(g)). Furthermore, under s 15(6), the LEA/governors must take:

"such steps as are reasonably practicable to secure that every person who is known to them to be a parent of a registered pupil at the school is—
(a) informed of the vacancy and that it is to be filled by election;
(b) informed that he is entitled to stand as a candidate, and vote, at the election; and
(c) given an opportunity to do so".

Letters to parents informing them of vacancies and setting out election arrangements should in appropriate cases be in languages other than English (see DES Circular 7/87, Annex 9, para 16).

There may be problems in determining who is eligible to vote as a parent. A person with actual custody of a child or young person is to be treated as a "parent" for this purpose (see EA 1944 s 114(1)). Thus it is possible for there to be more than two persons eligible to vote as parents of one registered child! LEAs and governors are advised that they are "not required to track every person who might qualify under the . . . definition of a parent, but . . . cannot rule ineligible anyone known to them to be a parent" (DES Circular 7/87, para 12).

It is for the responsible authority (ie, the LEA or governors) to decide whether candidates should be nominated, and if so, by how many persons. It may also choose the method of election, for example first past the post or some form of proportional representation. Guidance on these and other matters relating to the conduct of elections, including what

School government

constitutes a secret ballot, is given in DES Circular 7/87, Annex 9—*The Conduct of Governor Elections*. An extract appears in Appendix 4 (see page 298).

If it is alleged that an election of parent governors was carried out in a defective manner, complaint should be made to the Secretary of State under EA 1944 s 99 rather than via judicial review in the High Court (*R* v *Northampton County Council ex parte Gray (1986)*).

5. Appointment

Where appointment of a governor is required (see above), the clerk must give written notice of the vacancy to the appointing authority so that the authority may fill it (Education (School Government) Regulations 1989 reg 18(1)). When the appointment is made, the authority must inform the clerk of the name and usual place of residence of the person it has appointed (reg 18(2)).

6. Governorship

(a) Term of office

Governors, other than those who are *ex officio*, hold office for not more than four years in county, controlled and maintained special schools (E(No 2)A 1986 s 8(2)). However, a governor may resign his/her office at any time (s 8(4)) or may become disqualified (s 8(3) and see below). A teacher governor may not continue as such once s/he ceases to be employed at the school (Education (School Government) Regulations 1989 reg 15). Where there is an excess of governors, a paring down in the size of the governing body may be required (E(No 2)A 1986 s 14). Governors may be re-appointed or re-elected after the expiry of their term (*ibid* s 8(3)).

In GM schools, elected governors are to hold office for four years (ERA 1988 s 56(1)), and foundation or first governors generally for such term as is specified in the instrument or articles of government, being not fewer than five nor more than seven years (*ibid*, s 56(4) and (5)). Similar rules to

113

those in the 1986 Act relating to serving a further term, resignation and disqualification are laid down for GM schools (*ibid*, s 56(6), (7), (9)).

(b) Disqualification

Governors in county, voluntary and maintained special schools may be disqualified from holding office only in the circumstances laid down in regs 5–8 (and 15 (above)) of the Education (School Government) Regulations 1989 (reg 4). In GM schools, the instrument of government is to make provision for the circumstances in which a person is to be disqualified (ERA 1988 s 56(9)).

The first rule concerning disqualification aims to prevent a person from holding office as a governor on more than four governing bodies (reg 5(1), (2) and (5)). An *ex-officio* governor of more than four schools must designate four or fewer at which he wishes to continue as a governor (reg 5(3)).

A person may also be disqualified from holding or continuing to hold office as a governor if s/he is adjudged bankrupt or has made a composition or arrangement with creditors. In either case the governor must give notice of that fact to that clerk to the governing body (reg 6(1)). In most cases the disqualification will cease on the person's discharge from bankruptcy or on annulment of the bankruptcy order (reg 6(2)). In the case of a composition or arrangement with creditors, the disqualification ends after five years, or after the debts are paid in full (if sooner) (see reg 6(3)).

An important aspect of disqualification concerns criminal convictions (excluding convictions outside the UK for offences involving conduct which would not amount to an offence in the UK: reg 7(4)). A governor with relevant convictions must give written notice of them to the clerk to the governors (reg 7(3)). Convictions which disqualify a person from holding, or continuing to hold, office as a school governor are (reg 7(1) and (2)):

    (i) a conviction (in the UK or elsewhere) within the five years before election or appointment or while a governor, in respect of which a sentence of imprisonment (whether suspended or not) of not less than three

School government

months, and without the option of a fine, has been imposed;
(ii) a conviction as above, within the previous twenty years, for which a sentence of imprisonment of at least two and a half years has been passed;
(iii) a conviction plus fine within the previous five years, or since being appointed or elected, for causing nuisance and disturbance on school premises (including those of a GM school) contrary to the Local Government (Miscellaneous Provisions) Act 1982 s 40 (as amended) (see page 275 below).

A person is also disqualified from continuing to hold office as a governor if, without the consent of the governing body, s/he has not attended any governors' meeting for the previous twelve months or more (reg 8). However, s/he may be re-elected or re-appointed to office (*ibid*).

(c) Resignation or removal—notice and other requirements

The clerk to the governing body must be given written notice of (i) resignation or (ii) removal of a governor. Notice should be given by, in the case of (i), the governor concerned, and in the case of (ii), by those removing the governor (reg 17). Moreover, the governor concerned must be informed by the appointing authority of the proposed removal and the reason for it, and should be given an opportunity to reply in writing to the complaint made against him/her (*R v Brent LBC ex parte Assegai* (1987)).

Appointing authorities (governors or LEAs) have the power to remove from office, where relevant:

(i) any foundation governor of an aided school
(ii) any school governor other than:
- a co-opted governor who is not a co-opted foundation governor;
- an elected or appointed (by E(No2)A 1986 s 5) parent governor or elected teacher governor;
- an *ex-officio* governor (s 8(5) – see also EA 1944 s 21(1)).

The government hopes that the power of removal will be used "only in exceptional circumstances" (DES Circular 7/87, para 5.5.1.). But there have been complaints about the political manner in which the power has been exercised. For example, it has been alleged that Humberside LEA selected non-socialist governors for removal (*The Guardian*, 25 October 1989). In *R v Governors of Haberdashers' Aske's Hatcham Schools ex parte ILEA;* sub nom *Brunyate v ILEA* (1989), the Court of Appeal, and subsequently the House of Lords, held that a LEA cannot remove governors in mid-term solely because of their failure to promote the LEA's policies. The ILEA had removed two Conservative governors on a grouped governing body who had indicated that they were not prepared to support the LEA's policy concerning the future of the schools and an extended period of consultation thereon. In the House of Lords, Lord Bridge, giving the court's judgment, said (at 421) that to remove a governor because of his/her "non-compliance with the wishes (ie policy) of the authority is . . . a usurpation of the governors' independent function". Thus, as Woolf LJ had argued in the Court of Appeal in the instant case, the power to remove a governor was "limited to the extent that was necessary to prevent the policy of *the Act* being frustrated" (emphasis added). In *R v Trustee of the Roman Catholic Diocese of Westminster ex parte Andrews* (1989) (sub nom *Mars* in Div Ct: (1987))) the Court of Appeal, following the decision in *Brunyate*, held that the removal of two governors who would not support the trustee's scheme for reorganisation of the school had been an unlawful exercise of the power of removal.

7. Governors' meetings

(a) Requirement to hold a meeting

A governors' meeting must be convened at least once in every term (Education (School) Government Regs 1989 reg 12(1)), although it is becoming increasingly difficult for the necessary business to be completed in three meetings a year, even with referral to sub-committees, and most governing bodies can expect to meet more frequently. (The governing body of a *new* school need meet "as often as occasion may require" (reg 12(2)).) A meeting may be requisitioned by any three members of the governing body (reg 12(3)).

In some cases the power to make a decision may be delegated to a member of the governors, the head teacher, or a committee (regs 25 and 26). (See page 123 for further discussion of delegation.) A further provision empowers the chairperson or, if s/he cannot be contacted, the vice-chairperson, to make decisions without the other governors where "a delay... would be likely to be seriously detrimental to the interests of the school, or to the interests of any registered pupil at the school, his parent, or a person employed at the school" (reg 23(1) and (2)). "Delay" is defined as "a delay for a period extending beyond the date preceding the earliest date on which it would be reasonably practicable for a meeting of the governing body to be held" (reg 23(3)).

(b) Convening a meeting

The clerk to the governors convenes the meeting, although in doing so s/he must comply with any direction given by the governors, at their previous meeting, or by the chairperson or, in his/her absence, the vice-chairperson (reg 19(1)). At least seven days before the date of the meeting, a written notice of the meeting, signed by the clerk, and a copy of the agenda, should be given to every member of the governing body, the head teacher (assuming s/he is not a governor), and the chief education officer (reg 19(2)). However, a lesser period of notice of the meeting (plus agenda) may be given where the chairperson or, in his/her absence, vice-chairperson so directs —on the ground that there are matters requiring urgent consideration (reg 19(2)). The written notice and agenda must either be sent to, or left at, the usual place of residence of those entitled to receive them (reg 19(3)). The fact that a member did not receive a written notice does not invalidate the proceedings of the meeting (reg 19(4)).

In an aided or special agreement school, if a decision is to be taken at a meeting to rescind or vary a resolution carried at a previous meeting, such matter must be included as a specific item of business on the agenda for the meeting (reg 20). Otherwise there is no restriction on the contents of the agenda.

(c) Election of a chairperson and vice chairperson

Generally speaking the governors must elect a chairperson and vice-chairperson from their number at the first meeting in the school year (reg 9(1)). A subsequent casual vacancy may be filled at the next meeting after it occurs (reg 9(2)). A teacher governor is ineligible for election to either office (reg 9(5)). The chairperson or vice-chairperson may resign from office at any time (written notice to be given to the clerk) (reg 9(3)).

If the chairperson is absent from the meeting, the vice-chairperson must take the chair. If neither the chairperson nor vice-chairperson is in attendance at a meeting, the other members present may elect one of their number (apart from a teacher governor) to chair the meeting (reg 9(4)).

(Separate provisions govern chairpersons and vice-chairpersons of temporary governing bodies: see reg 10.)

(d) Quorum

Generally the quorum for a meeting of the governing body is (reg 13(1) and (2)):

- (i) three governors, or, if greater, one-third of the total membership (rounded up where necessary); or
- (ii) the quorum specified in the instrument of government for the school, if greater than (i) above, provided that it is not more than two-fifths of total membership (rounded up where necessary).

However, a larger quorum is required in a small number of prescribed circumstances, namely: appointment of parent governors under E(No 2)A 1986 (eg because there were fewer parents standing for election than the number of vacancies); co-option of non-foundation governors; co-option of temporary teacher governors; appointment of a committee with delegated functions (under reg 26—see below) (reg 13(3)). The quorum in these cases is to be three-quarters of the governors entitled to vote on these particular matters (*ibid*).

(e) The meeting

(i) Attendance and participation

Public access to governors' meetings is not specifically

barred. The governing body is left with a discretion whether anyone who is not one of those entitled to attend (one of its number, a headteacher non-governor, and the clerk to the governors) should be admitted to the meeting (reg 21).

In certain cases or circumstances any person present at a meeting, including those present by right, may be required to withdraw from the meeting or required not to take part in consideration or discussion of certain matters; sometimes s/he may simply have no right to vote on the matter (reg 14). In any event, the governors are to have an unrestricted right, when conducting a disciplinary hearing or appeal in relation to a pupil's or teacher's or other employee's alleged conduct, to allow such persons and others—the pupil's parent, the person making the allegation, or a material witness—to attend the meeting and be heard (reg 14(4)).

The Schedule to the Education (School Government) Regulations details "the only circumstances" in which withdrawal may be required (reg 14(2)). (It was held that the pre-1987 version of the regulations did not contain an exhaustive list of such circumstances (*Lockett* v *Croydon LBC* (1986)), hence the specific limitation incorporated into the 1987, and now 1989, regulations.)

The first situation where withdrawal is necessary relates to pecuniary interest. Anyone present who has such an interest, whether direct or indirect, in any "proposed contract or other matter" being considered by the governors must disclose that fact as soon as possible. S/he must take no part in the consideration or discussion of that matter and should withdraw from the meeting while the said matter is being considered—unless the governors decide otherwise. S/he must not vote on the matter or on any question relating to it (para 2(1)). What constitutes a direct or indirect pecuniary interest for this purpose is carefully defined. Certain changes have been made from the previous (1987) version of the regulations. Note that a person is to be taken to have a direct or indirect pecuniary interest if a "relative" (including a "spouse"—"includes a woman who lives with a man as his wife": reg 3(a)) to his knowledge has such an interest (para 2(3)).

An indirect pecuniary interest would arise if, for example, a proposed contract for the benefit of the school was to be with a company or other organisation of which the governor was a member (with securities in it), or a partner, or an employee (with securities in it) (para 2(2)).

Governors are nowadays taking major decisions affecting the conduct of their schools. Such decisions can clearly have a major impact on the teaching staff. The governing body includes teacher governors and generally also the head teacher. The Schedule lists the circumstances in which the teacher governors and head teacher (whether a governor or not) shall *not* be deemed to have a direct or indirect pecuniary interest (para 2(4)):

(a) an interest in a contract or other matter which is a greater interest than that of the generality of teachers at the school (note that conflict of interest concerning employment matters is covered elsewhere—see below);
(b) the contract or other matter relates to the governors' exercise of their functions relating to the curriculum or management of the school's budget share following financial delegation; or
(c) the decision being considered relates to whether or not to initiate the procedure for changing to grant-maintained status or to pass a first or second resolution for opting out (see Appendix 1). This confirms the decision of the Court of Appeal in *R* v *Governors of Small Heath School ex parte Birmingham City Council* (1989). In that case, decided under the previous version of the regulations, which did not refer to this particular category of decision, it was held that there was no pecuniary interest because there was no evidence that the financial position of the teacher governors would alter if the school became grant-maintained. The court distinguished a previous case, *Bostock* v *Kay* (1989), in which it was held that four teacher governors had a direct pecuniary interest in the outcome of proposals to turn the school into a City Technology College (CTC). The Court of Appeal in *Small Heath* said that a change to GM status was far less fundamental than a change to CTC. In the latter circumstance the school would cease to exist and would be replaced by a completely new

institution; staff might not be re-engaged, and if they did they might have to work longer hours, although for greater pay.

Governing bodies (or a selection panel thereof) may also have to consider the appointment, transfer, promotion or retirement of staff. If such appointment etc relates to a governor or his/her relative (including spouse—as above) the governor in question should take no part in the proceedings and should not vote. Indeed, s/he should not be present at all, unless the governors decide otherwise (para 3). Such restrictions on participation also apply if the governors are to consider the transfer, promotion, retirement, dismissal or suspension of a member of staff (teaching or otherwise), where one of the governors (or his/her relative) could be a candidate for any vacant post arising from the decision on the matter (para 4). A decision under the 1981 version of the regulations, admittedly concerned with appointment rather than promotion *per se*, is relevant here: *Noble* v *ILEA* (1984). P, a senior teacher, applied for a deputy headship at his school. He was interviewed by the governors. K, a teacher governor at the school was present at the meeting. K voted in favour of P's appointment. P was recommended for the post and received a formal offer from the LEA which he accepted. The LEA subsequently tried to repeat the selection process, but without K who should not have been on the panel because he was eligible to be considered for P's post if P was appointed to the deputy headship. P tried to force the LEA to the contract he had accepted. The Court of Appeal found in favour of the LEA.

The remainder of the Schedule relates principally to withdrawal during consideration of disciplinary matters or the admission of pupils. A pupil or his parent must withdraw from a meeting if the admission of or disciplinary action against the pupil or against another pupil where the aforementioned pupil was involved in the incident, is being considered (para 5(1)(a) and (b)). A relative of the pupil other than a parent has, if in attendance, to disclose the relationship as soon as practicable after the commencement of the meeting (para 6). A person making allegations which might lead to disciplinary action against a pupil or teacher or other employee at the school must also withdraw, as must a witness of any alleged incident (para 5(1)(c), as qualified by para 5(2)—which enables the chief education officer or his/her representative to attend but not vote). The person against whom the disciplinary action is brought—a teacher or other employee or the clerk to the governors—must also withdraw (para 5(1)(e)).

In all these cases in para 5(1), the person concerned must withdraw during discussion or consideration of the matter in question and may not vote.

If the governors are hearing an appeal in respect of any disciplinary matter, anyone previously concerned with the matter, other than in the capacity as a governor, must not take part in consideration of the appeal or any vote relating to it (para 5(1)(d)). This often results in the head teacher having to withdraw. However, s/he may nevertheless attend, but may not vote, in cases involving dismissal of staff (ERA 1988 Sch 3 para 8(9); Education (School) Government Regulations 1989 Sch para 5(2)). Nevertheless, it is, as the DES has put it, "in the interests of natural justice . . . when a head has, for example, previously suspended [a] member of staff, [that] he should withdraw while the governing body considers its decision" (Letter to Chief Education Officers and others re: *The Education (School Government) Regulations 1989*, 31 August 1989).

Finally, the Schedule deals with cases where the governors are considering various matters relating to staff employed at the school, namely, their conduct, continued employment at the school, and the appointment of successors (para 7). (There appears to be some overlap but not inconsistency with para 5(1)(e).) Whether a governor or not, the member of staff should, unless the governors permit otherwise, withdraw from the meeting while consideration and discussion of the matter are taking place. If the member of staff has governor voting rights, s/he may not exercise them in respect of this matter.

(ii) Decisions: voting

Regulation 14(1) states: "Any question coming before the governing body of a school shall be decided by a majority of the members thereof voting on the question at a meeting of the governing body". If equal numbers of votes for and against are cast, the chairperson is to have a second or casting vote.

(iii) Minutes and record of persons present

Minutes of meetings are to be recorded in a minutes book and must be signed at the meeting, or at the next one, by the chairperson (reg 14(5)). If the minutes are entered on loose leaves, each sheet must be initialled by the chairperson (*ibid*). The chief education officer can, on request, insist on the LEA being furnished with a copy of the signed minutes of a meeting of the governing body (reg 14(6)). A record must be kept of governors and head teacher present at a meeting (reg 22).

As soon as they are ready, the draft minutes (if approved by the chairperson) or signed minutes of a meeting, plus a copy of the agenda and reports or other papers considered at the meeting, are to be made available at the school to persons wishing to inspect them (reg 24(1)). However, certain material may be excluded from them before being made available—that relating to: a named teacher or other person employed at, or proposed to be employed at the school; a named pupil or possible future pupil; "any matter which, by reason of its nature, the governing body are satisfied should be dealt with on a confidential basis" (reg 24(2)). Note that temporary governing bodies of new schools are excepted from these requirements concerning publication of minutes etc (reg 24(3)).

8. Delegation

(a) Introduction

The introduction of a detailed legal framework for delegation of decision-making to committees and individuals was the principal area of change which the revised Education (School Government) Regulations 1989 made. Under previous legislation (which is still in force but has been added to considerably) delegation was expressly empowered in only two cases. Under E(No 2)A 1986 the governors can delegate to the head teacher responsibility for any sum of money made available to the governors by the LEA under s 29(1)(b) for expenditure on books, equipment, stationery etc (s 29(1)(d)). Also, the selection of permanent staff (other than a head or deputy head teacher) can be delegated to the head teacher and/or one or more governors (s 38(6)— and now ERA 1988 Sch 3 para 2 in the case of schools with delegated budgets).

Section 8(7) E(No 2)A 1986 (as amended by ERA 1988 s 116) now empowers the Secretary of State to make regulations providing for the establishment, by governing bodies, of committees of governors and/or others and for the delegation of functions of governing bodies to committees, individual governors and the head teacher. As noted above, these regulations have now been made and came into force on 8 September 1989 (the Education (School Government) Regulations 1989, Part III). The government has said that these provisions are needed:

> "because of the greatly increased powers of governing bodies, which may render it impracticable for all decisions to be taken by the governing body . . . and the fact that governors may develop a particular interest or expertise in certain areas, such as finance, the curriculum or staffing, and . . . some decisions in those areas could most efficiently be taken by a small group of such governors" (DES Consultation Document, *Amendments to the Education (School Government) Regulations 1987,* May 1989, para 29).

The changes also permit the governors to invite experts on various matters to assist them in their decision-making. (Such experts would not have voting rights.)

Note that the provisions on delegation do not apply in grant-maintained schools. However, the articles of such schools may make provision for the establishment, by the governing body, of "committees or other bodies of persons" to carry out such functions as may be determined by or under the articles (ERA 1988 s 58(4)).

(b) Delegated functions

The regulations divide governors' functions into three categories:

(i) those which may not be delegated;
(ii) those which may be delegated to a committee only;
(iii) those which may be delegated to a committee, a member of the governing body or to the head teacher.

(i) Functions which may not be delegated

These are shown in the table below; the various functions are discussed elsewhere.

Functions which may not be delegated by governing bodies (Reg 25(2))

Duty to hold a meeting at least once a term (reg 12).

Election of a chairperson and vice-chairperson of governing body (regs 9 and 10).

Appointment or co-option of governors (E(No 2)A 1986 ss 3–6).

The power of delegation itself (reg 25(1)).

Functions relating to school admissions (EA 1980 ss 6–8 and ERA 1988 ss 26–32).

Various curricular matters in E(No 2)A 1986 ss 18 and 19 (as amended), including consideration of LEA curriculum policy, aims of secular curriculum for school, control of secular curriculum (subject to s 18(5)), decision as to whether sex education should form part of secular curriculum for the school.

Responsibilities in relation to the basic curriculum, National Curriculum and collective worship and religious education, standing advisory council on religious education etc (ERA 1988).

Responsibilities concerning the manner in which sex education is to be provided and governing the treatment of political issues and activities (E(No 2)A 1986, ss 44–46).

The provision of information (ERA 1988 s 22(1)).

Policies on charging for education and on remissions (ERA 1988 s 110).

Times of school sessions and the dates of school terms and holidays (E(No 2)A 1986 s 21(2) and (4), as amended).

Statement of governing body's general principles concerning pupil discipline (E(No 2)A 1986 s 22(b)(i)).

Approval of governing body's annual report to parents under E(No 2)A 1986 s 30.

Initiation of procedure for acquisition of grant-maintained status etc (ERA 1988 s 60).

Governors' role in discontinuance of voluntary schools (EA 1944 s 14) or in relation to their establishment or alteration (EA 1980 s 13).

Governors' role in relation to approval of school premises (EA 1980 s 14).

(ii) Functions which may be delegated only to a committee

In two situations functions may be delegated to a committee, constituted in the prescribed manner (under reg 26 – see below).

Functions which may be delegated by the governors only to a committee (Reg 25(3) and (4))

Dismissal of member of staff and appeals relating thereto (ERA 1988 Sch 3 para 8).

Re-instatement of excluded pupils and appeals arrangements relating thereto (E(No 2)A 1986 ss 24–26).

(c) Committees

Save as otherwise provided in the regulations, the constitution, membership and proceedings of the committee to which functions have been delegated is to be determined by the governing body (reg 26(1) and (2)). Most of the provisions of regs 14, 19, 22 and 24 and the Schedule, which relate to proceedings and minutes of, and withdrawal from, meetings of the governing body (see above), apply also to committees (reg 26(7)). Persons who are *not* members of the governing body may be included on a committee, but, as indicated above, shall have no voting rights (reg 26(3)).

Special provisions apply in the case of committees with delegated functions relating to (i) dismissal of staff (under reg 25(3)) and (ii) re-instatement of pupils (under reg 25(4)):

(i) Dismissal

The committee must include not fewer than three members of the governing body. Where this committee is taking an initial or preliminary decision in a dismissal case, no member of it may sit on the committee which hears any appeal (reg 26(5)(a)). The membership of the appeal committee must comprise no fewer in number than that of the committee taking the first decision (reg 26(5)(b)). However, if there are fewer than six governors qualified for membership of one or both committees, or it is not practicable for there to be at least three governors on them, the committees may include fewer than three governors (*ibid*).

(ii) Re-instatement of a pupil

The committee must include not less than three governors, none of whom may be the head teacher (reg 26(6)).

Disqualification etc: The provision of regs 6 and 7 relating to disqualification from membership of governing bodies on the grounds of bankruptcy and possession of criminal convictions (see above) apply also to membership of delegated committees (reg 26(7)). Note that the House of Lords recently held that a police officer who was an elected parent governor could serve on an appointments committee without being in breach of police regulations (*R* v *Chief Constable of Gwent* (1989)). It had been argued that such involvement might be viewed by the public as interference with a police officer's impartial discharge of his professional duties; but their Lordships felt otherwise.

(d) Reporting action or decisions

The person or committee to whom delegation has been made must report any action or decision taken to the governing body at their next meeting (reg 27).

9. Accountability and liability of governors

(a) Governors' annual report and annual parents' meeting

Accountability has been an important aspect of the conduct of school government under the post 1986 and 1988 Act regimes. Among the provisions concerned with this are those requiring the governors to prepare an annual report to parents and to arrange an annual meeting with parents at which the content of the annual report and the discharge by the LEA, head teacher and governors of their various functions in relation to the school may be discussed (E(No 2)A 1986 ss 30 and 31). These provisions are considered in Chapter 4 (see pages 140 and 147).

(b) Liability

Governing bodies are protected against personal liability for any act done in good faith for the purposes of expenditure of a school's delegated budget (ERA 1988 s 36(6)). This and other aspects of governors' liability following financial delegation were discussed in Chapter 1.

When the governors of a school with a delegated budget

School government

enter into a contract they do so on behalf of a LEA, which is therefore liable under it (see DES Circular 7/88, para 183). But given the independent functions of governors under education law (as emphasised by the House of Lords in *Brunyate* v *ILEA* (1989) (*op cit*)), it has become increasingly difficult to argue that in general they act in the capacity of agents for the LEA.

Leaving aside the protection available to them when dealing with delegated budgets (above), governing bodies may be liable for negligence in respect of certain activities carried on at the school for which they are responsible (eg using the school premises for a special event and not making safe arrangements). Premises liability is set to become a complex issue given the division of responsibility for maintenance of buildings between LEAs and governors following financial delegation (see Chapter 1).

Where governors are liable for negligence, such liability will be joint and several. In other words, the negligent action of one governor acting in his/her capacity as such may render all governors personally liable as well as the governing body as a whole. In some cases, a governor who is liable may be able to claim a contribution under the Civil Liability (Contribution) Act 1978 (ss 1 and 2) from another governor who, for example, perpetrated the negligence. From time to time, individual governors might have to act on their own initiative. As Lord Bridge said in *Brunyate* v *ILEA* (1989) (at page 420), "individual governors, so long as they hold office as such, have both the right and the duty to exercise the function of their office independently in accordance with their own judgement". (On joint torts, see *Street on Torts*, 8th ed (1988), pages 526–533.)

As noted in Chapter 1 (see page 56), LEAs have been required to arrange insurance cover for any personal liability in negligence towards staff or third parties incurred by governors in the exercise of their responsibilities. Such arrangements are to form part of the delegation scheme submitted by the LEA for approval by the Secretary of State (DES Circular 7/88, paras 86 and 186).

Where a member of staff is negligent, the employer may be vicariously liable if the act or omission occurred, *inter alia*, while the employee was acting in the course of his/her employment. Where the governors are the employers—for example in voluntary aided schools or grant-maintained schools—they will need to ensure that insurance cover is arranged. They must also comply with ss 2 and 3 Health and Safety at Work Etc Act 1974 (see Chapter 9). In schools covered by delegation schemes, governors will have responsibility for certain health and safety matters (DES Circular 7/88, paras 189 and 191).

Governors also have responsibilities under the Sex Discrimination Act 1975 and Race Relations Act 1976 (see Chapter 5) in respect of which they could incur liability.

10. Disputes with the LEA

Provision was made in the Education Act 1944 for the resolution of disputes between governors and LEAs; in its amended form the relevant provision (s 67(1)) states:

> "Save as otherwise expressly provided by this Act, any dispute between a [LEA] and the governors of any school with respect to the exercise of any power conferred or the performance of any duty imposed by or under this Act, may. . . be referred to the Secretary of State; and any dispute so referred shall be determined by him".

This provision is additional to many others dealing with disputes over particular matters where the Secretary of State is to decide the issue—for example, over the instrument of government for a voluntary school (see E(No 2)A 1986 s 2(5)–(7)). The Secretary of State may also use powers in EA 1944 ss 68 and 99 where the governors or LEA are acting or proposing to act unreasonably (s 68) or in default (s 99). (These powers are discussed in Chapter 4; see page 158.)

Until recently, LEAs have been able to exert considerable control over schools. LEA policy, as determined by its education committee (after being forged in sub-committee), has shaped local provision. But while their strategic role is set to continue (see Audit Commission, *Losing an Empire, Finding a Role—the LEA of the future* (1989)), they are increasingly having to share their diminishing powers and responsibilities. It is possible to envisage that as their powers are stripped away, some LEAs will fight a rearguard action resulting in a short disputatious era in education administration. As in the past, many of these disputes will result in litigation.

One possible area of conflict, highlighted in two cases which both received considerable media attention, has been removed. Section 24(1) Education Act 1944 gave the final say on dismissal of teaching staff at county schools (and of teachers, other than those employed to give religious instruction, at controlled schools) exclusively to the LEA. In two cases, both involving alleged racist remarks by serving head teachers, the LEA chose to ignore a recommendation by the governing body against dismissal of the member of staff concerned. In the first of these cases, *Honeyford* v *Bradford City Metropolitan Council* (1986), the court held that the articles of government of the school had to be construed in the light of s 24(1) under which the LEA had a residual power to dismiss. In the second case, *McGoldrick* v *Brent LBC* (1987), the school governors unanimously decided that there was no evidence to substantiate allegations of racist remarks by an infants' school head teacher, Miss McGoldrick. She had been suspended by the LEA but the governors demanded her re-instatement. The LEA disciplinary sub-committee subsequently, and unexpectedly, confirmed Miss McGoldrick's suspension at a meeting to which neither she nor her representative was invited. The sub-committee decided to hold a full investigation into the allegations and informed Miss McGoldrick of this. At this stage she commenced legal proceedings. In the High Court, Roch J held that the disciplinary sub-committee could not rehear the case and that the governors' findings of fact should stand. The Court of Appeal held that the sub-committee was bound to follow the governors' findings only if those findings supported disciplinary action, for that was what the articles of government and disciplinary code contemplated. Moreover, s 24(1) of the 1944 Act gave the final say on dismissal exclusively to the LEA.

Section 24(1) was repealed by the E(No 2)A 1986 Sch 6, but the LEA retained the final say on dismissals (E(No 2)A 1986 s 35), subject to consultation with the governors and (unless s/he was being dismissed) the head teacher (*ibid* s 41(1)). However, under ERA 1988 Sch 3 para 8, once a financial delegation scheme is in operation the governors will have the final say on dismissals (see Chapter 1).

11. Expenses

Travelling expenses and subsistence allowances may be paid to governors of county, voluntary and maintained special schools if the LEA makes a scheme for this purpose (E(No 2)A 1986 s 58(1)). The scheme can differentiate between different categories of school in the level of support offered, but not between different categories of governor of the same school (s 58(2)). LEAs may also pay travelling expenses and subsistence allowances to their representatives on the governing bodies of independent schools or special schools not maintained by them (s 58(6)(b)). No other allowances may be paid to a governor (s 58(7)).

In a grant-maintained school, the governing body may pay its members such travelling, subsistence, "*or other*" allowances as may be determined by a scheme for this purpose approved by the Secretary of State (ERA 1988 s 55(5)).

12. Information and training

LEAs must provide every governor of a county, voluntary and maintained special school with a copy of the instrument and articles of government for their school and such other information as they consider appropriate for a school governor (E(No 2)A 1986 s 57(a)). No charge may be made to governors for the supply of this information.

LEAs must also secure that "such training as the authority consider necessary for the effective discharge of [their] functions" is made available (without charge) to every governor (s 57(b)). LEAs have been expected to include arrangements for governor training in their proposed schemes for financial delegation (DES Circular 7/88, para 148). Whilst governors' training is not covered by the Local Authority Training Grants Scheme it has been funded (at the rate of 70 per cent) under Education Support Grants paid under the Education (Grants and Awards) Act 1984. In 1989–90, £4. 9m has been made available, specifically for training on LMS (local financial management of schools—see Chapter 1), and support at a comparable level has been promised for 1990–91 and 1991–92 (DES Circular 7/88, *op cit*, para 150).

13. Control of school session times and term and holiday dates

Under the E(No 2)A 1986 s 21, governing bodies of aided and special agreement schools were to determine the times at which the school session was to begin and end on any day, and the dates and times at which school terms and holidays were to begin and end. In county, controlled and maintained special schools, control of such matters lay with the LEA.

Section 115 ERA 1988 substituted a new s 21 for the old one. The position in aided and special agreement schools is unchanged (s 21(4)). In county, controlled and maintained special schools the LEA must determine term and holiday dates, but the governing body is to determine the starting and finishing times of school sessions (s 21(2)). A governing body which proposes to change session times may institute the changes only at the start of the school year. They must provide opportunities for discussion of the proposals at the annual parents' meeting and must consult the LEA and parents (both of whom are entitled to three months notice of the changes). Details of the proposals are to be provided in the governors' annual report; the LEA can insist on its comments being appended to the report.

A draft circular offering guidance on, amongst other things, the amount of teaching time recommended for schools, was issued in the summer of 1989 (*Length and Control of School Sessions: Draft Circular* (May 1989)). The draft circular states that minimum hours of secular instruction which are required to be given, under the Education (Schools and Further Education) Regulations 1981, as amended (eg at least four hours per day for children over eight), are to be scrapped because they bear little relation to current practice. The *minimum* weekly hours proposed in the circular vary from 21 for 5–7 year olds, 23.5 for 8–13 year olds and 25 for 14–15 year olds (see para 10). Guidance on how this time is to be allocated is set out. No change is proposed in the requirement (currently in reg 10(2) of the 1981 Regulations) that a school year should consist of 380 half-day sessions. Publication of the final version of the circular has, at the time of writing (January 1990) been delayed. Many replies to the draft circular were received, and a number of changes to the circular can be expected.

A further change concerns the power (formerly in EA 1944 s 21(2), now in E(No 2)A 1986 s 21(5)) to require a pupil in attendance at a school to receive secular instruction or training other than on the school premises. In county, controlled and maintained special schools this power rested with the LEA. Now the governors of these schools, as well as those voluntary aided and special agreement schools, are to have this power, under their articles.

Chapter 4

Parents as consumers: information and choice of school

1. Information

A considerable amount of information about the new legal regime affecting schools especially in the area of the curriculum, is currently being made available to governors and parents by the DES. Most parents have received a copy of *Our Changing Schools*, published by the Department last year. Governors and head teachers have been receiving a regular *ERA Bulletin*. All governors are being issued with a loose-leaf (for updating) *Governors' Guide*. Head teachers have been sent *National Curriculum: From Policy to Practice* (1989) in addition to a vast array of circulars and statutory instruments. The Secretary of State has a duty to send to "persons having a special interest in education" copies of proposed Orders relating to the National Curriculum and relevent documents referred to in them (ERA 1988 s 20). But LEAs, governors and head teachers have onerous legal duties to provide various forms of information to parents and others.

(a) Admissions

The Education Act 1980 (s 8(1)) requires LEAs and governing bodies to publish annually particulars of the arrangements:

    (i) for the admission of pupils to maintained schools;
    (ii) for the provision of education at schools maintained by another LEA or not maintained; and

(iii) made for enabling a parent to express a preference for a particular school (under s 6(1) of that Act) and to appeal against the appropriate authority's decision on admission to a school (under s 7(1)).

Other information which the 1980 Act requires to be provided includes the *admission number,* ie the standard number applicable to admissions in a school (s 8(3)(a), as substituted by ERA 1988 s 31(2)) (see Admissions below) and the policy followed in deciding admissions (s 8(3)(c)). Regulations made under s 8 require the publication of various forms of information about schools, which parents might wish to consult when exercising their right to express a preference for a school (see below).

Where *grant-maintained* schools are concerned, the articles of government must require the governing body to publish, for each school year, details of admissions and appeal arrangements (ERA 1988 s 58(5)(f)).

(b) Educational policy and provision

The Secretary of State has a power, in s 22(1) of ERA 1988, to make regulations requiring LEAs, and governing bodies and head teachers of maintained schools, to make certain forms of information available "either generally or to prescribed persons, in such form and manner and at such times as may be prescribed". This information may relate to the educational provision and syllabuses followed at maintained schools, and to the educational achievements of pupils (s 22(2)) (but not the result of an individual's assessment, under the National Curriculum or otherwise (s 22(5))). The information may also convey the contents of various documents—reports and policy statements such as the LEA's statement of curricular policy; the governors' statement of how, if at all, the LEA's statement should be modified; the governors' statement of curricular policy for their school; and the governors' annual report (s 22(3)). Regulations may authorise charges for the provision of documents supplied (s 22(6)) (see below).

Regulations have been made (the Education (School Curriculum and Related Information) Regulations 1989) which amend the Education (School Information) Regulations

1981, as previously amended. LEAs and governing bodies are placed under a duty to ensure that head teachers comply with any regulations made under s 22(1) (s 22(7)). The regulations impose a regime for the supply of information to parents and between the various authorities. They do not, as yet, cover pupils' achievements and individual schools' performances under the National Curriculum, although further regulations are planned for 1990.

(i) LEA information to be sent to parents of prospective pupils

The information which falls under this heading is *policy and arrangements in respect of primary and secondary education* (Education (School Information) Regulations 1981, as amended, Sch 1). Under this category, LEAs must, in advance of a school year and (except where the information relates exclusively to primary education or special educational provision) at least six weeks before parents may express a preference for a school, send parents of prospective pupils information about their schools and make it available at schools, libraries and LEA offices (reg 5). The information is to include schools' names and addresses, numbers on the roll and religious affiliation (if any). Also to be included are statements of LEA policy on such matters as examination entry, special educational needs and charging and remission of charges.

(ii) Information for inclusion in a school's "prospectus"

Certain types of information about individual schools must be published by a LEA or by or on behalf of the governors of an aided or special school. This information must be published in a "school prospectus", which must be made available to parents on request and for reference by parents and others (reg 6, as amended).

The main categories of information surviving from the original version of the 1981 Regulations, and set out in Sch 2, include:

    (a) the name of head teacher and chair of governors;
    (b) the classification of the school;

(c) the arrangements for visits by parents of prospective pupils;
(d) the arrangements for pupils with special needs and in respect of pastoral care, discipline and education in general at the school;
(e) the requirements as to uniform and dress;
(f) GCSE, A and AS level examination results (of year groups) and policy on examination entry (see para 15);
(g) starting and finishing times of the school day.

A requirement to publish, in addition to (a)–(g) above, details of curriculum content and organisation was also included in the 1981 Regulations, and referred to matters such as subjects offered, sex education and arrangements for careers guidance. Under amendments, this part of the regulations remain in force in Wales only, and in England a new regulations (4A, inserted by the Education (School Curriculum and Related Information) Regulations 1989 reg 3(2), in force from 1 January 1990 (*ibid* (Amendment) Regulations 1989)) applies. The new regulations require much more detailed information than hitherto to be made available.

Information concerning the curriculum for inclusion in school prospectuses in England

Governing body's statement of curricular policy and indication of how, if at all, LEA's statement on curricular policy should be modified (county, controlled or maintained schools); or governors' statement of curricular policy or indication (if such is the case) that no such statement has been made (aided or special agreement schools).

Summary of the content and organisation of sex education when it forms part of the secular curriculum.

Details of time set aside for teaching during the school day.

Dates of school terms and half-term holidays for the next school year.

Details of curriculum content and organisation: how foundation subjects and RE organised, other subjects and cross-curricular themes included in curriculum, how subject choices may be constrained.

List of approved external qualifications for which pupils of compulsory school age may be prepared at the school and titles of syllabuses for them[a].

List of external qualifications, and names of syllabuses associated with them, for pupils over compulsory school age.

Particulars of careers guidance and arrangements for work experience by pupils.

Details of the complaints procedure established by the LEA under ERA 1988 s 23 (see below) (county, voluntary and maintained special schools other than special schools in hospitals).

Arrangements for inspection and obtaining copies of documents which have to be made available to parents etc[b].

---

[a] ERA 1988 s 5, Education (Prescribed Public Examination) Regulations 1989
[b] Education (School Curriculum and Related Information) Regulations 1989, as amended by the Education (School Curriculum and Related Information) (Amendment) Regulations 1989.

Grant-maintained schools: The 1981 Regulations, as amended, do not apply to grant-maintained (GM) schools. However, each GM school will be required by its articles of government to publish a prospectus and include in it information equivalent to that required under the Regulations (ERA 1988 s 58).

(iii) Information to be published with the governing body's annual report to parents

School governors in LEA-maintained schools and grant-maintained schools must prepare, and, where reasonably practicable, distribute to parents copies of, an annual report (E(No 2)A 1986 s 30; ERA 1988 s 58(5)(j)). The report must set out the manner in which they have exercised their various functions, the dates of the beginning and end of each term and of half-term holidays, and a summary of any changes to the school prospectus (Education (School Curriculum and Related Information) Regulations 1989 reg 4(1)). Note that the articles of government must:

(a) enable the governors to produce their report "in such language or languages (in addition to English) as they consider appropriate" (E(No 2)A 1986 s 30(3)a)); and
(b) require them to "produce it in such language or languages (in addition to English and any other language in which the governing body propose to produce it) as the local education authority may direct" (s 30(3)(b)).

So far as GM schools are concerned, ERA 1988 is silent as to the matters covered by (a) and (b) above.

The governors' annual report is among the matters to be laid for discussion at the annual parents' meeting (required by E(No 2)A 1986 s 31—see below). DES Circular 8/86 explains that the report "is intended to be a straightforward factual document for reference by parents of pupils at the school and to inform the annual meeting" (para 10(c)).

(iv) Documents and information to be available for public access

"Public access" information falls into two distinct categories:

(a) Statements of curricular policy which LEAs and governors are required to prepare under the E(No 2)A 1986, as amended (see Chapter 7). Copies of these statements must be available to head teachers, governors and LEAs (Education (School Curriculum and Related Information) Regulations 1989 reg 5(1)–(4)); and, in turn, head teachers must make any such

documents available to any persons wishing to inspect them (reg 5(5)).
(b) The head teacher of every maintained school must make available on request prescribed types of information "at all reasonable times" (but not in relation to nursery classes in primary schools) (reg 6(1) and (2)).

The head teacher *must*, on request, supply a copy of any document within (a) above, and *may* supply a copy of a document (other than one subject to copyright) within (b) (reg 7(1)). S/he may make a charge, not exceeding the cost of producing the copy (reg 7(2)).

Information to be made available at school to parents and others "at all reasonable times" on request

Relevant statutory instruments, departmental circulars and administrative memoranda relevant to Chapter I Part I of the ERA 1988 (the curriculum)[a].

Any published Her Majesty's Inspectorate reports relating to the school.

Schemes of work in current use at the school.

Syllabuses followed at the school.

Arrangements for complaints under ERA 1988 s 23 (see below) or under the articles of government of a grant-maintained school.

The agreed syllabus for RE adopted by the LEA and, in the case of a voluntary school, the arrangements for RE in that school as specified in its trust deed or other document.

---

[a] The Secretary of State has given an undertaking that enough copies of these documents will be sent to schools for the purposes of public access (DES Circular 14/89, *The Education*

(School Curriculum and Related Information) Regulations 1989, para 25).

(v) Provision of statistical information to the LEA and/or Secretary of State

Close monitoring of curricular provision at each school is provided for by new legal requirements, most of which came into force on 1 August 1989 (Education (School Curriculum and Related Information) Regulations 1989, as amended, regs 8–11 and Schs 1 and 2). They require head teachers and governors to compile, on a *pro forma* or suitable alternative (Sch 1, and see the detailed guidance in DES Circular 14/89, Annex BI), detailed statistical information on the curriculum (the "Annual Curriculum Return"), with, on a separate form, details of provision for pupils excepted from the National Curriculum (NC) (Sch 2). The forms must be sent to the LEA (or, in the case of a GM school, to the Secretary of State) by 30 June each year—starting with June 1990 (1991 in the case of pupils excepted from the NC because they have special educational needs) (reg 8 and Sch 2). The information must be sent to the Secretary of State by 30 September each year (reg 11). There is no requirement to make any of this information available to parents.

(c) Translation of documents

Translation of documents may be necessary in the following circumstances:

> "If it appears requisite to an education authority or, as the case may be, the governing body of a maintained school, that any such document should be translated into a language other than English, it shall be so translated and the translated document shall be published or made available in such manner as appears to the governing body to be appropriate" (Education (School Curriculum and Related Information) Regulations 1989 reg 13(2)).

(d) The keeping, disclosure and transfer of pupil records

The law is contained in the Education (School Records) Regulations 1989, and applies to LEA-maintained schools, special schools (maintained or not) and grant-maintained schools. The duty to keep and transfer records came into force on 1 September 1989. The provisions dealing with disclosure come into effect on 1 September 1990.

(i) "Curricular record"

The regulations apply to a pupil's "curricular record". This is defined as "a formal record of a pupil's academic achievements, his other skills and abilities and his progress at school" (reg 4(1)). Where disclosure is concerned, "other educational records" relating to the child, including a "teacher's record", are to be treated as part of the pupil's curricular record (reg 7). The Circular on the regulations (17/89) explains that "other educational records" (a phrase not defined in the regulations) refers to "any other information which schools might find it helpful to keep for their own purposes" even though they are not legally required to do so (para 16). Included, as mentioned above, is information contained in a "teacher's record". This is defined as "any record kept at the school by a teacher other than a record kept and intended to be kept solely for that teacher's own use" (reg 7(2)). No guidance on how the distinction between what is or is not intended for the teacher's own use is offered by the Circular, and the regulation is bound to cause some confusion as well as leaving the matter to be decided by individual teachers, which is probably not what the regulations intended.

(ii) Duty to keep curricular records

School governing bodies are required to ensure that in respect of every registered pupil there is a curricular record and that it is updated at least once a year (reg 6(1)(a)).

(iii) Disclosure

Those entitled to disclosure: The regulations provide that an "entitled person" may, on making a request in writing, see a pupil's record and receive a copy of it (provided s/he is willing to pay the cost of producing it). Where appropriate, the record should be provided in a language other than

English—at no extra cost to the entitled person (reg 14). Access to the record must take place within fifteen days of receipt of the request.

The following are entitled persons (reg 4(1)):

(a) the parent of a pupil, where the pupil is aged under sixteen;
(b) the pupil or his/her parent where the pupil is aged sixteen or seventeen;
(c) the pupil, if aged eighteen or over.

Various persons might have rights as parents for this purpose, including those who do not have day to day care of the pupil—a separated parent, a divorced parent with joint legal custody, a legal guardian, or a foster parent. Local authority social services departments or voluntary organisations in which parental rights have been vested may also qualify (See DES Circular 17/89, *op cit*, para 22).

Correction and removal of inaccuracies: If the entitled person (above) submits a written notice to the school pointing out any alleged inaccuracies in the record, the governing body must either correct the record accordingly, or leave it as it is but append the parent's notice to it (reg 6(1)(c)).

Exceptions to the duty of disclosure: A number of exceptions to the general rule on disclosure are prescribed. Most are concerned with situations where disclosure might be detrimental to the child (see below).

Duty to disclose educational records: exceptions (regs 9–13)

1. Information originating from a person who is not employed by the LEA, nor a teacher, nor an educational welfare officer.

2. Information which would reveal its source (except where the source is the pupil or person referred to in 1 (above)).

3. Where disclosure would, in the opinion of the holder, "be likely to cause serious harm to the physical or mental

health or emotional condition of the pupil or any other person".

4. Where, in the opinion of the holder, the information "is relevant to the question whether the pupil to which it relates is or has been the subject of or may be at risk of child abuse".

5. A reference given by a teacher in respect of a pupil's application to a school or to further or higher education.

6. Educational records which are data for the purposes of the Data Protection Act. (The regulations apply to the keeping, disclosure and transfer of manual records only.)

7. Statements of special educational needs under the Education Act 1981.

8. Information relating to an individual pupil's assessment under the National Curriculum or otherwise—other than where disclosure is to the pupil's parent.

9. Any report prepared for the purposes of proceedings to which the Magistrates' Courts (Children and Young Persons) Rules 1988 (as amended) apply.

10. Information as to the racial group to which a pupil belongs, the language spoken in his home, and his/her religious persuasion—except to an "entitled person".

11. Anything recorded before 1 September 1989.

(iv) Transfer

When a pupil changes school or moves to a college or other institution the person responsible for the conduct of that institution is entitled to receive, without charge, the pupil's records or a copy thereof on request in writing (reg 6(1)(d)). Educational records kept before 1 September 1989 should also be transferred, if the governors consider it appropriate (reg 6(5)). On a change of school, details of the pupil's temporary exception (if any) from the National Curriculum should be transferred as well.

(v) Appeals

The governing body must make arrangements for parents to appeal against any decision relating to disclosure, transfer, correction or supply of a copy (reg 8). Nothing in the Education (School Government) Regulations 1989 prohibits the delegation of the hearing of appeals to a committee of governors. It is advisable (in the interests of natural justice) that neither the head teacher nor teacher governors hear such appeals.

(e) Defamation

Untrue statements which are defamatory could appear in school reports. A defamatory statement is one which might tend to lower the plaintiff's reputation in the eyes of right thinking members of society. If it is written, such a statement would be libellous (if untrue) and the plaintiff might recover High Court damages, without having to prove loss. It is probable that references and testimonials are covered by the defence of "qualified privilege"—provided the statement was made without malice. Malice might arise where, for example, the writer knows that what s/he is writing is untrue or where s/he is motivated by spite.

(f) The Data Protection Act 1984

The Data Protection Act 1984 regulates the keeping of *computerised* data. Schools should be registered with the Data Protection Registrar as data users—this is the LEA's or governors' responsibility. Failure to register is a criminal offence.

Data users must indicate to the Data Protection Registrar that they hold information and the purpose for which it is held. The Act establishes "data protection principles" (s 2) which require, *inter alia*, such data to have been lawfully obtained, relevant, accurate, and kept for no longer than is necessary. The data must only be used and disclosed for the purpose for which it was obtained (s 5).

Subject to certain exceptions, individuals (including pupils) have the right of access (s 21) to the information personal to them and may insist on amendments and deletions in appropriate cases (s 24). Data users must make appropriate security arrangements and may be liable for damage caused as a result of loss or unauthorised disclosure of data (s 23). Pupils are entitled to see the marks on which their examination results are based, although disclosure may be delayed until forty days after they are published, or five months after the request, whichever is the earlier (s 35). (See further, M Staunton, *Caught in the Act*, TES 29 November 1985.)

(g) Annual parents' meeting

The articles of most maintained schools require their governing bodies to hold a meeting once every school year—the "annual parents' meeting"—which shall be open to:

" (a) all parents of registered pupils at the school;
 (b) the head teacher; and
 (c) such other persons as the governing body may invite" (E(No 2)A 1986 s 31(1)).

(The articles for grant-maintained schools must make similar provision, although the meeting is to be open to parents and governors' invitees, and not expressly the head teacher (ERA 1988 s 58(5)(k)).)

Teachers, other than the head teacher, have no legal right to attend the annual parents' meeting, unless invited by the governors to do so. The official guidance is that there "may . . . be a case for inviting a few non-governor members of the teaching and non-teaching staff to the meeting" (DES Circular 8/86, para 13(b)).

The meeting is intended to consider the governors' report and the discharge by the governors, head teacher and LEA of their functions in relation to the school (E(No 2)A 1986 s 31(2)). The government believes that these meetings should "give the whole parent body the opportunity to become more closely involved in the life of the school, to mutual benefit" (DES Circular 8/86, para 13), although, realistically, the meeting could be a small element only of parental involvement.

2. Admissions

New arrangements for admissions to county and voluntary *secondary* schools will come into operation on 4 August 1990 (ERA 1988 Chapter II; ERA (Commencement No 1) Order 1988; DES Circular 11/88). The new arrangements are designed to enable popular schools to admit as many pupils as their legal limit allows them to, rather than the limit the LEA has set (perhaps with a view to spreading pupil numbers evenly around the authority's schools).

The Education Reform Act 1988 also makes provision for new admission arrangements in *primary* schools, but only when the Secretary of State issues an Order bringing the provisions into effect in relation to these schools. This has not yet been done, and there are no immediate plans for extending the new arrangements to these schools. (Separate provisions govern admissions arrangements in *grant-maintained* schools (see below, page 152).)

Whatever the timetable for the introduction of the new admissions arrangements in particular school sectors, the Secretary of State:

> "hopes that admission authorities will give full recognition to the expression of parental preference with immediate effect and will not turn away eligible applicants to their schools unless those schools are physically full" (DES Circular 11/88, para 1).

Note that no charge may be made for admission to any maintained school, including one which is grant-maintained (ERA 1988 s 106(1)).

(a) Admissions limit—"the standard number"

Every school will have a "standard number", and the authority responsible for admissions to the school must not restrict its intake below that number (ERA 1988 s 26(1)). Authorities responsible for admissions may, however, decide to have an admissions total *higher* than the relevant standard number (s 26(3)) (see below).

Parents as consumers: information and choice of school

(i) What is the "standard number"?

It is to be whichever is the greater of the following two numbers:

    (a) The "appropriate pre-commencement number" (s 27(1)(a)) ie "in the case of a secondary school . . . the standard number applying to the school under section 15 of the 1980 Act in relation to the age group in question in the school year immediately preceding the commencement year" (s 27(2)(a)). This normally means the total number of pupils admitted to the relevant age group in the whole of the school year 1979–80 (DES Circular 11/88, para 8). The school and LEA will already know this number.

    (b) The "number of pupils in that age group admitted in the school year immediately preceding the commencement year" (s 27(1)(a)). So, if admissions in 1989-90 exceeded the standard number under s 15 EA 1980 (above), the 1989–90 admissions figure would be the new "standard number".

"Relevant age group" is defined in s 32(2) (and see also DES Circular 11/88, para 9). Note that admissions of pupils at ages other than the normal age or ages of admission do not count towards a standard number.

(ii) Increasing admission levels

Admissions in excess of the standard number may be permissible in two situations:

First, the authorities responsible for admissions may, subject to certain requirements (including the duty under E(No 2)A 1986 s 33 to consult over varying admissions arrangements) admit pupils in excess of the standard number, *provided the buildings are adequate to accommodate the new number* (see Education (School Premises) Regulations 1981—Chapter 9). The DES Circular 11/88, para 10 advises that schools are not required to expand physically to meet demand and that if the LEA or governors wish to enlarge the premises so that they may accommodate more pupils, proposals for school changes should be published in the normal way (see page 33).

Secondly, a proposal may be made by (a) the governors, if the LEA is the admissions authority, or (b) the LEA, if the admissions authority is the governing body, for:

"fixing as the number of pupils in any . . . age group it is intended to admit . . . a number which exceeds both—
(a) the relevant standard number; and
(b) any number fixed or proposed to be fixed for that purpose by the authority responsible for detemining the arrangements for admission of pupils . . ." (ERA 1988 s 26(4)).

The proposer may make a formal application (in writing) to the admissions authority, asking for a higher admissions limit and specifying how many should be admitted (s 26(6)). If the admissions authority does not reject the proposal in writing within two months of the day after it was received, the authority must adopt it (s 26(7)). If the admissions authority does so object, the proposer has twenty-eight days in which to make an application to the Secretary of State to increase the relevant standard number (s 26(8)). The information the Secretary of State would wish to have before him when considering a proposal to increase the standard number (under his power in s 27(5)) is set out in DES Circular 11/88, para 13. On an application to increase the standard number the Secretary of State may refuse to make the order, or order the number to be increased to that proposed, or, after consultation with the LEA and governing body, set the number at a lower number than that proposed (s 27(7)).

(iii) Physical capacity (secondary schools)

There is a standard form to be used in calculating a school's physical capacity (Annex A to DES Circular 11/88). The form should be completed and submitted to the Secretary of State with any application for a variation in the standard number. In the case of proposals to reduce the standard number, the completed form should accompany the published proposals and be made available for inspection by relevant parties. Further guidance, including advice as to completion and submission of the form, is in the DES Circular 11/88, paras 21-27, and is set out on the *pro forma* itself.

(iv) Reductions in admissions limits—setting a lower standard number

Applications for a reduction in the standard number may be made, but only by the authority responsible for admissions (s 28(1)). The appropriate authority must first consult the LEA or governors (as appropriate) (s 28(8)). The Secretary of State may make an order only if he considers that:

> "reduction is necessary, having regard to any reduction in the school's capacity to accommodate pupils as compared with its capacity at the beginning of the school year to which the current standard number first applied in relation to that age group" (s 28(7)).

The DES Circular 11/88 para 14 explains that reduction in the standard number would be necessary if:

" (a) the amount of accommodation available at the school at the time the standard number was determined is no longer physically available, or
 (b) the use to which the accommodation has subsequently been put has reduced the school's capacity to accommodate pupils, or
 (c) admitting pupils up to the existing standard number would lead to the school having to exceed the number of pupils for whom accommodation could be provided under the current school premises regulations".

It will be important for the admissions authority to assess the likely demand for places at the school in question. As the Circular states, if the level of demand is likely to be short of the standard number, authorities "may consider it unnecessary to seek a reduction, believing they can safely have an admission limit which will not in practice be reached" (*ibid*).

Any proposal to reduce the standard number must be published by the admissions authority together with a statement of the effects of the proposals. Regulations give details relating to the publication of proposals (Education (Publication of Proposals for Reduction in Standard Number) Regulations 1988). If objections to the proposals are raised by ten or more local government electors, or by the governing body or LEA, etc (s 28(3) and (5)), the admissions authority must refer them, within specified time periods, to the Secretary of State. The Secretary of State may reject outright or confirm the proposals, or he may set a higher standard number than that proposed (s 28(6)). (For further information, see DES Circular 11/88, paras 14-20.)

(v) Primary schools

For the purposes of defining admission numbers for primary schools, children admitted to a primary school for nursery education must be disregarded. Their admission will be deemed to take place when they are transferred to a reception class. Children aged between four and a half and five years are now included in the standard number (s 29). The standard number will thus reflect the actual numbers at the school more accurately than under EA 1980. No date has as yet been fixed for the new admissions arrangements to become operative in primary schools.

(vi) Keeping the standard number under review

The admissions authority is required to

"keep under review any standard numbers . . . having regard to any change in the school's capacity to accommodate pupils as compared with its capacity at the beginning of the school year to which those standard numbers first applied" (s 27(8)).

(b) Admissions to grant-maintained schools

The articles of government for grant-maintained schools are to make provision "with respect to arrangements for the admission of pupils to the school and the policy to be followed in deciding admissions" (s 58(5)(b)). Admissions arrangements are to be "independent of, but similar in nature to, the arrangements operating for local authority schools in the area" and "consistent with the previous character of the school" (DES Circular 10/88). As stated previously, the articles of government must require publication of admissions arrangements and appeal procedures (ERA 1988 s 58(5)(f)). Published information should also contain the criteria to be applied in deciding on admissions where the school is over-subscribed. According to the Circular 10/88:

> "The Secretary of State will expect those criteria to be clearly expressed so that parents will have the fullest possible indication of their chance of succeeding in gaining a place for their child".

The admissions limit set by the governors must be not less than the approved admission number for the relevant age group which they intend to admit (ERA 1988 s 83(1))—ie the number of pupils in the relevant age group in the proposals for GM status (s 83(2)(a)). (Pupils intended to be admitted for nursery education shall be disregarded; those so admitted but now transferring to a reception class are to be included (s 83(2)(b) and (c)).) According to DES Circular 10/88, it is the Secretary of State's intention that the admissions limit will normally be set at the physical capacity of the school. The approved admission number may be varied with the approval of the Secretary of State (s 83(3)).

(c) The exercise of parental preference

A parent is entitled to express a preference for a particular school for his/her child. The relevant provisions (which do not apply to grant-maintained schools or city technology colleges) are in the Education Act 1980, as amended. LEAs must make arrangements for such a preference to be expressed and for the parent(s) to give reasons (s 6(1)). Subject to the conditions in s 6(3), LEAs and governors have a duty to comply with any preference expressed.

Before the 1980 Act, some parents sought to rely on s 76 of the 1944 Act (children to be educated according to the wishes of parents if it is "compatible with the provision of efficient instruction and training and the avoidance of unreasonable public expenditure"). But the courts showed s 76, which, incidentally, is still in force, to be somewhat limited in scope; parental wishes were only one of a number of factors to which LEAs had to have regard when exercising their powers and duties (*Watt* v *Kesteven County Council* (1955); *Wood* v *London Borough of Ealing* (1967); *Cumings* v *Birkenhead Corporation* (1972); *Smith* v *ILEA* (1978)).

Recently this position was re-affirmed in a Scottish case, concerned with the application of the identical provision in Scottish education legislation—the Education (Scotland) Act 1980 s 28(1). Parental wishes were only one of the factors to be taken into account when plans to close a school were being considered: *Harvey* v *Strathclyde Regional Council* (1989).

When LEAs need not comply with parental preference: Choice of school may be denied:

(i) "if compliance... would prejudice the provision of efficient education or the efficient use of resources" (EA 1980 s 6(3)(a)). If the admission of the pupil would not take admissions above the school's standard number for the relevant age group or any higher admissions number fixed for the school (see *Increasing admissions levels* (above)), such admission shall not be taken to "prejudice... resources" for the purposes of s 6(3)(a) (ERA 1988 s 26(9)) and the pupil could not be denied a place on this ground.

The "efficiency" requirements above apply not only to decisions in individual cases but also to broader policy decisions on admissions. In *R* v *Greenwich LBC ex parte Governors of John Ball Primary School* (1989), Greenwich's education committee approved an admissions policy which favoured children residing in the borough over and above those living in neighbouring Lewisham. Under relatively long-standing reciprocal arrangements between the boroughs, a number of children attending seven named primary schools in Lewisham had in the past been allocated places at Greenwich secondary schools. But the effect of Greenwich's new policy would have been removal of the opportunity for Lewisham children to attend Greenwich secondary schools. Greenwich's policy decision was declared invalid in the High Court (Parker LJ and Tudor-Evans J). Explaining the duty of the LEA, Parker LJ said:

"All parental preferences are to be complied with unless it is shown that compliance would prejudice efficient education. It was the same for children in or out of the area [see s 6(5)]. The schools admission policy should have been designed to create such a result... The policy was invalid for, far from advancing the purpose of the 1980 Act, it was seen and recognized to be a policy which did not further the purpose but went against the statute".

When the LEA appealed to the Court of Appeal, the appeal was dismissed (*The Times*, 27 December 1989), for the same reasons as had been given in the High Court's judgment. The Court also emphasised that "efficiency", as per s 6(3)(a), was not to be "the first source of an admissions policy" (*per* Lloyd LJ) but rather a basis for denying choice, otherwise presumed to be generally guaranteed by virtue of s 6(2), in an individual case. A LEA could adopt admissions criteria based on, for example, the presence of an applicant's siblings on the register of a school or proximity of the school to the applicant's home. Such criteria "could exist in a sound and lawful policy, whether or not the policy promoted efficient education". But in applying any such criteria laid down in its policy, the LEA was bound to comply with parental preference (s 6(2)) unless, *inter alia*, compliance would result in inefficiency (see also *R v S. Glamorgan Appeals Committee exp. Evans* (1984);

(ii) if, in the case of aided or special agreement schools, it "would be incompatible with any arrangements between the governors and the local education authority made under subsection (6)" (s 6(3)(b), as amended by ERA 1988 s 30(2)). Subsection (6) requires LEAs to make admission arrangements with the governors of these schools "for preserving the character of the school", where so requested by the governors. If agreement on the arrangements cannot be achieved by the LEA and governors, the arrangements shall be determined by the Secretary of State. The DES Circular 11/88, para 40 advises that:

> "the arrangements might, for example, safeguard the particular character of a church-aided school by stipulating what percentage of the intake has to be of the denomination concerned";

(iii) if entry to the preferred school is selective in terms of a child's ability and aptitude, and compliance would be incompatible with selection under these arrangements (s 6(3)(c))—even if the school is not full (see DES Circular 11/88, para 39).

(d) Criteria for admission

Parents should be informed of the policy on admissions—details must be published by the LEA or, in the case of aided, special agreement and grant-maintained schools, the governors (EA 1980 s 8, and ERA 1988 s 58(5)(b)). The criteria applied by LEAs/governors usually include, in various orders of priority:

- attendance of siblings at the preferred school;
- distance of home from school;
- attendance at a particular "feeder" primary school;
- medical reasons;
- other social or domestic reasons.

DES Circular 11/88 states that LEAs and governors may apply "any reasonable criteria they wish for deciding which pupils should have priority of admission" subject to various legal requirements, such as the Race Relations Act 1976 and Sex Discrimination Act 1975 (para 49).

It is important for admissions authorities to avoid operating either an admissions policy or admissions criteria which are too rigid. Parker LJ put the matter succinctly in *R v Greenwich LBC ex parte Governors of John Ball Primary School* (1989):

> "Every council has to have some policy regarding school admissions, particularly in the case of over-subscription. The creation of the policy is a matter of discretion for the local authority but the discretion is not to thwart the law. A policy has to be prepared to consider exceptions".

(e) Appeals

(i) Schools other than those which are grant-maintained

The appropriate admissions authority—LEA or governors—must make arrangements for parents to appeal against the school allocated for their child (EA 1980 s 7). Authorities may have informal procedures for resolving disputes over choice of school. But these cannot override statutory rights of appeal.

Parents as consumers: information and choice of school

The appeal lies to an appeal committee constituted in accordance with Sch 2 to the 1980 Act. Guidance on procedure before, during and after the hearing is contained in a Code of Practice (not legally binding) drawn up by local authorities in association with the Council on Tribunals.

In relation to county and controlled schools each committee must have three, five or seven members drawn from LEA members (including any education committee members) and people who have experience in education, have knowledge of local education conditions or are parents of pupils registered at a schoo (but not the school in respect of which the appeal is being made) (Part I para 1(3)). Of LEA employees, only teachers are permitted to sit as appeal committee members, but not where the appeal relates to their own school (*ibid*). LEA members must not outnumber the other members by more than one (para 1(4)) and the chairperson of the appeal committee must not be a member of the education committee (para 1(5)). The Code of Practice on Appeals warns against the selection of a committee too large in number, in case this proves too daunting for appellants.

The constitution of the appeal committee is slightly different for voluntary aided and special agreement schools (para 2), although the number of panel members required is the same. The panel may include governors, may not include anyone employed by the governors or LEA otherwise than as a teacher, and must include sufficient persons drawn from a list compiled by the LEA to enable them to constitute half the appeal committee (excluding the chairperson). The chairperson may not be a governor.

In all cases the appellant must give notice of appeal setting out the grounds on which the appeal is made (para 5). The appellant can address the appeal committee and can be accompanied by a friend or be represented (para 6). The hearing must be held in private except where the LEA or governors direct otherwise (para 10). However, a LEA observer, or a member of the Council on Tribunals, may attend (*ibid*).

The matters that the appeal committee must take into account when reaching its decision include:

(a) any preference expressed by the parent(s) (under EA 1980 s 6);
(b) the arrangements for admission published in accordance with s 8 (para 7).

This does not, of course, preclude consideration of other relevant factors; the committee will, in any event, have to apply s 6(3) (above). The decision of the appeal committee is binding on the LEA or governors (EA 1980 s 7(5)). In the event of disagreement, the committee may decide by majority, with the chairperson having a second or casting vote in the event of equal voting (para 8). The committee's decision must be sent in writing to the appellant and LEA (or governors, in respect of an aided or special agreement school); the grounds for the decision must be stated (para 9).

(ii) Grant-maintained schools

In GM schools the appeal may be made to an appeal committee constituted in accordance with the instrument of government (ERA 1988 s 58(5)(d)). The DES Circular 10/88, para 62 emphasises that the appeal committee will have "independent representation". The appeal committees will, in common with those established under EA 1980 for LEA schools, fall within the supervisory jurisdiction of the Council on Tribunals (ERA 1988 Sch 12 para 12).

(f) Further action by parents

Sections 68 and 99 EA 1944 contain very important default powers which could be employed in relation to school admissions, but which have, in fact, been very sparingly used.

Section 68 empowers the Secretary of State, on a complaint by any person or on his own initiative, to give directions to LEAs or governors if he is satisfied that they have "acted or are proposing to act unreasonably" in respect of any power or duty under the Education Acts.

In *Secretary of State for Education and Science* v *Tameside MBC* (1977), the House of Lords held that the test of unreasonableness laid down by the Master of the Rolls in 1948 (Greene MR in *Associated Provincial Picture Houses* v

Wednesbury Corporation)—"unreasonable in the sense that the court considers it to be a decision that no reasonable body could have come to. . . not what the court considers unreasonable. . ."—was applicable to s 68.

Section 99 empowers the Secretary of State to give directions to a LEA or governors where he is satisfied that such body is acting in default of any duty under the 1944 Act. Such directions can be enforced by *mandamus* (a court order compelling a public body to carry out its duty).

As mentioned above, these powers are used very infrequently. Between 1977 and 1984, only three or four interventions in respect of school allocations were made under s 68 (D Bull, (1985) JSWL 189, 222). In 1988 the Secretary of State refused to use his powers when asked to do so by a group of white Dewsbury parents. They had objected to the decision of the LEA (from which the authority subsequently backed down) to allocate their children to a school the majority of whose pupils were of Asian origins. The courts seem unwilling to set aside Secretary of State's decisions and substitute their views for his, provided they are satisfied he has taken account of relevant factors and ignored irrelevant ones (see *Thameside*, above).

Other possible courses of action open to parents are:

(i) to apply (generally, but not exclusively, following unsuccessful reference to the Secretary of State—see *R v Northamptonshire County Council ex parte Gray* (1986) and *R v ILEA ex parte Ali* (1990)) for judicial review in the High Court (if, for example, the appeal hearing was not conducted in accordance with natural justice—eg, the parent was not given an opportunity to speak—or on the basis of the "unreasonableness" of the LEA or governors); or

(ii) to complain to the local commissioner for administration (ombudsman). A complaint that a woman who appealed to a Rochdale appeal committee had not been given an adequate opportunity to state her case and was frequently interrupted by the chairman was upheld (Complaint No 388/C/83).

Chapter 5

Equal opportunities

In the 1960s, the existence of a long-standing right to education for all citizens from the ages of five to eighteen, coupled with a duty on LEAs under the Education Act 1944 to ensure there was suitable provision, suggested that, in theory at least, the benefits of a sound education would be available to all. Certain reforms in that decade, such as the introduction of comprehensive schools, reinforced the notion of equality—even though concerns about standards, and the continuation of the private sector and grammar/direct grant schools, demonstrated that equality, if seen in terms of access to the various forms of provision, was far from absolute. At least in Britain the kind of struggle to establish equal rights to education that had occurred in the United States had never proved necessary. There it took a Supreme Court ruling (in *Brown* v *Board of Education* (1954)) to set the southern states in particular on the road to racial desegregation of schools under the law. (For analysis of *Brown* and its aftermath, see MG Yudof et al, *Educational Policy and the Law*, 2nd ed (1982), Chapter 5.) Nevertheless, in Britain it was increasingly felt that recognition for the principle of equal opportunities should appear in legislation, as it had under the European Convention on Human Rights, although, especially where sex discrimination was concerned, the impetus arose chiefly from concern about discrimination at work rather than inequality of educational opportunity. Discrimination on the grounds of race and sex became unlawful under the Race Relations Acts 1965 and 1968 (see now the Race Relations Act 1976) and Sex Discrimination Act 1975.

Equal opportunities provisions also appear in both EC law (Directive 76/207, providing for equality between men and women in the provision of access to vocational training) and, as mentioned, in the European Convention on Human Rights 1950. Article 14 of the Convention forbids discrimination on the grounds of, *inter alia*, sex, race or colour in relation to the various rights guaranteed by the Convention, including, under Article 2 of the 1st Protocol, the right to education. Council of Europe Recommendation R(85)2, Principle II.3, calls for equality of access to education between men and women.

1. Sex Discrimination Act 1975

The Act outlaws direct or indirect discrimination against women on the grounds of sex or marital status as well as victimisation of a person who has complained of an infringement under the Act. The Act refers to discrimination against women, although by virtue of s 2(1) it applies also to discrimination against men.

(a) Defining discrimination

Direct discrimination falls under s 1(1)(a) of the Act. It involves treating a woman "less favourably" on the ground of her sex. (The sex of the complainant must be a "substantial cause" of the less favourable treatment: *James* v *Eastleigh Borough Council* (1989) (CA) per Sir Nicholas Browne-Wilkinson V-C.) Indirect discrimination arises if a person applies to a woman:

> "a requirement or condition which he applies or would apply equally to a man but—
> (i) which is such that the proportion of women who can comply with it is considerably smaller than the proportion of men who can comply with it, and
> (ii) which he cannot show to be justifiable irrespective of the sex of the person to whom it is applied, and
> (iii) which is to her detriment because she cannot comply with it" (s 1(1)(b)).

(Note that the giving of careers advice by LEAs is also covered by the Act (s 15(2)).)

There is no need for the discrimination to have been intentional:

> "The intention or motive of the defendant to discriminate, though it may be relevant so far as remedies are concerned (see s 66(3) of the 1975 Act (below)), is not a necessary condition to liability; it is perfectly possible to envisage cases where the defendant had no such motive, and yet did in fact discriminate on the grounds of sex" (per Lord Goff in *Equal Opportunities Commission* v *Birmingham City Council* (1989)).

(b) Discrimination by the responsible body under section 22

Under s 22 Sex Discrimination Act 1975, direct or indirect discrimination on the ground of sex is unlawful if committed by a LEA (or governors) ("the responsible body") in relation to:

- the admission of a pupil to an educational establishment;
- what is provided at the school (the "benefits, facilities and services"); and
- exclusion "or other detriment".

(It might reasonably be supposed that "detriment" refers here to some form of punishment akin to exclusion rather than a wholly different form of detriment (see *De Souza* v *Automobile Association* (1986) which deals with the phrase "or other detriment" in the Race Relations Act 1976).)

Responsibility under s 22 rests with the appropriate "responsible body"—ie the governors or LEA, depending on which is responsible for the particular function in question. Institutions must be designated under the Sex Discrimination (Designated Institutions) Orders 1975 and 1980, made under s 24 of the Act (as amended by ERA 1988). The proprietor of an independent school is also a "responsible body". In a grant-maintained school the responsible body is the governing body (s 22, as amended by ERA 1988 Sch 12 para 15).

Discussion of discrimination within schools ensues below, but it may be noted here that in a co-educational school discrimination could occur in relation to subject choices,

Equal opportunities

since this clearly falls within the definition of "benefits, facilities or services".

(c) LEA discrimination under s 23

Section 23(1) requires LEAs to carry out without discrimination on the grounds of sex those of their functions under the Education Acts not covered by s 22. An example would be s 8 Education Act 1944, discussed in Chapter 1, which requires LEAs to ensure that there are, in their area, primary and secondary schools which are "sufficient in number, character and equipment" to afford all pupils appropriate and desirable opportunities for education. In the view of the Equal Opportunities Commission (*Formal Investigation Report: West Glamorgan Schools* (1988)) the opportunities for girls, in a LEA's schools as a whole, would have to be no less favourable than for boys.

(d) The general duty under s 25

A further duty, in s 25, rests on LEAs and any other bodies which are responsible bodies under the Act "to secure that facilities for education provided by [them], and any ancillary benefits or services, are provided without sex discrimination". There is clearly some overlap between the s 25 duty and the duties in ss 22 and 23. Indeed, a specific instance of discrimination may fall foul of s 25 and either of these other sections, although, unlike the other sections, only the Secretary of State may enforce s 25 (see below). In *Equal Opportunities Commission* v *Birmingham City Council* (1989) (HL), Lord Goff explained the relationship between, on the one hand, ss 22 and 23 (above), and on the other s 25. His Lordship could see "no reason why these two sections should not, in the field of education, embrace all cases of unlawful discrimination as such by [LEAs]" (at 775). So what is the purpose of s 25? His Lordship felt its purpose was rather different from that of the other two sections. It was intended:

> "not to outlaw acts of discrimination as such, but to place on ['responsible'] bodies a positive role in relation to the elimination of sex discrimination. The idea appears to

have been that such bodies are, so to speak, put on their toes to ensure that sex discrimination does not occur in areas within their responsibility" (at 776).

Guidance issued by the Equal Opportunities Commission (*Formal Investigation Report: West Glamorgan Schools* (1988) Appendix B) states that in order to assess whether there has been a breach of the s 25 duty it is necessary to consider:

(i) whether educational provision has been planned on the principle of equality of opportunity for pupils of both sexes;
(ii) whether the actual provision made is in accordance with the equality principle;
(iii) whether the actual provision made results or is likely to result in any act of unlawful sex discrimination.

Note that the duty in s 25 does not apply to the admission of pupils to single sex schools (see below).

(e) Specific aspects of provision

(i) Single sex schools

Single sex schools are popular with some parents, often on cultural or religious grounds. (See SM Poulter, *English Law and Ethnic Minority Customs* (1986), pages 191–195 for discussion of the legal and policy issues.) It is not unlawful to discriminate in relation to admission to a single sex school (s 26(1)). A single sex school which admits members of the opposite sex in comparatively small numbers to particular courses of instruction or teaching class groups (eg a single sex school which has a mixed sixth form) is regarded as a single sex school for this purpose. There are also special provisions permitting discrimination where selection of one sex or the other is necessary because the school is changing from a single sex to a co-educational school (s 27, and Education (Schools and Further Education) Regulations 1981, as amended).

But where a LEA provides single sex schools, it has to do so in such a way that its policy does not result in one sex being treated more favourably. For example, in *R v Secretary of*

State for Education and Science ex parte Keating (1986), Taylor J found unlawful a LEA's decision to close the only single sex boys school in its area while continuing to maintain two single sex girls schools. In another case, *Equal Opportunities Commission* v *Birmingham City Council* (1989) (HL), more places were available to boys (540) than to girls (360) in the LEA's voluntary aided single sex grammar schools, there being five such schools for boys and three for girls. One result of this was that as selection for admission to these schools was based on ability, on average a girl would have to achieve higher examination marks than a boy to gain a place. The LEA had a definite equal opportunities policy, but could do nothing about the inequality here because the governors of the schools insisted on selection by ability. The High Court, Court of Appeal (Woolf LJ dissenting) and the House of Lords in turn held that there was discrimination. In the House of Lords, Lord Goff said that discrimination resulted not from any supposed disadvantage resulting from the denial of selective education to a higher proportion of girls than boys—on the basis that education under a selective system might be better than under a non-selective system—but rather, it flowed from the denial of choice. Unfortunately, this particular issue in Birmingham has yet to be resolved. In October 1989 the governors of Handsworth Grammar School for boys voted against admitting girls, leaving the LEA in a difficult position. The chairman of the city's education committee feared further intervention by the Equal Opportunities Commission (*The Times*, 18 October 1989). Subsequently, so it appears, parents and governors of one of the boys' grammar schools in question contemplated pursuing a change to grant-maintained status for the school in order to avoid its becoming co-educational.

(ii) Sex discrimination in schools

Discrimination can occur in relation to subject choice and the way that subjects are taught. More often than not, such discrimination occurs unintentionally (Equal Opportunities Commission, *Formal Investigation Report: West Glamorgan Schools* (1988)). Despite positive efforts to eradicate it, including repeated emphasis on equal opportunities in DES guidance (eg DES Circular 2/76) and reports (eg *Science Education in Schools* (1982)), there is evidence that it is still a problem. For example, in the recent formal investigation into discrimination in West Glamorgan schools (*op cit*) the Equal Opportunities Commission found conclusive evidence of discrimination in relation to access to classes for craft, design and technology. Separate curricular provision for boys and girls, which was the problem in West Glamorgan, is surprisingly commonplace (*Secondary Schools. An Appraisal by HMI* (1988), page 43). The Equal Opportunities Commission (1988, *op cit*, page 47) explains that the Sex Discrimination Act 1975 "does not prohibit separate facilities for boys and girls within a co-educational school, provided that the facilities afforded to each sex can justifiably be regarded as equal". Although this implies a wider, qualitative, concept of "equality", such as that appearing in the Equal Pay Act 1970 and regulations thereunder, it is clear that the 1975 Act is concerned principally with equal access to specific learning opportunities across the curriculum. Thus, schools are advised that:

> "Equal opportunities does not mean that all pupils will study all subjects on offer, but it does mean that they should have an equal chance to study all such subjects. Care should be taken in the structuring of the time-table to make this choice real, particularly with respect to non-traditional subjects. The way in which options are devised is of crucial importance."

Discrimination might also occur in the way that classes are organised. In one case, a primary school in Bromley, faced with shortage of space for a fourth year class, sent only boys up to this class. The LEA admitted contravention of the Act, and three girls affected by the authority's decision were awarded compensation of £500 by the county court (*Debell and Teh v Bromley LBC* (1984)—cited in Milman, *Educational Conflict and the Law* (1986), page 52).

In limited circumstances, segregated physical education might be lawful—"where the physical demands of a particular competitive sport would place girls at an undue disadvantage. Thus inter-sex rugby could quite justifiably be banned" (Milman and de Gama, *Sexual Discrimination in Education: One Step Forward, Two Steps Back?* (1989) (1)

JSWL 4, 12). However, barring boys from netball or girls from soccer would, most probably, be unlawful (*ibid*).

(f) Enforcement

For breaches of s 22 or s 23, redress may be sought in the county court, where, in these cases, *High Court* remedies, eg unlimited damages, are obtainable (ss 62 and 66). Before proceedings can be brought (there have in fact been very few cases: Pannick, *Sex Discrimination Law* (1985), page 306), the complainant must give notice to the Secretary of State who then has two months to consider the complaint (s 66(5)). (Pannick, *op cit*, regards this as anomalous in the context of sex discrimination law as a whole.) Damages, which can include an amount for injury to feelings, cannot be awarded if indirect discrimination was unintentional (s 66(3)). Complaint to the Secretary of State under ss 68 and 99 EA 1944, on the ground that the responsible body is acting (or proposing to act) unreasonably or has acted in default of its duty, is also possible, and, indeed, is the only way of enforcing the duty under s 25 (s 25(4)). If the complaint is upheld by the Secretary of State, s/he can issue directions to the responsible body to desist from the discriminatory practice.

The power of the Equal Opportunities Commission to bring or assist with proceedings has assisted the enforcement of the Act. In the *Birmingham* case (above), for example, the court was able to make a declaration that the LEA's arrangements for secondary education were unlawful. The Equal Opportunities Commission is recognized by the court as having *locus standi* (ie a legitimate right to bring the case) for this purpose.

The Commission can also conduct a formal investigation (s 57) and, if it does so, must make any recommendations it considers necessary or expedient, and prepare a report (s 60).

It is not clear whether complaints of sex discrimination under the curriculum fall within the scope of the statutory complaints procedure which LEAs (and governors of grant-maintained schools) have to establish under ERA 1988 s 23 (see Chapter 7). The procedure applies, *inter alia*, to "any . . . enactment relating to the curriculum" (s 23(1)(a)(ii)). If this includes complaints of sex discrimination in relation to curricular provision, then s 23(2) of the 1988 Act will presumably apply. This states that before a complaint falling within s 23(1) of that Act can be considered by the Secretary of State, it must have first been taken through the statutory complaints procedure.

2. Race Relations Act 1976

In provisions parallel to those covering sex discrimination (above), the Race Relations Act 1976 provides that direct or indirect discrimination (ie less favourable treatment) in education on the grounds of "colour, race, nationality or ethnic or national origins" (ss 1 and 3(1)) (but not religion—see *Nyasi* v *Ryman Ltd* (1988)) is unlawful:

(a) under s 17 (non-admission or the terms of admission to a school, access to benefits, facilities or services at the school, exclusion or other detriment) (LEA or governors responsible, as appropriate, see table in s 17);
(b) under s 18 (the carrying out by a LEA of any of its functions under the Education Acts); and
(c) under s 19 (general duty in public sector of education—facilities for education and/or any ancillary benefits or services).

Sections 17–19 are identical in scope to ss 22, 23 and 25 Sex Discrimination Act 1975 (above).

There are some exceptions to these basic requirements—positive discrimination in the form of greater access for an ethnic or racial group to certain educational facilities because of its special educational needs, is permissible (s 35).

There is also a general duty on local authorities to carry out their various functions, which include provision of education, with due regard to the need to eliminate racial discrimination and promote equality of opportunity and good relations between persons of different racial groups (s 71). Anti-racism strategies have been adopted by a large number of LEAs. These are very important, although care must be exercised in the pursuit of such initiatives, as the report of the inquiry into the fatal racial attack in Burnage High School in Manchester (the MacDonald Report—*Murder in the Playground*) concluded. Schools and LEAs should have regard to the Commission for Racial Equality's recent guidance (*Code of Practice for the elimination of racial discrimination in education*, December 1989). This highlights the need for the avoidance of discrimination in school admissions, teaching, assessment, discipline, careers advice and work experience placement. In the *Code's* foreword, the Secretary of State for Education, John MacGregor, reminds LEAs and schools of their "important responsibility to work towards the promotion of equality of opportunity for the different ethnic groups who are part of our national life".

(a) Specific issues

(i) Dress

Insistence by a school or LEA that a particular form of dress and no other be worn by pupils could amount to indirect racial discrimination under s 1 of the Act, although it would be a defence for the governors or LEA to show that the requirement is "justifiable" under s 1(1)(b)(ii). The proportion of, for example, girls of Asian origin belonging to a particular ethnic group who "can comply" with a condition that they should wear skirts for school may be less than the proportion of girls of other (eg non-Asian) groups who can so comply. Although the former are physically able to comply, they may be unable for cultural reasons to do so—trousers or *shalwar* being required dress.

In *Mandla* v *Dowell Lee* (1983) a head teacher of a private school had refused to admit a Sikh boy unless he went without his turban and had his hair cut. The wearing of the turban was alleged to be inconsistent with the school's policy on uniform and its policy of de-emphasising religious and cultural differences. The House of Lords decided that the ban on the boy was discrimination and that discrimination for the reasons given was not "justifiable" under the terms of the statute—because it had to be "justifiable" irrespective of the race, colour, ethnic origins, etc, of the person to whom it applied (*per* Lord Fraser, at 1070). (The court also decided that Sikhs were a racial group; recently gipsies and rastafarians were held to be racial groups: *Commission for Racial Equality* v *Dutton* (1989); *Dawkins* v *The Crown Suppliers* (1990).)

Restrictions on type of dress could possibly be "justifiable" indirect discrimination on public health or safety grounds (eg wearing of jewellery in school). The safety argument was put forward by Altrincham Girls Grammar school to justify the suspension of two Muslim girls, aged fourteen and fifteen, for wearing traditional head scarves contrary to school rules. The governors, accused by some of unlawfully discriminating, subsequently acceded to the girls' request to wear the head coverings. The compromise reached was that the scarves would be in the school's colour of navy and would be tucked inside the girls' collars.

Justification based on practical inconvenience may be insufficient (see Poulter, *English Law and Ethnic Minority Customs* (1986), pages 181–188). In *Steel* v *Union of Post Office Workers* (1978) it was held that a discriminatory condition or requirement would have to be justified "by the need—not the convenience—of the business or enterprise". The necessity test in *Steel* was further articulated in *Rainey* v *Greater Glasgow Health Board* (1987). In *Ojutiku* v *MSC* (1982) the emphasis had been on whether reasonable people would find the condition "sound and tolerable". But in the recent case of *Hampson* v *Department of Education and Science* (1990) Balcombe LJ said that 'justifiable' requires an objective balance between the discriminatory effect of the condition and the reasonable needs of the party who applies the condition". It is difficult to apply this "reasonable necessity" test, laid down in these employment cases, to education. The principal "needs" of a school would comprise the provision of a sound curriculum and the maintenance of discipline, health and safety. It is hard to imagine any situation, except perhaps, where there is a risk to health or safety (see above), in which racial discrimination in a school would be "justifiable". If, of course, it *can* be shown that a condition or requirement which has a discriminatory effect is on balance justifiable irrespective of that effect, then it would not be unlawful under the Act. In any event, the question of restrictions on type of dress is for the LEA or, rather, the governors of a school to consider carefully and objectively. The onus is on the discriminator to show that the condition is justifiable and, moreover, justifiable irrespective of race, ethnic origins, etc (*Mandla, op cit*).

(ii) Language and culture

So far as the language in which pupils are taught is concerned, the fact that it is not a pupil's mother tongue would not be a ground for complaint under the Act (Poulter, *op cit*, page 177). However, claims that language such as Urdu, Punjabi, Bengali, modern Greek, Turkish and Arabic should at least be offered as subjects by schools have partly been met. These, and a few other languages, can be offered as modern languages under the National Curriculum provided one of the prescribed modern languages (French, German, Spanish etc) is available as an alternative (Education (National Curriculum) (Modern Foreign Languages) Order 1989) (see Chapter 7, page 201).

The Commission for Racial Equality has advised that the placement of children for whom English is their second language in separate centres, and their removal from mainstream schooling, would constitute indirect discrimination (Commission for Racial Equality, *Code of Practice for the elimination of discrimination in education* (1988), para 32). There is a particular risk of indirect discrimination in methods of assessing pupils' abilities, resulting from cultural bias. The *Code of Practice* advises (at para 44) that:

> "Indirect discrimination in assessment will occur if the criteria or procedures applied are culturally biased and result in lower assessments being given to a considerably higher proportion of pupils or students from particular racial groups and those criteria cannot be justified on educational grounds. Culturally biased assessment criteria are those that assume a uniformity in children's cultural, linguistic, religious and lifestyle experiences".

(iii) Collective worship and religion

This is considered in Chapter 7; page 212 *et seq.*

(b) Enforcement

In relation to a complaint of breach of s 17 or s 18, civil proceedings may be instituted by a complainant in a designated county court (s 57), within six or eight months of the discrimination (s 68). Notice must be given to the Secretary of State, as under the Sex Discrimination Act (above) (s 57(5)). Damages awarded may take account of, *inter alia*, injury to feelings but cannot be awarded if the indirect discrimination was unintentional (s 57(3)). Complaint to the Secretary of State under ss 68 and 99 Education Act 1944 is also possible (see Sex Discrimination Act— enforcement (above, page 167)). Whether or not proceedings have been brought in respect of a breach of s 19, the Commission for Racial Equality can, following the carrying out of a formal investigation (under s 48), issue a non-discrimination notice requiring the person in breach to desist from the discriminatory act(s) and to inform the Commission of the completion of changes in practice required in response to the notice (s 58(2)).

Where the claim is for breach of s 19 only, civil proceedings are not possible (see s 19(4)), and complaint lies to the Secretary of State under ss 68 or 99 EA 1944. The Commission for Racial Equality cannot issue a non-discrimination notice in s 19-only cases, but should refer any such cases of which it becomes aware to the Secretary of State (s 58(6)).

3. Assistance for the financially disadvantaged

Every pupil in England and Wales has the right to a free education (but see the rules on charging for education introduced by ERA 1988, discussed in Chapter 7). But there are expenses associated with the upbringing of children that are a consequence of a child's attendance at school and which can prove extremely burdensome for many parents, especially those who are on low incomes. In order that pupils from poorer families are not educationally disadvantaged as a consequence of their parents' impecuniosity, the law has provided for free milk, school meals and transport, and a framework for the provision of grants and education allowances. Provision is not, however, generous.

(a) School milk and meals

Mrs Margaret Thatcher attracted the nickname "milk-snatcher" for proposing the Bill which became the Education

Equal opportunities

(Milk) Act 1971. This Act, in effect, relieved LEAs of the duty to provide milk for a child after the school year in which s/he reached the age of seven. Only children at the infants stage, or at a special school, or who needed milk for health reasons, were entitled to school milk. LEAs had the *power* to provide milk to older pupils, but had to charge for it. The Education Act 1980 restated LEAs' power to provide milk, meals and other refreshments. But it stipulated that they were to be provided free of charge only to pupils whose parents were in receipt of supplementary benefit or family income supplement ("FIS") (s 22(2)). In all other cases LEAs could make "such charges as they think fit", although they could remit charges "if, in the particular circumstances of any pupil or class or description of pupils, they consider it appropriate to do so" (s 22(3)(b)).

Free provision is, following the introduction of s 77(2) Social Security Act 1986, restricted to pupils who are, or whose parents are, in receipt of income support (the replacement, along with the social fund, for supplementary benefit—which was abolished in April 1988). Family credit (FC) has replaced FIS as the main social security benefit intended for those families dependent on a low wage, and the government has sought to deflect the criticism that the lack of entitlement to free school milk and meals for those receiving FC will cause hardship, by pointing out the higher rate of benefit paid under FC than under FIS.

LEAs are required to ensure that there are such facilities as they consider appropriate for the consumption of any meals or other refreshments brought to the school by pupils (EA 1980 s 22(1)).

(b) Transport

LEAs are under a duty to make appropriate arrangements for the provision of free transport for the purpose of facilitating the attendance of pupils at schools, including boarding schools (EA 1944 s 55(1)). As shown in Chapter 6, a parent is not obliged to send his/her child to school if "the school . . . is not within walking distance . . . and no suitable arrangements have been made by the LEA for [the child's] transport . . . " (EA 1944 s 39(2)(c)). "Walking distance" is defined as two miles, or three miles if the child is aged eight or over, measured by the "nearest available route". (For judicial interpretation of this, see *Rogers* v *Essex County Council* (1986) and *George* v *Devon County Council* (1988), discussed in Chapter 6.) Section 55(3) (added by E(No 2)A 1986 s 53, following the *Rogers* decision) provides that:

> "In considering whether or not they are required [under s 55(1)] ... to make arrangements in relation to a particular pupil, the local education authority shall have regard (amongst other things) to the age of the pupil and the nature of the route, or alternative routes, which he could reasonably be expected to take".

The introduction of grant-maintained schools has necessitated further amendment to s 55—the addition of a further sub-section ((4)), which provides that transport arrangements made by a LEA under s 55(1) must include:

> "provision for pupils at grant-maintained schools which is no less favourable than the provision made in pursuance of the arrangements for pupils at schools maintained by a local education authority" (added by ERA 1988 s 100(3)).

Transport for pupils not covered by s 55(1) *may* be paid for, in whole or part, by the LEA (s 55(2)).

(c) Grants and allowances

The payment of grants and allowances falls under a variety of provisions.

(i) Payment of expenses

Payments to enable pupils to participate in educational activities, including those taking place outside school hours, and scholarships, may be provided by LEAs (EA 1944 s 81; Scholarships and Other Benefits Regulations 1977 as amended), provided that any such payment is warranted by virtue of low parental income. Payment could cover the cost of fees at an independent school. A LEA would act illegally if it fetters its discretion by precluding consideration of exceptional circumstances with regard to payment of fees under this discretionary power (*R* v *Hampshire Education Authority ex parte J* (1985)).

(ii) Clothing

LEAs may provide clothing (which includes footwear) to, *inter alia,* pupils who are:

- boarding at educational establishments maintained by the LEA;
- in maintained nursery schools or classes; or
- in respect of whom special educational provision is made and the LEA is providing board and lodging otherwise than at a maintained educational institution. (Education (Miscellaneous Provisions) Act 1948, as amended, s 5.)

Clothing may also be provided to those who do not fall into the above categories but who attend a maintained school or special school (including one that is not maintained) and would not be able to take full advantage of the education provided at the school because of the inadequacy or unsuitability of their clothing. Arrangements may also be made with the proprietor of a non-maintained school which is not a special school for such provision to pupils. Clothing for use in physical training may also be provided, to pupils at maintained schools.

Where the recipients are granted ownership of the clothing, the LEA may charge for it as much as the parents can bear without financial hardship (s 5(6); Education (Provision of Clothing) Regulations 1980).

(iii) Board and lodging

In fulfilment of its duty to provide an education for a child, a LEA may make arrangements for board and lodging if it is necessary to enable the child to attend the school that best suits his or her educational needs, including any special educational needs. LEAs have a duty to pay the fees and expenses for a child to attend a special school if, for example, it decides that a child's special educational needs will be met at such a school (Education (Miscellaneous Provisions) Act 1953 s 6). Where board and lodging is provided but is not necessary for the pupil to receive an education suitable to his or her age, ability and aptitude, the parent may be required to pay as much as he or she can afford without financial hardship.

(iv) Educational Maintenance Allowances

Educational Maintenance Allowances ("EMAs") are paid by LEAs in respect of pupils who have reached the end of their period of compulsory schooling but are staying on at school (Scholarships and Other Benefits Regulations 1977, as amended, reg 4(e)(i), made under EA 1944 s 81). The payments must be required to prevent or relieve financial hardship and must be related to the pupil's parents' means (reg 6). They are generally paid to the parents rather than the pupil. LEAs have discretion as to both the method of assessment of need and the amount paid. The result is a considerable disparity in levels of provision across different LEAs (see Burghes and Stegles, *No Choice at 16* (1983), published by Child Poverty Action Group). Most awards are very low.

Nevertheless, the importance of these allowances in encouraging participation in education beyond the age of sixteen has long been recognized (eg House of Commons Expenditure Committee (Education and Arts Sub-Committee) *Third Report* 1974 HC306). They were seen as essential to attract those with special educational needs to continue in education (*Warnock Report* (1978), para 10. 103). In the light of the current inadequacy of EMA provision, various proposals for an improved, national system have been made over the years; but all would involve considerable amounts of additional public expenditure, and reform has been resisted by government.

Discretionary (or "minor") awards may also be made (EA 1962 s 2, incorporated into the EA 1980 s 19 and Sch 5). They are payable in respect of persons over compulsory school age attending a full- or part-time course, other than a course of secondary education or a course "designated" for mandatory awards. They are usually paid direct to the young person concerned.

Chapter 6
Pupils—attendance and discipline

1. Registration

Pupils' names will be registered at a school on the first day they attend—in the *admissions register*. (Their parents' names and address(es), and certain other information, must also be recorded.) Thereafter, their attendance and failure to attend will be recorded in the *attendance register*, of which there must be one for each form or class. The rules concerning the keeping of this register are laid down in the Pupils' Registration Regulations 1956, as amended (eg by SI 1988 No 1185), made under EA 1944 s 80. Responsibility for the maintenance of the register rests with the proprietor of the school, which in county, voluntary and grant-maintained schools means the governors (EA 1944 s 114(1), as amended by ERA 1988 Sch 12 para 7).

(a) What must be shown on the register?

Guidance on the marking of attendance registers is at present a matter for the discretion of LEAs. Their guidelines are usually printed on the inside cover of the register. Apparently, these guidelines are of variable quality (HMI *Attendance at School,* Education Observed 13 (1989), para 13). The law says the following information must be shown:

- The names of all pupils in the class and a record (in ink, with alterations clearly identifiable) of their attendance at the beginning of each morning and afternoon session. (This does not apply to boarders at independent

schools.) Pupils receiving medical or dental treatment on a particular day should be marked present unless in hospital (Pupils' Registration Regulations 1956, *op cit*);
- "the name and address of every person known to the proprietor of the school to be a parent of a pupil at the school" (EA 1944 s 80(1A));
- "against the entry on the register of the particulars of any parent who has actual custody of the pupil, an indication of that fact and a note of at least one telephone number at which the parent can be contacted in the event of an emergency" (reg 3(2)(c)).

(b) Legal significance of the register

If is often said that the register "is a legal document". What this emphasises is the importance of the register as evidence of non-attendance when legal action is brought against parents, and the fact that failure to comply with the regulations concerning registers amounts to a summary offence (level 1 fine, Criminal Justice Act 1982) (EA 1944 s 80(2), as amended). Registers must be retained for three years after their period of use.

(c) Returns

LEAs have their own systems for monitoring school attendance. In any event, the law requires schools to make returns to their LEA indicating absences of named pupils, of two weeks or more, without medical certification, and the cause of absence where this is known (reg 7).

2. School attendance

(a) Parents' legal duty to cause child to receive education

"It shall be the duty of the parent of every child of compulsory school age to cause him to receive efficient full-time education suitable to his age, ability and aptitude and to any special educational needs he may have either by regular attendance at school or otherwise" (EA 1944 s 36).

Compulsory school age means aged betwe[en ... and] sixteen. A parent does not *have* to send his/[her child to] school until the beginning of the first term after [s/he has] reached his/her fifth birthday. The law provides [that a young] person may not leave school until after one of th[e two official] leaving dates—(i) the end of the spring term, if s[/he became] sixteen between 1 September and 31 January, a[nd (ii) the] Friday before the last Monday in May, if s/he became sixteen between 1 February and 31 August (Education Act 1962 s 9, as amended by the Education (School Leaving Dates) Act 1976 s 1).

Efficient has never been defined, but would have to be considered both in conjunction with *suitable* and in the context of the provisions of the National Curriculum. In other words, the quality of education provided must be of a suitable standard, bearing in mind the need for the requirements of the National Curriculum to be satisfied.

Full-time is not defined in the Act, but the Education (Schools and Further Education) Regulations 1981 (reg 10) at the moment prescribe at least three hours of secular instruction per day for classes of under-eights and four hours for over-eights, in schools operating a five day week. However, the government plans to revoke these rules and replace them with guidance on (extended) minimum teaching hours for pupils of different ages.

Regular attendance is not defined, but is generally taken to mean frequent attendance at times prescribed by the governing body (E(No 2)A 1986 s 21(2), added by ERA 1988 s 115) (formerly the LEA), not including times of arrival after the register has closed (*Hinchley* v *Rankin* (1961)).

Or otherwise permits parents to make their own arrangements for their children's education, including home schooling. LEAs may be entitled to inspect the child's home in such a case (*R* v *Surrey Quarter Sessions Appeal Committee ex parte Tweedie* (1963)). Many LEAs question the suitability of the curriculum likely to be provided by parents, and the introduction of the National Curriculum renders this type of education extremely questionable in a legal sense.

Note that governors have a power to require a pupil at a school to attend for secular instruction and training other than on school premises (EA 1944 s 21(5)).

reach of s 36—school attendance procedures

Although various strategies are being devised for improvement of school attendance (see HMI *Attendance at School, Education Observed* 13 (1989), Chapter 7)—from closer monitoring to the rewarding of attendance—the legal framework remains important.

If a parent is failing to comply with his/her s 36 responsibilities, the LEA must serve a notice requiring the parent to satisfy the authority within a specified time (being not less than fourteen days) that the child is being properly educated in accordance with s 36 (EA 1944 s 37(1)). If the parent does not satisfy the LEA, the authority must serve a school attendance order ("SAO") in the prescribed form. The procedure, as amended by EA 1980 ss 10 and 11, is set out in the chart on pages 182 and 183. Note that there is a separate procedure for children with special educational needs (see below). Non-compliance with a SAO is a punishable offence (EA 1944 s 40—see page 184). Once made, the SAO remains in force until the child has ceased to be of compulsory school age, unless revoked by the LEA (EA 1944 s 37(7)). Once there has been a prosecution in respect of non-compliance with a particular SAO, no further prosecution may be brought in respect of that order (*Enfield LBC* v *Forsyth* (1987)).

(c) Non-excused absence of children with special educational needs

There is a separate procedure governing enforcement of attendance of children with special educational needs in respect of whom the LEA maintains a statement under EA 1981 s 7 (see Chapter 8) (EA 1981 ss 15 and 16).

The main difference from the procedure in s 37 (as amended by EA 1980) above is that parents are permitted to name a school for inclusion in the SAO (s 15(2)), and it must be included unless the Secretary of State directs otherwise (s 15(3)). But if the LEA considers that the named school is unsuitable in respect of the child's age, ability, aptitude or special educational needs, or that the efficient use of resources might be prejudiced if the child attends that school, the authority may, after giving due notice, apply to the Secretary of State for a direction determining which school is to be named in the order (s 15(4)). There is no appeal from the Secretary of State's decision, and the child must be admitted to the named school. (This applies also to grant-maintained ("GM") schools—s 15(7), added by ERA 1988 Sch 12 para 27.)

A request by a parent for the revocation or amendment of a SAO which is in force must be complied with unless the efficient use of resources would be prejudiced, or it would be unsuitable having regard to the child's age, ability, aptitude and special educational needs, or the proposed change is "against the interests of the child" (s 16(2)). A parent can ask the Secretary of State to make "such direction . . . as he thinks fit" if the authority fails to comply with a requested revocation or amendment (s 16(3)), and the LEA must insert any named school into the SAO in place of the one it had included (s 16(5)). (The Secretary of State can now name a GM school in the SAO—s 16(6), added by ERA 1988 Sch 12 para 28.)

(d) Absence of registered pupils—s 39

Unless one of the excuses laid down in s 39(2) applies, a parent commits an offence for failing to ensure the regular attendance of a child registered as a pupil at a school (EA 1944 s 39(1)). The excuses are:

(i) sickness (the child's not the parent's) (s 39(2)(a));
(ii) unavoidable cause, being a cause affecting the child and generally involving an emergency (s 39(2)(a); see *Jenkins* v *Howells* (1949) and *Jarman* v *Mid-Glamorgan Education Authority* (1985));
(iii) day of religious observance (s 39(2)(b));
(iv) "The school . . . is not within walking distance . . . and no suitable arrangements have been made by the LEA for [the child's] transport . . . or for boarding accommodation" (s 39(2)(c)).

Walking distance is defined as two miles, or three miles if the child is eight or over, *measured by the nearest available route* (s 39(5)). A route does not cease to be *available* simply because it would not be possible for an unaccompanied child

THE LAW RELATING TO SCHOOLS

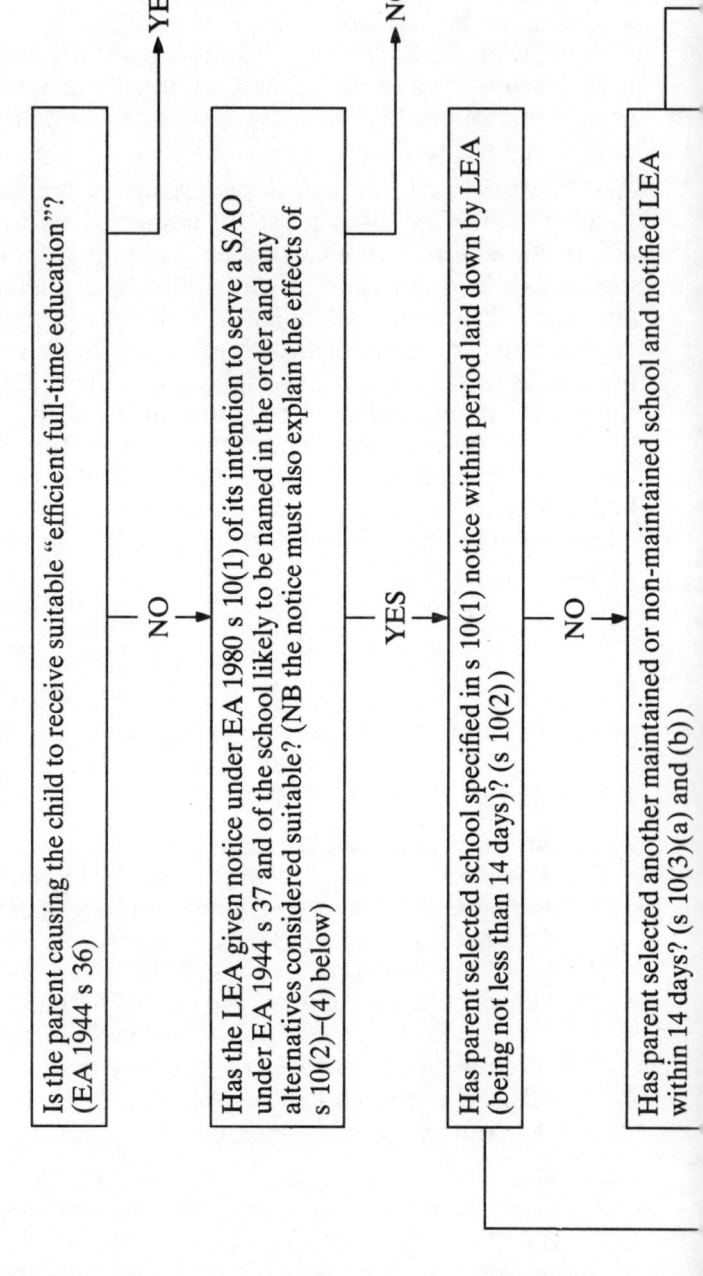

Procedure leading to possible service of a school attendance order

Pupils—attendance and discipline

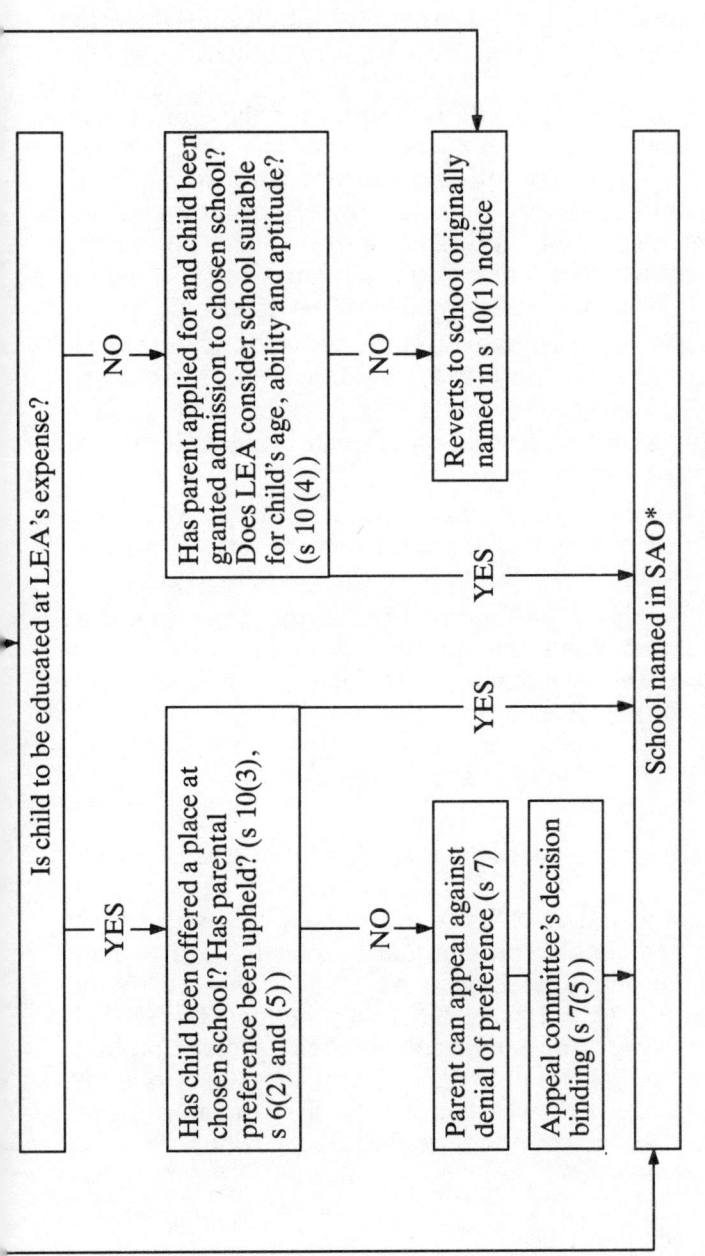

to walk it without risk of danger (*Rogers* v *Essex County Council* (1986) (HL)). In furtherance of his/her duty to ensure a child attends school, a parent should, where reasonably practicable and prudent to do so, accompany a child to school when it would be unsafe for the child to go unaccompanied (*George* v *Devon County Council* (1988)). However, in deciding whether to provide transport for a child, LEAs must now have regard (amongst other things) to "the age of the pupil, and the nature of the route, or alternative routes, which he could reasonably be expected to take" (EA 1944 s 55(3) added by E(No 2)A 1986 s 53).

The courts have refused to extend the list of excuses (*Spiers* v *Warrington Corporation* (1954)), unduly strain their interpretation of it (eg *Happe* v *Lay* (1977)) or apply international law (the European Convention on Human Rights) (*Jarman* v *Mid-Glamorgan Education Authority* (1985)).

Section 39(1) creates an *absolute offence* (*Crump* v *Gillmore* (1969)), which means that a parent cannot rely on his/her lack of knowledge of the child's absence as a defence.

Pupils may be absent with permission during term time for the purposes of going on an annual holiday with their parents (two weeks maximum) (Education (Schools and Further Education) Regulations 1981 reg 12).

(e) Court action in non-attendance cases

(i) Criminal proceedings in the magistrates' court

Failure to comply with a SAO and breach of s 39 (above) render a parent liable, on summary conviction, to a fine (level 3 on the Criminal Justice Act 1982 scale—currently £400 maximum) (EA 1944 s 40(1) as amended by Sch 15 Children Act 1989). Fines imposed generally average around £50, but the actual amount depends on local factors and, more importantly, on whether it is a first or subsequent offence. Proceedings may be brought by a LEA only.

(ii) Child care proceedings

Once the relevant parts of the Children Act 1989 come into

effect, there will be a new system for dealing with truancy cases. For the time being, the Children and Young Persons Act 1969 ("CYPA 1969") will continue to apply.

The Children and Young Persons Act 1969: Before instituting proceedings under s 40(1) (above) an authority must:

> "consider whether it would be appropriate, instead of or as well as instituting the proceedings, to bring the child in question before a juvenile court under Section 1 of the Children and Young Persons Act 1969" (EA 1944 s 40(2)).

An order under CYPA may be made if a child:

> ". . . is of compulsory school age within the meaning of the Education Act 1944 and is not receiving efficient full-time education suitable to his age, ability and aptitude and to any special educational needs he may have" (CYPA 1969 s 1(2)(e)),

provided that the court considers that he is in need of *care and control* which he is unlikely to receive unless such an order is made (s 35, as amended). *Care* here relates not only to the child's physical well-being but also, so far as s 1(2)(e) is concerned, to his educational needs (*Re S (A Minor) (Care Order: Education)* (1977)). Generally a supervision order is made, but a full care order is a possibility.

The court sometimes adjourns the proceedings indefinitely, to allow parents a further opportunity to comply with their legal duty, avoiding the need for an order. The legality of this adjournment system, pioneered in Leeds magistrates' court and adopted elsewhere, has been questioned (Grenville, *School Attendance: Supervision by the Courts* (1988) 18 Fam Law 488); but the system is claimed to be effective in re-establishing attendance (Hullin *et al,* (1987) 17 Fam Law 324).

The Children Act 1989: The specific grounds for taking a non-attending child into care under CYPA 1969 (above) will disappear once the Act comes into effect. In non-attendance cases an *education supervision order* ("ESO") will be possible. An ESO will be made in favour of a LEA (the authority in whose area the child concerned is living or will live, or in whose area the child will go to school (s 36(7))). The order will be possible only if the court is satisfied "that the child is of compulsory school age and is not being properly educated" (s 36(3)). Before applying for the order the LEA will have to consult the local authority social services committee (s 36(8)).

The supervisor (educational welfare officer) will be required to:

>   advise, assist and befriend, and give directions to—
>   (i) the supervised child;
>   (ii) his parents; and
>   (iii) any person who has parental responsibility for him

in such a way as will ensure that the child is "properly educated" (Sch 3 para 12(1)). The supervisor will give directions to the parents (or persons exercising parental responsibility), but will have to take steps to ascertain and, so far as is reasonably practicable, take into account, their wishes and feelings and those of the child (para 12(2) and (3)). Sanctions may be imposed for non-compliance with an ESO's directions. In particular, persistent failure to comply with such directions is a criminal offence, although there are limited defences—for example, that the parent has taken "all reasonable steps" to comply or that the direction is "unreasonable" (para 18). The LEA must inform the local authority (social services department) of such failure. (For a critique of the ESO, see N Harris, *Supervision of Truants: Whose Role?* (1989) 19 Fam Law 404.)

The Children Act 1989 has also made changes to criminal proceedings under EA 1944 s 40(1). The power to imprison has been removed, and LEAs must, before prosecuting, consider whether ESO procedure should be invoked instead of, or as well as, prosecution (EA 1944 s 40(2A)).

(iii) Wardship

It is possible for a wardship order in the High Court to be made in a case involving truancy, although the courts seem reluctant to interfere—because, as they see it, compulsory education has been placed by Parliament squarely within the ambit of a LEA's discretion (*Re Baker* (1961)). It is almost certain that a parent would be unable to obtain a wardship order as a means of, in effect, overturning a care order in a truancy case (effect of *A* v *Liverpool City Council* (1982) and *W* v *Hertfordshire County Council (1985)*).

3. Discipline

(a) Introduction

The importance of discipline in schools is not only its contribution to effective educational provision; it also helps protect pupils from bullying, which appears to be a major problem at the present time. Various measures may be taken within a school to improve standards of discipline (see the Elton Report, *Discipline in Schools* (1989)). Their selection may be left to the good sense of a school, provided that due regard is given to the constraints imposed by the law.

(b) Responsibility for disciplinary matters

The conduct of a county, controlled and maintained special school is to be "under the direction of the governing body" (E(No 2)A 1986 s 16(1)). This includes pupil discipline. But in the 1986 Act there are also more specific rules dealing with discipline, placing day to day responsibilities in the hands of head teachers:

"The articles of government for every county, voluntary and maintained special school shall provide—
 (a) for it to be the duty of the head teacher to determine measures (which may include the making of rules and provision for enforcing them) to be taken with a view to—
  (i) promoting, among pupils, self-discipline and proper regard for authority;
  (ii) encouraging good behaviour on the part of pupils;
  (iii) securing that the standard of behaviour of pupils is acceptable; and
  (iv) otherwise regulating the conduct of pupils;
 (b) for it to be the duty of the head teacher, in determining any such measures—
  (i) to act in accordance with any written statement of general principles provided for him by the governing body; and
  (ii) to have regard to any guidance that they may offer in relation to particular matters;

(c) for it to be the duty of the head teacher to make any such measures generally known within the school;
(d) for the standard of behaviour which is to be regarded as acceptable at the school to be determined by the head teacher, so far as it is not determined by the governing body;
(e) for it to be the duty of the governing body and the head teacher to consult the local education authority, before determining any such measures, on any matter arising from the proposed measures which can reasonably be expected—
   (i) to lead to increased expenditure by the authority; or
   (ii) to affect the responsibilities of the authority as an employer;
(f) for the power to exclude a pupil from the school (whether by suspension, expulsion or otherwise) to be exercisable only by the head teacher" (s 22).

Note that under the Education (School Government) Regulations 1989, the governors cannot delegate to the head teacher, nor to anyone else, the role of agreeing their written statement on pupil discipline.

(c) Exclusion of pupils

If a head teacher wishes to exclude a pupil, s/he must act in accordance with the strict legal framework laid down in the Education (No 2) Act 1986. The Act states that once a head teacher has decided to exclude, s/he must:

(i) without delay—
  - inform the pupil's parents (if the pupil is under eighteen) of the period of exclusion (including where the exclusion was originally for a fixed or indefinite period and the head teacher subsequently decides to make it permanent) and the reasons for it; and
  - inform the parents, and the pupil himself if eighteen or over, of the right to make representations about the exclusion to the governing body and the LEA;
(ii) without delay inform the LEA of his/her decision

(including the period of exclusion in relevant cases) and the reason for it—
- if it will involve exclusion for an aggregate of more than five days in any one term, or the pupil would miss an opportunity to take a public examination; or
- if a fixed or indefinite period of exclusion is to be made permanent. (E(No 2)A s 23. See further DES Circular 7/87, paras 5.12.6–5.12.18.)

(d) Reinstatement of an excluded pupil

The E(No 2)A 1986 contains rather complex provisions dealing with reinstatement—giving, amongst other things, wider powers to governors than previously. (Note that when governing bodies or their delegates are considering any disciplinary matter relating to a pupil, they should bear in mind the rules on withdrawal from meetings and voting laid down in the Education (School Government) Regulations 1989 (discussed in Chapter 3).)

(i) County, controlled and maintained special schools

The articles of government must contain the requirements as to reinstatement laid down in s 24. These may be summarised thus:

Permanent exclusion: Once informed of a permanent exclusion, the LEA must consider, after consulting the governing body, whether the pupil should be reinstated. If it decides s/he should be, it should give an appropriate direction to the head teacher. If it decides not to reinstate, it must inform the pupil (if aged eighteen or over) or his/her parent (s 24(a)). The head teacher is bound by any direction made under s 24(a) (s 24(f)). If the governors order the reinstatement of a pupil who had been excluded from the school for an aggregate of five days in any term or for any period during which he would have taken a public examination and who has been permanently excluded, the head teacher must comply with the order (s 24(b)). (As to LEA and governors' orders conflicting, see "conflicting directions" below.)

Indefinite exclusion: Here the LEA is under a duty:

"where the governing body do not intend to direct the

head teacher to reinstate the pupil or the authority consider that he should be reinstated by a date which is earlier than that determined by the governing body as the date by which he is to be reinstated—

(i) to direct that he be reinstated immediately; or
(ii) to direct that he be reinstated within such period as may be specified in the direction" (s 24(c)).

The LEA must first consult the governing body (but see (iii) below).

The head teacher is under a duty to comply with a LEA direction under s 24(c) (s 24(f)). But such a direction shall cease to have effect if the head teacher decides that the exclusion should become permanent (s 24(e)).

Section 24(b) (above) (reinstatement of pupil excluded for aggregate of five days etc ordered by governors) applies to indefinite exclusion also, save that in such a case reinstatement xkmay be ordered by the governors or the LEA (s 24(b)).

Fixed term exclusion: Reinstatement here may be ordered by the governors or LEA. (Where the LEA proposes to order reinstatement, it must first consult the governors (s 24(d)).) The head teacher must comply with the order, provided that the pupil has been excluded for more than five school days (in aggregate) in any school term or in circumstances in which the pupil will miss the opportunity to take a public examination (s 24(b)).

Conflicting directions: Where the directions of the LEA and governors conflict, the head teacher must "comply with that direction which will lead to the earlier reinstatement of the pupil" (s 24(g)).

Duty to inform: The governors and LEA are required to inform each other and the parents of the pupil (and the pupil if eighteen or over) of any order as to reinstatement under s 24.

(ii) Voluntary aided, and special agreement schools

Rules similar to those applicable in the schools in (i) above apply to aided and special agreement schools (s 25), with one significant difference—the corresponding duty to that in s 24(a) (compliance with order to reinstate) in cases of permanent exclusion rests with the governing body and not the LEA (s 25(a)).

(iii) Common provisions

Governing bodies cannot delegate to an individual consideration (under ss 24 and 25 (above)) of whether to direct the reinstatement of an excluded pupil or the consideration of representations made in exclusion cases (Education (School Government) Regulations 1989 reg 25(4)), but may delegate such matters to a committee of at least three governors (excluding the head teacher) (reg 26(6)).

(e) Appeals

Arrangements for appeals against failure to reinstate in cases of *permanent exclusion only* must be made. These arrangements must be made by the LEA, in the case of county, controlled and maintained special schools (E(No 2)A 1986 s 26(1)), and by the governing body in the case of aided and special agreement schools (s 26(2)). Appeals may be made by the pupil him/herself, if aged eighteen or over, and in other cases by the parent(s).

In the case of county, controlled and maintained schools, the governors may also appeal—if the LEA has ordered the reinstatement of a permanently excluded pupil.

Appeal lies to an appeal committee—the same committee that hears appeals concerning school admissions (see page 157). The decision of the appeal committee is binding (s 26(5)).

(i) Information about the appeal right

Since 1 September 1988 the articles of government have required the LEA, in the case of county, controlled and maintained special schools, and the governors, in the case of aided and special agreement schools, to inform the parents (or pupil, if eighteen or over) of their right of appeal when informing them of the decision on reinstatement (E(No 2)A 1986 Sch 3 paras 1 and 2). If it is the *governors* that are appealing, the parent (if the pupil is aged under eighteen) or pupil (if aged eighteen or over) must be informed of the right to make representations to the appeal committee (*ibid*, para 3(2)). (Note that reinstatement ordered by the LEA is suspended for seven days whilst the governors decide whether or not to appeal (Sch 3 para 3(1)).)

(ii) Procedure

Written notice, setting out the grounds of appeal, must be given (para 6). Appeals should be disposed of "without delay" (para 9). All parties can attend, be represented and offer oral or written submissions (paras 7 and 8). (Governors with a personal involvement in the case must withdraw.) Detailed guidance on the conduct of hearings is contained in a 1988 Annex to the Code of Practice on Appeal Committees (para 18), which recommends that given the contentious nature of most cases a set procedure (which is spelt out) is followed. The appeal committee's decision must be communicated in writing to the pupil (if aged eighteen or over) or to the parent (if the pupil is aged under eighteen). The appeal hearing must generally be held in private, but LEA observers or members of the Council on Tribunals are entitled to be present (para 13).

(f) Discipline in grant-maintained schools

The provisions of E(No 2)A 1986 relating to exclusion of pupils, cited above, do not apply to grant-maintained schools. Although ERA 1988 does not expressly say so, pupil discipline will undoubtedly be one of the matters dealt with by these schools' articles of government. The articles are to made provision as to "the functions to be exercised in relation to the school" by the governors, head teacher etc, and for delegation of those functions (ERA 1988 s 58(5)(a)). The articles are also to provide for arrangements for appeals against:

> "any decision or action taken by the governing body, or by any persons authorised under the articles to take any decision or action of the kind in question, in relation to—
> (i) . . .
> (ii) the permanent exclusion of any pupil from the school" (s 58(5)(d)).

Their articles are to enable joint arrangements for this

purpose to be made between governing bodies of two or more GM schools (*ibid*).

(g) Corporal punishment

(i) Independent schools

Despite the general ban on the use of corporal punishment in State schools (E(No 2)A 1986 s 47—see below), it may still be inflicted in independent schools, but certainly not independent schools funded under the Direct Grants Regulations 1959, schools maintained by the Ministry of Defence and central government funded city technology colleges and colleges for the technology of the arts (s 47(5)(a)(iii) and the Education (Abolition of Corporal Punishment) (Independent Schools) Regulations 1987 and (Amendment) Regulations 1989). In independent schools where corporal punishment may still be used, it may not be given to any pupil whose fees in respect of attendance are paid by a local authority or education authority (Scotland) or the Education Board (Northern Ireland) (s 47(6)(b) and (7), and the Education (Abolition of Corporal Punishment) (Independent Schools) (Prescribed Categories of Persons) Regulations 1989).

The cases sanctioning the use of corporal punishment in schools have, since 15 August 1987, been relevant to independent schools only. In such schools, as in others before this date, corporal punishment may be inflicted on most pupils (see above) provided it is not excessive or improperly motivated (*R* v *Grey* (1666); *R* v *Hopley* (1860); *Ryan* v *Fildes* (1938); *R* v *Gilchrist* (1961); etc)—otherwise the teacher may be guilty of an assault and could be made the defendant in a prosecution or civil suit. However, inflicting corporal punishment where the parents are philosophically opposed to it is a breach of the European Convention on Human Rights (*Campbell and Cosans* v *UK* (1982)). Corporal punishment may also be "torture or . . . degrading treatment or punishment" contrary to Article 3 of the Convention. The European Commission on Human Rights has awarded compensation to certain persons against whom corporal punishment has been inflicted by teachers at school (*The Times*, 25 September 1987).

(ii) Public sector schools

Corporal punishment in State schools, including grant-maintained schools, is no longer lawful (E(No 2)A 1986 s 47)—other than where it is necessary:

"for reasons that include averting an immediate danger of personal injury to, or an immediate danger to the property of, any person (including the pupil concerned)" (s 47(3)).

No specific offence of "unlawful corporal punishment" is created by s 47 (s 47(4)); the section merely seems to remove a defence of lawful chastisement in any proceedings brought against a teacher. "Corporal punishment" means, for the purposes of the section,

"anything (done) for the purposes of punishing the pupil concerned (whether or not there are also other reasons for doing it) which, apart from any justification, would constitute battery" (s 47(2)).

A battery is a physical interference with the person of another (including the clothes s/he is wearing) without his/her consent. Consent is implied in certain situations—for example, during sporting activities (within the rules of the sport and not excessive) or when attracting someone's attention.

(On an attempt, before the 1986 Act, by a LEA to ban corporal punishment in schools, see *R* v *Manchester City Council ex parte Fulford* (1984).)

(h) Detention

The legal limits set on the power to detain a class, or individual pupils, derive from the following:

(i) *R* v *Hopley* (1860) (above) which holds that punishment must be reasonable and moderate, and not "for the gratification of passion or rage, or . . . excessive in its nature or degree, or . . . protracted beyond the child's powers of endurance" (*per* Cockburn CJ).

(ii) The tort of false imprisonment, from which a teacher may claim exemption only if acting lawfully (*Fitzgerald* v

Northcote (1865)—detention for improper reason is false imprisonment). A teacher acts *in loco parentis*, and detention by a parent of his/her own child is unlawful if it is "for such a period or in such circumstances as to take it out of the realm of reasonable parental discipline" (*per* Lane LCJ in *R v Rahman* (1985)).

(iii) The overriding duty on teachers for the safety of pupils (see Chapter 8). Therefore parents should be notified in advance if younger pupils are to be detained or if the detention is going to be for more than five to ten minutes.

(i) Confiscation of property

Confiscation is not unlawful, and in some cases is a necessity eg if a pupil has a dangerous object or weapon. These items, or drugs, or obscene material, should be handed to the police as soon as possible. Deliberate destruction by a teacher of a confiscated item could lead to criminal or civil liability, unless, perhaps, the destruction was necessary in the immediate interests of safety. Retention by a teacher of confiscated items for his/her own use may amount to theft (Theft Act 1968 s 1). To avoid any possible liability, the item should be returned to the pupil or his/her parent at an early opportunity—preferably at the end of the school day.

(j) Breakdown of discipline: LEAs' reserve power

LEAs are empowered to:

> "take such steps in relation to any county, controlled or special school maintained by them as they consider are required to prevent the breakdown, or continuing breakdown, of discipline at the school" (E(No 2)A 1986 s 28(1)).

The power can be exercised only if, in the LEA's opinion, the behaviour of pupils, or the action taken by them or their parents is such that "education of any pupils is, or is likely in the immediate future to become, severely prejudiced" (s 28(3)). Just what form of action Parliament expected LEAs might decide to take in these circumstances is not at all clear.

Chapter 7

The curriculum

1. Introduction

The school curriculum is undergoing significant change at the present time. Certain reforms, such as the introduction of the GCSE examination and syllabuses, have occurred without changes being required to the legal framework of education. But the Education Reform Act 1988 has made it possible for the government to institute sweeping reforms to the school curriculum. It has resulted in further reductions in LEA control of curricular matters, building on previous Acts (as far back as the Education Act 1980) in this respect. More importantly, it has given England and Wales its first ever National Curriculum.

2. Basic principles

The general duty resting with the Secretary of State for Education to "promote the education of the people of England and Wales" (EA 1944 s 1) and on LEAs to "contribute towards the spiritual, moral, mental and physical development of the community" (EA 1944 s 7) are unaffected by recent reforms. But there is now a specific overall duty resting on the Secretary of State, LEAs, governing bodies and head teachers (of public sector schools), to exercise their functions with a view to securing that the curriculum of a school:

"is a balanced and broadly based curriculum which—

(a) promotes the spiritual, moral, cultural, mental and physical development of pupils at the school and of society; and
(b) prepares such pupils for the opportunities, responsibilities and experiences of adult life" (ERA 1988 s 1(1) and (2)).

This is referred to as the "whole curriculum", which goes beyond the National Curriculum. It also "goes far beyond the formal timetable", involving:

". . . a range of policies and practices to promote the personal and social development of pupils, to accommodate different teaching and learning styles, to develop positive attitudes and values, and to forge an effective partnership with parents and the local community" (National Curriculum Council, *Circular No 6* (1989), para 6).

There is an important cross-curricular aspect to the "whole curriculum", involving the inculcation of various skills and emphasising themes such as economic and industrial understanding, careers education and guidance, environment education, health education and citizenship. Such themes "make links between different parts of the curriculum" and may be taught through other subjects (*ibid*, paras 15 and 16).

(On the application of s 1 (the "whole curriculum") to pupils with special educational needs, see National Curriculum Council *A Curriculum for All* (1989), and Chapter 8 of this book.)

3. Control of the secular curriculum

LEAs were granted control of the secular curriculum by EA 1944 s 23. But this section was repealed by E(No 2)A 1986 (Sch 6). Now the "determination and organisation of the secular curriculum" is in the hands of the head teacher (s 18(5)). However, s/he must ensure that the curriculum is compatible with the governors' policy on sex education (see below) and the LEA's statement on curricular policy—as modified by the governors' own statement on the curriculum for the school. The head teacher must also ensure that the curriculum is compatible with other enactments relating to education, "including, in particular, those relating to children with special educational needs" (s 18(6)(c)). (The major statutory duty concerns implementation of the National Curriculum—see below.)

The above provisions apply to county, voluntary controlled and special agreement schools. In voluntary aided schools control of the secular curriculum is placed in the hands of governors, although they must have regard to, *inter alia*, LEA curricular policy (s 19(1) and (2)).

LEA autonomy over the curriculum has been reduced to such an extent that their absolute control extends only to term and holiday dates, and only in county, controlled and special agreement schools. LEAs continue to be responsible for an inspection and advisory service.

4. Statements of curricular policy (secular)

(a) The LEA's statement

The LEA is obliged to publish and keep under review its policy on secular provision, and must consider the range and balance of curriculum to content (E(No 2)A 1986 s 17(1) and (2)).

(b) The governors' statement

The governing body must make and keep up to date a statement of curricular policy for the school—referring to content and organisation and whether sex education should form part of the secular curriculum (s 18(1) and (2)). When considering these matters the governors are required to have regard to the LEA's statement and to representations made to them by persons connected with the community served by the school and by the chief officer of police (s 18(3)).

5. The "basic curriculum"

"The curriculum for every maintained school shall comprise a basic curriculum which includes—

The curriculum

(a) provision for religious education for all pupils at the school; and
(b) a curriculum for all registered pupils at the school of compulsory school age (to be known as 'the National Curriculum') . . ." (ERA 1988 s 2(1)).

6. The National Curriculum

The National Curriculum comprises "core" and "other foundation" subjects (see Charts 1 and 2 below). LEAs, governors and head teachers are under a legal duty to ensure that the National Curriculum is implemented in their schools (ERA 1988 s 10(2)), once brought into effect by the Secretary of State (see pages 204–205 for commencement).

(a) Assessment

There is to be compulsory assessment of pupils, at ages seven, eleven, fourteen and sixteen—ie at or near the end of each key stage. Formal assessment at ages seven and eleven will occur early in relation to the three core subjects. Teachers' own continuous assessments will also form an important part of the new system.

The Act empowers the Secretary of State to prescribe assessment arrangements (s 4(2)(c)). Parents are to be informed of the results of their child's assessment. Aggregated results across key stages will be published, enabling comparisons between schools to be made. Work in the development of tests, "Standard Assessment Tasks", is being carried out under the direction of the Schools Examination and Assessment Council (SEAC). Attainment targets (ATs) may be grouped into "profile components" for the purposes of reporting achievements. Teachers will be expected to keep a record of each pupil's progress in relation to each AT throughout the child's period of schooling; records of achievement will chronicle individual pupils' attainment within the National Curriculum. (For publication of results, see above, page 138.)

Chart 1 **The National Curriculum**

I. Core subjects	II. Other foundation subjects
(ERA 1988 s 3(1)(a))	(ERA 1988 s 3(1)(b) & (c))
Mathematics, English and Science and Welsh in Welsh-speaking schools)	History, Geography, Technology, Music, Art, PE and a modern language* (in secondary years 1–3 or equivalent) (and Welsh in non-Welsh speaking schools in Wales) *See Chart 2 below

	I and II each to have:	
"Attainment targets"	"Programmes of study"	"Assessment arrangements"
"the knowledge, skills, and understanding which pupils of different abilities and maturities are expected to have by the end of each key stage"	"the matters, skills and processes which are required to be taught to pupils of different ablilities and maturities during each key stage"	"the arrangements for assessing pupils at or near the end of each key stage for the purpose of ascertaining what they have achieved in relation to the assessment targets for that stage"
(ERA 1988 s 2(2)(a))	(ERA 1988 s 2(2)(b))	(ERA 1988 s 2(2)(c))

The attainment targets (ATs) and programmes of study (PS are being prescribed by Order—several such Orders have already been made (eg Education (National Curriculum) (Attainment Targets and Programmes of Study in Mathematics, Science and English) Orders 1989 and English (No 2) and Technology 1990). The Act permits the ATs and PS to be set out in a separate document published by HMSO, provided the Order makes appropriate reference to it (s 4(4)). One example is *Science in the National Curriculum* (1989) (ISBN 0 11 2706673). ATs and PS are prescribed for different "key stages" of compulsory schooling (see Chart 3, below).

Chart 2 Prescribed modern languages (National Curriculum key stages 3 and 4)

I. Languages unconditionally specified as foundation subjects:

Danish, Dutch, French, German, Greek (Modern), Italian, Portuguese and Spanish.

II. Languages which may be offered as foundation subjects provided that the school also offers pupils the opportunity of studying one or more of the languages in I. above:

Arabic, Bengali, Chinese (Cantonese or Mandarin) Gujerati, Hebrew (Modern), Hindi, Japanese, Punjabi, Russian, Turkish and Urdu.

Source: The Education (National Curriculum) (Modern Foreign Languages) Order 1989 (in force 1 August 1989).

Chart 3 **The "key stages"**

Stage 1 ages 5–7	From attainment of compulsory school age to the end of the school year that the majority of pupils in the class reach the age of seven
Stage 2 ages 8–11	From the school year when the majority of pupils in the class reach the age of eight until the end of the year in which the majority reach the age of eleven
Stage 3 ages 11–14	From the school year when the majority in the class reach the age of twelve to the end of the year that the majority reach the age of fourteen
Stage 4 ages 15–16	From the school year when the majority in the class reach the age of fifteen to the year when the majority cease to be of compulsory school age

(ERA 1988 s 3(3))

(b) Reports to parents

Under legal requirements expected to be introduced in 1990, schools will have to ensure that parents receive an annual report on their child's progress in relation to the various components of the National Curriculum. (For discussion, see *SEAC Recorder* (1989) No 3, page 7.) Some teachers feel that the scope of this report will be too narrow to give a true indication of the child's developing ability.

(c) Exception from the National Curriculum

Exception from the National Curriculum may be possible, under three separate provisions:

The curriculum

(i) If the head teacher thinks fit, individual pupils' education can be excepted from the National Curriculum (ERA 1988 s 19(1))—in circumstances prescribed by regulation and for a certain period (not more than six months at a time). The child's parents, the LEA and the school governors are to be given information on this (including reasons) by the head teacher. Parents have a right of appeal to the governors against the head's direction (or any revocation or variation of it) (ERA 1988 s 19(7)–(10)). The head must comply with the governors' ruling in such a case.

Regulations have been made under s 19—the Education (National Curriculum) (Temporary Exceptions for Individual Pupils) Regulations 1989, which came into force on 1 August 1989. For exemption, the head teacher must consider that it is inappropriate for the child to follow the National Curriculum for the time being and that *either:*

(a) circumstances giving rise to that opinion are likely to change within the next six months; or
(b) the pupil may have special educational needs requiring modification of the NC, and temporary exception is necessary while those needs are assessed.

If the head's direction is given under (a) it is called a "general direction", and if under (b) it is a "special direction". A general direction could be necessary, for example, in respect of a recently immigrated child who speaks little English and who needs intensive language support (see DES Circular 15/89, *The National Curriculum: Temporary Exceptions for Individual Pupils*).

(ii) Where a child has special educational needs for the purposes of the Education Act 1981, any special educational provision specified in a statement under s 7 of that Act (see Chapter 8) *may* include provision excluding the application of the National Curriculum or modifying it in his/her particular case (ERA 1988 s 18). This is clearly intended to exempt a child for a longer period than under (i)(b) ("special direction" case).

(iii) There is also a wide discretionary power to provide by regulation for all or part of the National Curriculum not to apply, or to apply in a modified form, in specific cases (ERA 1988 s 17). So far this power has only been used to dis-apply, with regard to pupils in Wales at key stage 1 who receive more than half their teaching in Welsh, the requirements concerning the implementation of the National Curriculum relating to English (Education (National Curriculum) (Exceptions) (Wales) Regulations 1989).

(d) Implementation

The phasing in of the National Curriculum began on 1 September 1989. The Secretary of State is obliged to introduce it "as soon as it is reasonably practicable (taking first the core subjects and then the other foundation subjects)" (ERA 1988 s 4(1)). Chart 4 shows which parts of the National Curriculum are to be operational by September 1991.

Chart 4 Introduction of the National Curriculum in England and Wales—initial stages[a]

From 1 September 1989:

In key stages 1–3, all core and foundation subjects are to be covered for a reasonable amount of time during the week—sufficient to constitute 'worthwhile study'[b]

In the first year of key stages 1 and 3, Maths and Science attainment targets and programmes of study.

In the first year of key stage 1, English attainment targets and programmes of study.

From 1 September 1990:

In the first year of key stage 4 all core and foundation subjects are to be covered for a reasonable amount of time during the week (as above).

The curriculum

In the first year of key stage 2 and first two years of key stage 3 (in the case of Maths and Science) and first year of stages 2 and 3 (in the case of English), attainment targets and programmes of study.

In the first year of key stages 1–3, Design and Technology attainment targets and programmes of study.

From 1 September 1991 (provisional):

In the first year of key stages 1–3, Geography and History attainment targets and programmes of study.

^a The National Curriculum is being introduced under ERA 1988 s 10(3) and various Orders, including those relating to the attainment targets and programmes of study (referred to above) and ERA Commencement Orders Nos 5 and 6 1989.
^b The Secretary of State is prohibited by ERA 1988 s 4(3) from prescribing periods of time or proportions of school timetables to be allocated to programmes of study.

(e) The Curriculum and Assessment Councils

The Curriculum and Assessment Councils are responsible for advising on the content of the National Curriculum.

The proposed National Curriculum attainment targets, programmes of study and assessment arrangements must all be referred to the *National Curriculum Council* (there is also a Curriculum Council for Wales) as must any proposed changes to arrangements in operation. The National Curriculum Council must consult governing bodies and LEAs over such matters and make recommendations. At the end of the day the Secretary of State has complete discretion over the ATs and PS for each subject, provided he gives reasons for failing to follow any of the National Curriculum Council's recommendations (see ERA 1988 ss 20 and 21).

The National Curriculum Council (and Curriculum Council

for Wales) has not less than ten and not more than fifteen members, appointed by the Secretary of State. Membership must "include persons having relevant knowledge or experience in education" (ERA 1988 s 14(2)). The National Curriculum Council has a wide range of essentially advisory functions (see s 14(3)).

The functions of the *School Examinations and Assessment Council* (SEAC) include keeping all aspects of examinations and assessment under review and advising the Secretary of State on these matters (ERA 1988 s 14(4)). The powers and organisation of the SEAC are set out in ERA 1988 Sch 2.

(f) Complaints

The Education Reform Act 1988 requires LEAs to establish complaints procedures for the consideration and disposal of complaints about various curricular matters, including the implementation of the National Curriculum and decisions about whether to grant exemption from its requirements in individual cases (s 23(1)). The complaints procedure, which covers a wide range of duties and which may be invoked by parents, is explained later in this Chapter (see page 222).

7. Political issues

Under the Education (No 2) Act 1986, LEAs, head teachers and governing bodies are required to forbid the pursuit, at a school, of:

(a) "partisan political activities" by junior school pupils (the side note refers to "political indoctrination"), and

(b) with reference to pupils at all stages, "the promotion of partisan political views in the teaching of any subject in the school" (s 44(1)).

Also, teachers must not make arrangements for junior pupils to engage in partisan political activities off the school premises (s 44(2)). Finally, LEAs, head teachers and governing bodies must take reasonable steps to secure that:

"... where political issues are brought to the attention of pupils while they are—
(a) at the school; or
(b) taking part in extra-curricular activities which are provided or organised for registered pupils at the school by or on behalf of the school;
they are offered a *balanced presentation of opposing views*" (s 45, emphasis added).

These provisions were a response to what the government saw as an unbalanced treatment of issues, or politically motivated selection of issues for coverage, by teachers in some LEA schools—especially those offering "Peace Studies" or where pupils were allegedly being radicalised by "left-wing" teachers.

The question of what is or is not a "political" issue is important. It would seem to be appropriate to extend its meaning beyond the merely party political. Nuclear power or "green" issues can clearly be political, depending on the context in which they appear.

8. Sex education

(a) Must sex education be provided?

The Education Acts impose no *specific* duty on schools or education authorities to provide sex education. But it features in the National Curriculum "attainment targets" for Science. The DES Circular 11/87 on sex education in schools states (at para 7) that although a governing body is free to decide that sex education should not be provided at a school (which, in fact, seems doubtful given its inclusion in the Science attainment targets), the Secretary of State expects that governors will accept that "schools have a responsibility to their pupils to offer at least some education about sexual matters". In any event, it would not really be possible for schools adequately to "prepare ... pupils for the ... responsibilities and experiences of adult life", as required by ERA 1988 s 1(2)(b), without providing sex education.

Governors are required to consider whether sex education

should form part of the *secular* curriculum of a school (E(No 2)A 1986 s 18(2)(a)). It may be the government's wish that sex education be taught as part of the school's religious curriculum, if this is what the governors want.

(b) Can a parent withdraw a child from sex education lessons?

On the face of it, parents have no right to withdraw their children from sex education lessons. However, it is possible that a parent may have such a right by virtue of EA 1944 s 76, which states that provided that inefficiency in provision is not increased as a result, "children are to be educated in accordance with the wishes of their parents". The courts have considered the scope of s 76 (see Chapter 4), but not yet in this context.

It may be that a governing body decides that sex education should be taught as part of religious education; in such a case a parent would be able to invoke the provisions enabling him/her to withdraw the child from RE (see below).

In any event, schools have a discretion to permit parents to withdraw their children from sex education, and the DES Circular 11/87 on sex education advises schools to recognize the strong religious objections felt by some parents towards sex education and to bear these views in mind when exercising their discretion.

(c) Information about sex education

Under the Education (School Information) Regulations 1981 (see Chapter 4), LEAs and governors have a duty to include in the published information about their schools, "the manner and context in which education as respects sexual matters is given".

(d) What kind of sex education?

LEAs and governing bodies have, since 7 January 1987, been charged with a duty to:

> "take such steps as are reasonably practicable to secure that where sex education is given to any registered pupils

at a school it is given in such a manner as *to encourage those pupils to have due regard to moral considerations and the value of family life*" (E(No 2)A 1986 s 46, emphasis added).

At the *primary* school level, says the Circular, teaching should "aim to help pupils cope with the physical and emotional challenges of growing up and give them an elementary understanding of human reproduction" (para 15). In responding to pupils' questions, teachers should, the Circular advises, show "due consideration for any particular religious or cultural factors bearing on the discussion of sexual issues" (*ibid*). At *secondary* schools, sex education may be taught as part of biology or health education. But the Circular suggests that there are cross-curricular opportunities for tackling various emotional and ethical dimensions of the subject.

According to the government, s 46 is important in establishing a "moral framework" for sex education. Sex education, the government says, should present the facts and explain the law on sexual behaviour. But it should be:

> "set within a clear moral framework in which pupils are encouraged to consider the importance of self-restraint, dignity and respect for themselves and others, and helped to recognise the physical, emotional and moral risks of casual and promiscuous sexual behaviour" (para 19).

So far as "physical" risks are concerned, teaching about sexually transmitted diseases is obviously important.

The moral framework for sex education also involves emphasising the "value of family life". The Circular advises that schools should foster a recognition of the benefits of stable married and family life (para 19), but care should be taken to avoid upsetting pupils from one-parent families.

(e) Advice about contraception

The legal and ethical problems surrounding the giving of *contraceptive advice* highlighted by the *Gillick* case (1985) (in which Mrs Victoria Gillick had challenged the legality of the provision of advice about contraception given by doctors to under-age girls without parental consent) could well arise in a school situation. Teachers may be giving information about contraception as part of sex education lessons or possibly may be approached by individual pupils for advice. The Circular warns teachers never to allow their concern for the well-being of pupils to "trespass on the proper exercise of parental rights and responsibilities" (para 25). Teachers are also warned that the circumstances which the House of Lords felt justified doctors giving contraceptive advice, without parental knowledge or consent, to children under sixteen years old have no parallel in school education (para 26).

If a teacher is approached for advice by a pupil whom the teacher knows to be sexually active, the teacher should, according to the Circular, warn the pupil of the risks involved and the possibility that the pupil may be engaging in illegal sexual activity. The Circular suggests that in some cases the head teacher should be informed so that s/he can call upon the specialist support services. The Circular makes no mention of whether teachers should inform parents. An implication of the *Gillick* decision is that giving advice without parental consent could, in such circumstances, be illegal. On the other hand, teachers may feel compelled not to commit a "breach of confidence", given the importance of retaining the trust and respect of pupils.

Note that although the government believes that subjects like contraception and, indeed, abortion, would normally be covered by sex education, it accepts that the religious ethos of schools founded on specific religious principles will have a direct bearing on how these subjects are presented.

(f) Complaints about sex education

The curriculum complaints procedure, referred to earlier and considered more fully below (page 222), applies also to sex education.

9. Homosexuality

The government's concern about some teacher' alleged portrayal of homosexual relationships as "normal" resulted, controversially, in its forceful rejection of such teaching.

The curriculum

Paragraph 22 of the DES Circular on sex education (11/87, above) tells teacher that:

"There is no place in any school in any circumstances for teaching which advocates homosexual behaviour, which presents it as the 'norm', or which encourages homosexual experimentation by pupils".

The government has not sought to ban all references to homosexuality in the course of teaching. But it has reminded schools that unless the subject is handled with sensitivity by teachers when discussed in the classroom, "deep offence" might be caused to those, expecially members of various religious faiths, for whom "homosexual practice is not morally acceptable".

Section 28 Local Government Act 1988 (which inserts s 2A into the Local Government Act 1986) probably gives legal effect to the above guidance. It states that local authorities shall not:

"(a) intentionally promote homosexuality or publish material with the intention of promoting homosexuality;
(b) promote the teaching in any maintained school of the acceptability of homosexuality as a pretended family relationship."

The section applies to local authorities, rather than their employees, such as teachers. A local authority that failed to prevent a teacher from "promoting" homosexuality might be in breach of s 28.

It is clear that fears that certain works of literature (eg Mann's *Death in Venice*) might have to be taken out of the school curriculum—and possibly off examination syllabuses—because of s 28 were unfounded. But doubts remain about whether advertising that a teaching post in a LEA school is open to persons "regardless of their sexual orientation" might serve to "promote" homosexuality for the purposes of the section.

Once again, if parents have any objection, they can make use of the local complaints machinery (see below).

10. Collective worship and religious education

(a) Introduction

The Education Act 1944 requires provision of religious education and a daily act of collective worship for all pupils, and although many of the relevant provisions have been left intact, ERA 1988 has introduced significant and controversial changes—notably an emphasis on Christianity.

(b) The statutory advisory councils on religious education

Each LEA has been required to establish a *statutory advisory council on religious education* (with a somewhat appropriate acronym of SACRE) for its area. The council's function is to:

> "advise the authority upon such matters connected with religious worship in county schools and the religious education to be given in accordance with an agreed syllabus as the authority may refer to the council or as the council may think fit" (ERA 1988 s 11(1)(a)),

and to consider whether, on an application by the head teacher of a county school, it is appropriate for the requirement for Christian collective worship (see below) to apply in the case of that school, or in the case of any class or description of pupils at that school (ERA 1988 ss11(1)(b) and 12(1)).

The standing advisory councils are to consist of governors, representatives of Christian and other "principal religious traditions" in the area, the Church of England (except in Wales), teachers' associations and the LEA; they may also include co-opted members and a nominee of the governors of a grant-maintained school which is following an agreed syllabus adopted by the LEA (ERA 1988 s 11(3) and (4)). The phrase "principal religious traditions" is nowhere defined in the Act, nor is it explained in the relevant DES Circular (3/89). The LEA is required to take all reasonable steps to assure itself that a person seeking to represent a particular denomination on the SACRE is a true representative of that denomination (s 13(1)).

(c) Collective worship

Section 25 Education Act 1944, which provided for an act of collective worship at the start of each school day (and for religious instruction at each county and voluntary school) has been repealed with effect from 1 January 1989 (SI 1988 No 2271 Sch 1). In its place are carefully worded and rather more prescriptive provisions.

(i) What form of act?

Section 6 ERA 1988 provides that in each maintained school (including a grant-maintained school), on each school day, all children present at the school must take part in an *act of collective worship*—whether a single act of worship for all pupils or separate acts for different age groups or other school groups. "Worship" is not defined in the Act, but is defined in the OED with reference to a divine being or deity.

(ii) Whose responsibility?

Responsibility for making the necessary arrangements for the act of collective worship rests with the head teacher, after consultation with the school governing body, in the case of a county school, and vice versa in the case of a voluntary school. Generally the act of collective worship is to take place on the school premises; the governors can if they consider it desirable, make appropriate arrangements for it to take place elsewhere "on a special occasion" (s 6(4) and (5)).

(iii) The act to be of a broadly Christian character

The Education Reform Act 1988 states that the act should be "wholly or mainly of a broadly Christian character"—ie it should reflect "the broad traditions of Christian belief without being distinctive of any particular Christian denomination" (ERA 1988 s 7(1) and (2)—in force 1 August 1989, and one year later in the case of former ILEA schools). Note that, from time to time, acts of collective worship do not have to comply with the above requirements, provided most of them do (s 7(3)).

The requirement as to Christian collective worship applies only in LEA-maintained *county* schools. In *voluntary* schools the character and content of collective worship will continue to be determined by governing bodies. Where a school has been allowed to "opt out" of local authority control (and become a *grant-maintained school*) its position will be more or less the same as under its pre-opting out status (DES Circular 3/89 and ERA 1988 ss 6 and 84–88). *City Technology Colleges* and *Colleges for the Technology of the Arts* are exempt from the legal requirements regarding collective worship (and RE).

(iv) Alternative collective worship

The head teacher of a county school may, if s/he considers that alternative collective worship is appropriate in respect of the whole school or any class or description of pupils at the school, apply to the local SACRE to lift or modify the requirements for Christian collective worship where such pupils are concerned (s 12(1)). The right of parents to withdraw pupils from acts of collective worship (previously in the Education Act 1944) is re-enacted in ERA 1988 s 9(3) (and EA 1981 s 12(4) in the case of special schools), and DES Circular 3/89 (para 36) suggests that one factor which might inform a head teacher's decision concerning such an application could be the extent of such withdrawal. Perhaps another factor should be the extent of teacher withdrawal from acts of collective worship. Teachers' unions are predicting extensive opting out by teachers from acts of collective worship. Teachers have a right not to be discriminated against for exercising this right (see page 216).

Various circumstances are to be taken into account by the school when deciding on an appropriate act of collective worship under the provisions, including pupils' family backgrounds, ages and aptitudes, and what the SACRE has decided on the question of whether Christian collective worship is appropriate for the school or any class or description of pupils (ERA 1988 s 12(2)). SACREs must review their decisions on this matter within five years of their previous determination, or at any time if an application for review from the head teacher (after s/he has consulted with the governing body) is received (s 12(5)).

DES Circular 3/89, para 36 maintains that the purpose of the modification/exemption procedure is to:

"allow for acts of collective worship according to a faith or religion other than Christianity where for some or all of the pupils in a school the requirement that worship should be of a broadly Christian character is inappropriate".

One problem here, though, is that in schools of a multi-ethnic composition there might have to be a form of segregation for acts of collective worship. Segregation on the basis of religion often results in segregation by race. This could constitute unlawful discrimination under the Race Relations Act 1976 (s 1(2)), although s 41 of that Act permits discrimination in furtherance of compliance with any other enactment (in this case, ERA 1988). It is to be hoped that the kind of ecumenical spirit prevailing in many school assemblies at present can be preserved, at least in part, by virtue of the fact that not all acts of collective worship have to be of a broadly Christian character provided that in any school term most of them are.

Where approval has been granted for alternative acts of collective worship for particular pupils, such collective worship will have to take place on a daily basis. If, in any particular school, the numbers requiring alternative collective worship are very small, the SACRE may decide not to authorise it, and parents will simply have the option of withdrawing their children from the Christian act of worship. If alternative collective worship for a minority religious group *has* been authorised by the SACRE, the collective worship must "not be distinctive of any particular Christian or other religious *denomination* (but this shall not be taken as preventing that worship from being distinctive of any particular *faith*)" (ERA 1988 s 7(6)(b), emphasis added). In some schools, teachers will undoubtedly experience great difficulty in drawing the required distinction.

All approved worship, whether "alternative" or not, must be provided free of charge. But nothing in ERA 1988 prevents a school from allowing RE or worship in a particular faith or denomination to be given to individual pupils whose parents have withdrawn them from approved RE or collective worship (see DES Circular 3/89, para 42). This non-statutory provision need not be provided free of charge, according to an education minister (*Times Educational Supplement*, 5 January 1990).

(v) Opting out by teachers

Teachers in most State schools will retain the right contained in EA 1944 s 30, not to be discriminated against for failing to participate in acts of collective worship. (This right would not be affected should the school become grant-maintained.) Many teachers are, in fact, opposed to compulsory collective worship for pupils. The Circular (3/89, para 48) states that where there are, in a county school, insufficient teachers who are prepared to lead an act of collective worship, the head must take all reasonable steps to find suitable persons *not* employed at the school who would be willing to conduct such acts, perhaps initially taking advice from their LEA and SACRE. The same paragraph of the Circular also points out that "as now, there is nothing to prevent senior pupils leading acts of collective worship".

(d) Religious education

Sections 26–28 Education Act 1944, which make provision for religious instruction at all maintained schools, remain basically intact. But there have been certain amendments to the law (see ERA 1988 Sch 1)—for example, to incorporate references to the requirement in ERA 1988 s 2(1)(a) that religious education must form part of the basic curriculum at all maintained schools.

(i) Religious education syllabuses

Religious education does not form part of the National Curriculum and so will not be subject to prescribed national programmes of study, attainment targets and so on (see National Curriculum above). However, EA 1944 s 26(1) and Sch 5 as amended, provide for a *locally agreed syllabus* for religious education, drawn up by a "conference" convened by the LEA and constituted very similarly to SACREs. The conference may stipulate a local programme of study.

The curriculum

All religious education syllabuses adopted on or after 29 September 1988 must:

"reflect the fact that the religious traditions in Great Britain are in the main Christian whilst taking account of the teaching and practices of the other principal religions represented in Great Britain" (ERA 1988 s 8(3)).

The phrase "principal religions" is nowhere defined in the Act, and the "taking account" requirement is especially vague.

It is important to bear in mind that the requirement in EA 1944 s 26, that RE should not be given "by means of any catechism or formulary which is distinctive of any religious denomination", is preserved in the amended version of the section. However, the amended section goes on to state (in s 26(2)) that "this provision is not to be taken as prohibiting provision in a syllabus for the study of such catechism or formularies". So pupils can, subject to the parental right of withdrawal (see below), be required to learn about religions other than their own during RE lessons.

(ii) Parental rights

Parents may exclude their children from religious education at a school and have their children receive a particular form of such education away from the school premises but during school hours (ERA 1988 s 9(3) and (4)). It cannot be a condition of attendance at a maintained (including a grant-maintained) school that a pupil attends, or abstains from attending, any Sunday school or place of worship (s 9(1)).

(iii) Grant-maintained schools

Chapter I of ERA 1988, including, therefore, the provisions concerned with religious education discussed above, applies to GM schools. But there are several additional provisions which are relevant to religious education in these schools:

- s 84 (former county schools);
- s 85 (former controlled schools);
- s 86 (former aided and special agreement schools).

Under these provisions, the transition to GM status need not result in change to religious education (and collective worship, in the case of former county schools) in these schools.

However, it is possible for an application to be made by the governors of a GM school to the Secretary of State for approval of a significant change in the character of the school, including, where the school's trustees (if any) consent in writing to the change, "a significant change in the religious character" (s 89(1) and (2)). The procedure for a change in the character of a GM school, laid down in ERA 1988 s 89 and in the Education (Grant-Maintained Schools) (Publication of Proposals) Regulations 1989 reg 4, is discussed in Chapter 1. The effect of approval by the Secretary of State under s 89 is set out in s 87 and will depend principally on whether the change in religious education is or is not planned to result in its provision in accordance with the tenets of a particular religious denomination. If it *is*, religious education is to be either (a) in accordance with the tenets of the particular denomination in question, or (b) governed by the arrangements for aided or special agreement schools which have become GM, laid down in s 86(3). If, following the change, religious education is *not* to be denominational, then such education is to be governed by most of the provisions applicable to former county schools, laid down in s 84; the "appropriate agreed syllabus" (the definition in s 88(3) will apply, not that in s 84(7)), which has been adopted (or deemed adopted) under Sch 5 to EA 1944 (see above), is to be followed in such cases.

11. External qualifications and examinations

(a) External qualifications

Courses leading to qualifications authenticated by an outside body cannot be offered to pupils of compulsory school age unless the syllabus has been approved or meets approved criteria (ERA 1988 s 5(1)). Approval must be given by the Secretary of State or a "designated body" (ie one designated by the Secretary of State for this purpose). The SEAC has been given this role and has approved a number of syllabuses. DES Circular 11/89 explains approval arrangements.

(b) Examination entry

Pupils at maintained schools must be entered by the school for any public examinations for which they have been prepared by the school, unless either the parent requests in writing that the pupil should not be so entered or the governors determine that there are "educational reasons" for not entering him/her (ERA 1988 s 117(1) and (2)). Governing bodies are required to notify parents in writing of their determinations under s 117(2) "as soon as practicable" after such determination (s 117(5)).

12. Charging for education

The charging provisions in ERA 1988 have been in effect since 1 April 1989. HMI guidance has been issued, in the face of much confusion over the legal requirements.

(a) Lessons and materials

Section 61(1) Education Act 1944 provided that "No fees shall be charged in respect of admission to any school maintained by a local education authority, . . . or in respect of the education provided in any such school". So charging for music tuition, for example, was illegal (*R v Hereford and Worcs LEA ex parte Wm Jones* (1981)). But s 61 has now been repealed.

In its place are ss 106–111 ERA 1988. As previously, no charge is possible in respect of admission to a maintained school (s 106(1)). But charges are possible for education provided during school hours for *individual* music tuition. No charge may be made in respect of RE or the National Curriculum (of which music, as a foundation subject, is part), nor in respect of anything required as part of a syllabus for a prescribed public examination (see the Education (Prescribed Public Examinations) Regulations 1989) which is a syllabus for which the pupil is being prepared at the school (s 106(4)), nor for entry to the examination itself (s 106(5)). (The legal position as regards charging for examinations is considered further below). Charging for "materials, books, instruments or other equipment" (except, perhaps, in respect of individual music tuition), or for transport required for an incidental to non-chargeable provision, would be unlawful (s 106(6) and (7)). Nevertheless, parents may be invited to provide these voluntarily (s 118) in order to release resources from the school budget, as long as no child is put "at a disadvantage because of a parent's unwillingness or inability to contribute in this way" (DES Circular 2/89, para 15).

Moreover, parents may be required to pay for materials to be used by pupils to produce, in the course of education provided to them, an article which the parent or child wishes to keep. This clearly has implications for art and craft lessons. (Could parents be required to pay for paint and paper if the child or parent intends to keep the painting?) Home economics is another problem area—the Circular refers, in this context, to the cost of "ingredients".

(b) Public examinations

It was noted above that no charge may be made for entry to a prescribed public examination for which the pupil has been prepared by the school. But although the LEA or governors will generally be responsible for examination fees, they may nevertheless recover the amount of such fees from the parent of a pupil who "fails without good reason to meet any examination requirement for that syllabus" (s 108(1)). It is for the authority concerned to decide what is or is not a "good reason" for this purpose (s 108(2)). It would clearly be unreasonable for the LEA or governors to recover the fee where the pupil has simply failed the examination (however "failure" may be defined). The Circular (2/89, *op cit*) does not deal with examination failure, but advises that failure to complete necessary course-work or failure to sit the examination without good reason might constitute grounds for recovery of fee.

The curriculum

(c) School trips

Charges may be made for residential trips, provided that the number of am and pm school sessions spent away is less than 50 per cent of the number of half-days spent on the trip; and the trip involves at least one night away from the pupils' usual accommodation (s 107(3)–(6)). "Half day" is defined as "any period of twelve hours ending with noon or midnight on any day" (s 107(4)). The Circular (2/89) advises that if six or more hours in a half day are spent on a residential trip, the whole half day is to be counted as spent on the trip. In relation to classes in general, education provided partly in and partly out of school shall be treated as falling within school hours (and so attracting no charge) if at least 50 per cent of the time (including travelling) falls within school hours (s 107(1) and (2)). If more than 50 per cent falls outside school hours, then a charge may be made for the entire activity.

Optional extras

Where the lesson or public examination does not fall within the terms of s 106 (above) it is known as an "optional extra" for which the education, examination entry and transport (and board and lodging if the provision is a residential trip) may be charged for—provided the parents have agreed to such provision being made for their child (s 109(1) and (2)). A "regulated charge", up to, but not exceeding, the cost of providing the optional extra(s) to that child, can be made to a parent. Governors may, however, meet all or part of such costs from their own funds (s 109(10)).

Apparently, reasonable charges may be made by schools for the use, by pupils, of lockers. According to the Education Secretary, provision of lockers is extra-curricular; it is for "convenience" rather than a "necessity". The announcement was made after doubts arose over plans by a school in Brighton to charge pupils £3 a year for the hire of lockers to be purchased by the school's parent-teacher association (*Times Educational Supplement,* 26 January 1990).

If it is necessary, because there is no other suitable provision, for a child to be educated at a maintained (including grant-maintained) school as a boarder, parents will not have to bear the cost (s 111(2)–(4)). In any other case where a child is so educated, the LEA or governors have a discretion to remit up to 100 per cent of boarding charges, to avoid financial hardship to the parent (s 111(5) and (6)).

(d) LEA/governors' policy on charging

Governing bodies and LEAs are required to determine and keep under review a policy on charging for optional extras and board and lodging, including the circumstances where they would remit all or part of the charges (s 110(1) and (2)). The remissions policy must provide for a complete remission of a permitted boarding charge for a residential trip (under s 106(9)), in respect of pupils whose parents are in receipt of income support or family credit during any part of the period encompassed by the trip (s 110(3)). There is no requirement to remit on the grounds of parental income any other permitted charge, although there is nothing to stop governors and LEAs making provision for this in their policies.

13. Complaints

(a) Introduction

The Education Reform Act 1988 has imposed a duty on LEAs to make arrangements for the consideration of complaints about the curriculum in maintained schools (s 23). LEAs were required to institute their complaints systems on 1 September 1989 (or 1 April 1990, in the case of London boroughs taking over from the ILEA) (SI 1989 No 46 reg 3(2)).

(b) Which types of complaint should be covered?

The new machinery covers complaints relating to the National Curriculum, RE, collective worship and any other statutory provision on the curriculum—although statutory appeal rights (eg under the Education Act 1981 in a case of special educational needs) would have to be exhausted first. The complaint may relate to a governing body's or LEA's unreasonableness or failure to carry out its statutory duty.

The curriculum

Although the Secretary of State may intervene (under EA 1944 ss 68 and 99) if the governors or LEA are acting or proposing to act unreasonably or have not carried out their duty (see pages 158–159), he cannot interfere under these powers where there is a complaint concerning a curricular matter, unless it has first been dealt with under the local complaints machinery (ERA 1988 s 23(2)).

(c) What procedure should be followed?

There are no formal requirements concerning procedure. LEAs must devise whichever system they consider most suitable in their particular case. However the DES has issued guidance in Circular 1/89. This advises that concerns felt by parents over aspects of the school curriculum and related matters could often be disposed of by way of informal discussions between parents and teachers, including the head teacher, and that such discussions should, in any event, form the first stage in the "formal" complaints procedure.

(d) Complaint to the Local Commissioner for Administration

The existence of a new statutory complaints procedure does not preclude investigation of maladministration by one of the Local Commissioners for Administration. For example, Derbyshire County Council's practice of charging parents for "A" level field trips, and the authority's refusal to refund fees of up to £75 charged for certain trips, were condemned by a Local Commissioner in her report into the matter (see *The Times*, 8 July 1988). Commissioners' reports can put pressure on LEAs to improve practices, although a Commissioner's recommendations are not legally enforceable.

14. Copyright law

Copyright restrictions may affect the way teaching and learning materials are prepared. They thus can have an influence over the way the curriculum is delivered. With teaching increasingly being influenced by technology—computers, video, and so on—it is important to be aware of the way copyright law affects the new as well as the more traditional methods of teaching.

Copyright law takes up over 150 sections of the Copyright, Designs and Patents Act 1988, which is replacing the Copyright Act 1956.

(a) What is copyright?

Copyright is defined as a "property right" subsisting in:

"(a) original literary, dramatic, musical or artistic works,
 (b) sound recordings, films, broadcasts or cable programmes, and
 (c) the typographical arrangements of published editions" (s 1(1)).

Copyright protection applies only if certain requirements regarding the author (who must be a British citizen or other as prescribed) and the country in which the work was first published (the UK or other as prescribed) are satisfied (ss 1(3), 153 and 155).

First ownership of copyright generally rests with the "author" (ss 9 and 10) of the work (s 11(1) and (3)). Where a literary, dramatic, musical or artistic work is made by an employee in the course of his/her employment, his/her employer is the first owner, subject to any agreement to the contrary (s 11(2)). The Crown owns the copyright in works written by civil servants in the course of their duties and in Acts of Parliament (see ss 163 and 164).

Like any property right, copyright can be transferred by its owner. Where books are concerned, the usual practice is for the author to retain copyright in the text but to grant an exclusive right to print and publish the work to the publisher, under the agreement between them. The makers of broadcasts and films own a copyright in them which is separate from the copyright owned by the author. Copyright in "published editions" of works—typographical arrangements of them—belongs to the publisher.

The works etc in which copyright may be owned are defined in ss 3–8 of the Act. A "literary" work comprises any work, other than a dramatic or musical work, which is written, spoken or sung. A computer program is a literary work (s 3(1)). A "dramatic" work includes a work of dance or mime. Copyright does not subsist in a literary, dramatic or musical work unless and until it is recorded, in writing or otherwise (s 3(2)). "Artistic" works are defined as: graphic works, photographs, sculptures or collages, irrespective of artistic quality; works of architecture, whether buildings or models of buildings; and works of "artistic craftsmanship" (s 4). There are also definitions of sound recordings, films ("a recording on any medium from which a moving image may . . . be produced") (s 5), broadcasts (s 6), cable programmes (s 7) and published editions (s 8).

(b) Duration of copyright

Copyright in a work is not of unlimited duration. It subsists for prescribed periods, set out in ss 12–15. Where literary, dramatic, musical or artistic works are concerned, copyright expires fifty years after the end of the calendar year in which the author (or the last of known joint authors) dies (s 12(1) and (4)). (See s 12(2) and (4) for the position concerning unknown authorship.) The name purporting to be that of the author and appearing on the work when published or made, is presumed to be that of the author unless the contrary is proved (s 104(2)).

If the work is "computer generated", copyright subsists for fifty years from the end of the year in which it was made (s 12(3)). Crown copyright lasts for fifty years from the date at which the work was first published commercially (if the work was so published within the first seventy-five years after it was made) or, if not so published, for 125 years from the end of the calendar year in which it was made (s 163(3)). In the case of sound recordings, films and broadcasts, copyright subsists, basically speaking, for fifty years (ss 13 and 14)—running, where a broadcast is concerned, from the end of the year in which it was first made, not from any repeat broadcasts (s 14). Copyright in a typographical arrangement of a published edition subsists for twenty-five years (s 15). Although the copyright to Barrie's *Peter Pan* expired on 31 December 1987, all royalties from the work's public performance or commercial publication belong exclusively to the Hospital for Sick Children, Great Ormond Street, London (s 301, Sch 6).

(c) Infringement of copyright

Under copyright law, the copyright owner has the exclusive right to copy the work, issue copies of it to the public, perform, show or play the work in public, and make certain other uses of it (eg broadcasting) (ss 17–21). Anyone who, without the licence of the copyright owner, does any of these things, directly or indirectly and in relation to the work as a whole or *a substantial part of it*, infringes copyright (s 16(2) and (3)). The question of substantiality is one on which no guidance may be found in the legislation. It seems that it is a question to be determined as much by quality as by quantity (*Ravenscroft* v *Herbert* (1980)), so that if making a copy is worthwhile, in the sense that doing so perhaps obviates the need to purchase a copy of the work, the test of substantiality is satisfied.

Infringement of copyright may lead to the owner (or exclusive licence holder) pursuing the remedies available under ss 96–100 (or ss 101 and 102). The remedies are damages and/or injunction and/or delivery up of the infringing article (ss 98 and 99). Additional damages may be awarded to take account of the flagrancy of the breach and the benefit accruing to the defendant from the illegal copying, etc. Subject to certain strict conditions, infringing copies of works may be seized (s 100). A court may order the destruction or other disposal of infringing copies (s 114). In some cases, for example where a person sells copies commercially or makes an article to be used for making copies of a work with copyright protection, there can be criminal liability (s 107). Those responsible for, *inter alia*, the public showing or playing of a film or sound recording, or the public performance of a literary or dramatic work, may be guilty of an offence—if they had reason to believe that copyright would be infringed (s 107(3)).

This is the general position. But the infringement provisions are specifically modified in certain cases (s 16(4)), of which the most relevant to schools are: research and private study (s 29), education (ss 32–36) and libraries (ss 37–43).

(d) Research and private study

"Fair dealing" with a literary, dramatic, musical or artistic

The curriculum

work for the purposes of research or private study does not infringe any copyright in the work nor, in the case of a published edition, in the typographical arrangement (s 29(1)). "Fair dealing" is not defined in the Act, but would be taken to limit the usage to that which is justifiable for the purpose of the research or private study. If the usage might interfere with the normal commercial exploitation of the work, it might not amount to fair dealing.

Where the copying is by a librarian (including a school or college librarian—see below) it can amount to fair dealing only in specific defined circumstances (in ss 38 and 39—below) (s 29(3)(a)). If the copying is by any other person carrying it out on behalf of the student or researcher, there will be no fair dealing if the person doing the copying knows or has reason to believe that it will result in copies of substantially the same material being provided to more than one person at substantially the same time and for substantially the same purpose (s 29(3)(b)).

(e) Education

Although copyright legislation has traditionally relaxed some of its rules where schools are concerned, the scope for legal copying of published materials for use in teaching has been limited. There has, of course, been illegal copying on a wide scale. To schools experiencing shortages of learning resources, copying from works may at times seem the only answer. Some help has been offered by licensing, now dealt with by Chapter VII of Part I of the 1988 Act. Licensing schemes are expected to increase in number as a consequence of, for example, the growing competition in, and commercialisation of, broadcasting (see V Porter, *The Copyright Designs and Patents Act 1988: The Triumph of Expediency over Principle* (1988) 16 J Law & Society 340). In 1984 a successful licence agreement was reached between the Copyright Licence Agency and local authorities for copying from books, periodicals and journals in schools and colleges.

Copying, for use in instruction, of literary, dramatical, musical or artistic works, does not cause an infringement if the person copying is giving or receiving instruction and the copying *is not by means of a reprographic process* (s 32(1)). Copying, by a person giving or receiving instruction, of a sound recording, film, broadcast or cable programme, is also permissible, if being done for the purposes of instruction (s 32(2)).

Copying for the purposes of examinations, including the making of a reprographic copy of a musical score which a candidate will perform for an examination, will not infringe copyright (s 32(3) and (4)).

The legislation now permits multiple reprographic copying by educational establishments (or on their behalf) of passages from published works—for the purposes of instruction, provided that *not more than one per cent* is copied in any quarter (running from 1 January, April, July and September) (s 36(1) and (2)). However, such copying is not authorised where a licence is in force and the person doing the copying knows or ought to be aware of that fact (s 36(3)). Such a licence is of no effect in so far as it restricts the proportion of the work that may be copied to less than that authorised by s 36 (above). Recording of broadcasts and cable programmes for educational purposes at an educational establishment is also permissible under the Act or under a licence agreement, if one has been concluded (s 35).

The Act also enables extracts (a "short passage") from certain literary or dramatic works to be used in anthologies intended for use in educational establishments (and so described in their titles etc), provided that the anthology consists mainly of material in which no copyright subsists. It is necessary that the work from which the extract was taken is not intended for use in such an establishment. Also, no more than two extracts from copyright works by the same author may appear within a space of five years in the same publisher's collections (s 33).

Pupils, teachers and others (where the purpose is to instruct) may perform literary, dramatic or musical works without infringing copyright (s 34). The performance must be to an audience consisting of "teachers and pupils . . . and any other persons directly connected with the activities of the establishment". (Parents of pupils are not automatically to be taken to be directly connected with the activities of the establishment for this purpose: s 34(3).) If the performance is by persons other than teachers or pupils, it has to be at the relevant educational establishment (s 34(1)). The playing of a sound recording, film, broadcast or cable programme to such an audience does not amount to a showing of the work in public for copyright purposes (s 34(2)).

(f) Libraries (including school libraries)

Although the Act enables copying in libraries to take place without infringement, very tight restrictions apply. School libraries in all LEA-maintained and grant-maintained schools are amongst the classes of library covered (Copyright (Librarians and Archivists) (Copying of Copyright Material) Regulations 1989 reg 3(1) and Sch 1 para 3, referring to EA 1944 s 114, as amended).

Only the librarian may make and supply the copy under these provisions. A single copy of an article in a periodical may be made, but not more than one article from the same issue (s 38). Also, a single copy of no more than a "reasonable proportion of any work" may be made (s 39). In both cases the person for whom the copy is made must be either a student or researcher and must be required to pay the librarian "not less than the cost (including a contribution to the general expenses of the library) attributable to . . . production" (ss 38(2)(c) and 39 (2)(c)).

Regulations (*op cit*, reg 4(2)(a)) provide that the copy may not be supplied until the librarian has obtained a signed declaration (substantially in accordance with Form A set out in the regulations) from the person requesting the copy. The declaration states, *inter alia*, that the student etc has not previously obtained a copy of the same material from a librarian and that s/he will not use the copy for any purpose other than research or private study nor will s/he supply a copy of it to any other person. To prevent members of a class from obtaining individual copies of a work on their syllabus, thus defeating the restrictions against multiple copying, the librarian must be satisfied that the requirements of the person making the request and those of any other person are not similar (ie that, in effect, these persons are not following the same course of study for which the copy is required (*ibid*, reg 4(2)(b) and s 40)).

(g) The moral right

Finally, it may be noted that the Act recognizes the moral right of the author to ensure that his/her reputation is not sullied through the exploitation of his/her work by others (see especially ss 77–81). Basically speaking, this includes a right (i) to be identified whenever the work is performed in public, broadcast or published, and (ii) to object to derogatory treatment of one's work by others. There are exceptions to (i) and (ii). For example, neither apply to computer programs, and (ii) does not apply to literary work written for and published in newspapers, magazines or similar periodicals. So far as (i) is concerned, the author does not need to be identified when (by virtue of s 32(3)) his work may be used without infringement for the purposes of examination questions (s 79(4)(c)).

Chapter 8

Special educational needs

1. Introduction to the legislation

Local education authorities (LEAs) have a number of responsibilities concerning the identification and assessment of children with special educational needs and the provision of special education for such children. Most, but not quite all, of the duties are contained in the Education Act 1981 ("EA 1981") and the Education (Special Educational Needs) Regulations 1983, as amended. One of the notable features of this legislation, which was modelled on the recommendations of the Warnock Committee in 1978 (*Special Educational Needs*, Cmnd 7212), is the network of parental rights within it. But, above all, this is a complex area of the law, where interpretation is not always straightforward and specialist terminology is employed. Judicial decisions have removed some of the uncertainty concerning the precise meaning of the legal provisions.

The effectiveness of the 1981 Act has recently been examined by the House of Commons Social Services Committee and the key parts of it have been reviewed by the DES—leading to a revised circular. Although various aspects of practice and procedure are outlined below, the chief aim of this chapter is to explain the legal framework within which this important area of provision operates, including that relating to LMS and the National Curriculum.

2. Definitions

Unfortunately, the Act contains a rather complex set of inter-connected definitions.

(a) Learning difficulty

The starting point is "learning difficulty". Under s 1(1) of the Act, a child has special educational needs ("SEN") if s/he has a "learning difficulty which calls for special educational provision to be made for him".

"Learning difficulty" exists if a child has:

"(a) a significantly greater difficulty in learning than the majority of children of his/her age; or
(b) a disability which prevents or makes it difficult for him to make use of educational facilities of a kind generally provided in schools, within the area of the local authority concerned, for children of his age; or
(c) he is under the age of five years and is, or would be if special educational provision were not made for him, likely to fall within paragraph (a) or (b) when over that age" (s 1(2)).

Two contentious areas, (i) dyslexia and (ii) speech therapy have been held to give rise to a learning difficulty within (a) and (b) calling for special educational provision ((i) *R v Hampshire EA ex parte J* (1985); (ii) *R v Lancashire CC ex parte CM* (1989); cf *R v Oxfordshire EA ex parte W* (1986)).

Read together, the three subsections would seem to require that in order to fall within the Act a child must have a learning difficulty within s 1(2) (eg defective speech), being a difficulty/need which requires special educational provision.

(b) Special educational provision

Special educational provision is provision, for a child aged two or over, which is:

"additional to, or otherwise different from, the educational provision made generally for children of his age in schools maintained by the local education authority concerned" (s 1(3)(a))".

Section 1(3)(a) has been interpreted as meaning that even if each of a LEA's schools has, say, a deaf unit, such provision would still amount to "special educational provision" (*R* v *Hampshire EA ex parte J* (1985)). "Special educational provision" can thus be any generally available provision other than that made for what the judge in the above case (Taylor J) referred to as "the general run of normal children, to the normal majority". Hampshire LEA's argument, that any provision for children who were deaf, or partially blind, or disturbed etc, which was generally available in its schools was not special educational provision, was rejected by the court. Any educational provision for a child under two is special educational provision (s 1(3)(b)).

Note that a child is not to be taken as having a learning difficulty solely because the language (or form of language) in which he is, or will be, taught is different from a language (or form of language) which has at any time been spoken in his home (EA 1981 s 1(4)).

3. Integration

Although much special needs education is provided in special schools (described in Chapter 1—see page 9), the 1981 Act aims to ensure that, so far as possible, special educational needs are catered for in mainstream schools.

LEAs must, subject to certain conditions, ensure that special educational provision for children in respect of whom they hold statements under s 7 EA 1981 (see below) is made *in an ordinary school* (s 2). The conditions are:

> ". . . that account has been taken . . . of the view of the child's parent and that educating a child in an ordinary school is compatible with—
> (a) his receiving the special education that he requires;
> (b) the provision of efficient education for the children with whom he will be educated; and
> (c) the efficient use of resources" (s 2(3)).

Where a child with special educational needs is being educated in an ordinary LEA-maintained or grant-maintained school, there is a duty to ensure that the child "engages in the activities of the school together with children who do not have special educational needs" (s 2(7), as amended).

However, such integration must be compatible with the objects ((a)-(c) above) specified in s 2(3) and be reasonably practicable.

If the LEA considers that all or part of a child's education should be provided otherwise than at school, it can, after consulting the child's parent(s), make appropriate arrangements (s 3). Also, under a new section, 3A, added by the Children Act 1989 (Sch 12 para 36), a LEA may arrange for a child in respect of whom it maintains a statement of his/her special educational needs to receive education outside England and Wales. The LEA is entitled to meet all or part of any fees. This provision has become known as the "Peto" clause, after the Peto Institute in Hungary in which children with cerebal palsy receive specialist treatment not available in this country. By paying the fees, LEAs could now assist children whose parents lack the necessary means to attend for such treatment.

4. Identification and assessment of needs

Where there are grounds to suggest that a child has, or probably has, SEN which are such that special educational provision should be made for him/her (s 5(1) (a) and (b)), formal assessment will be necessary. Such children will probably have been identified through monitoring of pupils by the school. The revised DES Circular on *Assessments and Statements of Special Educational Needs* (22/89, which has replaced 1/83) advises teachers to keep full records of pupils' progress and stresses that the assessment arrangements under ERA 1988 will assist in the identification of pupils' SEN. Governors of county, voluntary and grant-maintained schools—and LEAs, in the case of nursery schools—must ensure that pupils with SEN are identified and that appropriate educational provision is made for them (s 2(5)(a) and (c)). They must also ensure that where the LEA informs the head teacher (or appropriate governor) that a child has SEN, the head teacher (or governor) makes those needs known to all who are likely to teach the child (s 2(5)(b)).

Only a certain proportion of children will have SEN which are such that the LEA should determine the special educational provision that should be made. Others' needs

Special educational needs

might be met through provision determined by the school—eg through remedial teaching.

Parents have no statutory right to object to the carrying out of an assessment, only the right to make representations when given notice of it (s 5(3)(d)) (see below).

Statutory assessment procedure

(i) Stage 1: Notice

The first stage is service of a notice on the parent or guardian informing him/her: that the LEA proposes to make an assessment; of the procedure that will be followed; of the name of the officer of the LEA from whom further information can be obtained; of the parents' right to make representations and submit written evidence (within a period stipulated in the notice, of at least twenty-nine days from the date on which the notice is served) (s 5(3)). The revised Circular advises that before the notice is issued:

> "every possible effort should be made to effect initial contacts between the teachers, or any other professional making the referral, and the child's parent" (para 33).

"Parent" is defined in EA 1944 s 114(1), as amended, which includes in the definition the person(s) with actual custody of the child and a guardian. Although the matter is not free from doubt, the Circular states (at para 36) that, for the purposes of the assessment procedure, LEAs should inform the following persons:

(a) both of the child's legal parents;
(b) any guardian appointed by deed, will or order of the court;
(c) any person with whom the child is living, whether or not a custody order is in force in that person's favour (eg a foster parent);
(d) the local authority, where the child is in care, or key worker, where the child is in a children's home;
(e) a voluntary organisation in whom the parental rights and duties have been vested by resolution.

(ii) Stage 2: Assessment

"When a local education authority have served a notice under subsection (3) above and the period specified in the notice . . . has expired, the authority shall, if they consider it appropriate after taking into account any representations made and any evidence submitted to them in response to the notice, assess the educational needs of the child concerned" (s 5(4)).

The LEA is required, when making an assessment of the child's SEN, to take account of parental representations and to seek advice from a variety of professional sources: educational, medical, psychological, and so on (EA 1981 Sch 1; Education (Special Educational Needs) Regulations 1983, regs 4–7). The advice should be in written form. When it is requested, a deadline should be set for its provision, because delay is not in the child's interests (DES Circular 22/89, para 38). The Circular recommends (Annex 1) that each professional adviser should provide details of:

(a) the child's relevant past and present levels of functioning. Reference would be made to his/her strengths and weaknesses, the influence of factors in the child's environment (home, school etc), and any relevant aspects of the child's past history;
(b) the aims to which provision for the child should be directed;
(c) the recommended facilities and resources to promote the achievement of these aims (in (b)).

"Educational advice" should be sought from the head teacher of any school which the child has attended at some time in the preceding eighteen months, says the Circular (para 40); if the head teacher has not taught the child within this period, s/he should consult a teacher who has. The head teacher of an independent school that a child is attending has no legal duty to provide such advice, although the draft version of the Circular urged such person's co-operation.

Note that the Circular suggests that "where practicable" the child should be helped and encouraged to participate in the assessment of his/her SEN (para 20).

(iii) Examination

An examination of the child will form a part of the assessment. It is here that the Circular's advice (at para 49) is particularly important:

> "the relations between professional advisers and parents during the process of assessment are of crucial importance. Parents should be encouraged to feel that they are partners in the process".

(Note that the draft Circular referred to parents as a "part of" rather than "partners in" this process.) To this end, the Act (Sch 1) requires the LEA to serve a notice on a parent before the actual examination, stating the place and time at which the examination will be held, the parent's right to be present at the examination, the officer from whom further information can be obtained and the parent's right to submit information to the authority. It is an offence for a parent, "without reasonable cause", not to comply with the requirements of such a notice if the child is of compulsory school age (Sch 1 para 2(4)). Parents have no right to attend any case conference which is called, but, as the Circular points out, there are advantages to their being invited there, in terms of maintaining their trust and co-operation (para 50).

5. Statementing

(a) When is a statement necessary?

Once an assessment (under s 5) of the child's educational needs has been made by the LEA, the authority:

> "shall, if they are of the opinion that they should determine the special educational provision that should be made for him, make a statement of his special educational needs" (s 7(1)).

(The statement can include a modification or exclusion of the National Curriculum in the child's particular case—see below.) The 1981 Act does not impose a duty on LEAs to maintain a statement under s 7(1) in respect of *every* child whose special educational needs are covered by the Act (*R v Secretary of State for Education and Science and Anr ex parte Lashford* (1988) (CA)). A distinction must be drawn between (i) a child who has special educational needs ("SEN") (for the purposes of the Act) and (ii) a child for whom statutory assessment is necessary because s/he has SEN *which are such that the LEA may consider that it should determine the special educational provision that should be made for him* (for the purposes of s 7(1)). The revised DES Circular emphasises that LEAs would be expected to prepare a statement for all children with severe or complex learning difficulties which require special provision, over and above that normally provided in ordinary schools, or where placement in a special school for all or most of the time is considered necessary (see paras 30 and 31). A statement would not generally be necessary in other cases.

(b) Form and content of statements

(Education (Special Educational Needs) Regulations 1983 reg 10, and s 7(1) of the 1981 Act.)

The statement is to include such matters as:

(i) the special educational needs as assessed by the LEA;
(ii) the special educational provision which the LEA considers appropriate to meet those needs;
(iii) the type of school (and name of any particular school) which the LEA considers appropriate for the child;
(iv) details of any non-educational provision which is considered necessary (note that LEAs are now empowered to make non-educational as well as educational provision for children with SEN (EA 1981 s 7(2), as amended by ERA 1988)).

The advice—educational, medical, psychological and other —and parental evidence, on which the LEA's decision was based, are to form part of the statement (1983 Regulations reg 10(1)(d)).

Detailed guidance on the form and content of statements is set out in the Circular, at paras 58–63.

(c) Procedure

Before making a statement under s 7, a LEA must supply the parents with a copy of the proposed statement and inform them of various matters (s 7(4)–(7)) including the arrangements for making representations if they disagree with all or part of it. The Circular emphasises that the language of the statement should be clear, concise and jargon-free (para 57). Parents have fifteen days to make representations or require the LEA to arrange a meeting with an officer to discuss the statement (s 7(4) and (7)). If the parents still disagree with any part of the assessment, they have a further fifteen days from the date of the meeting with the LEA officer in which to require the authority to arrange further meetings to discuss the relevant advice on which the statement was based (s 7(5)).

The LEA may then proceed to:

"(a) make a statement in the form originally proposed;
(b) make a statement in a modified form; or
(c) determine not to make a statement;
and shall notify the parent in writing of their decision" (s 7(8)).

In any case where a statement is made, the authority must serve on the parents not only a copy of the statement, but also notice of their right of appeal to an appeal committee under s 8(1) (see below) against the special educational provision specified in the statement; and "the name of the person to whom they may apply for information and advice about the child's special educational needs" (s 7(9)).

The LEA must arrange for the special educational provision specified in the statement to be made for the child (unless the parents have made suitable arrangements), making such provision in an ordinary school where possible (as required by s 2) (s 7(2)).

(d) Review/reassessment

Statements must be *reviewed* annually by the LEA, to ensure that provision is appropriate to a child's needs (EA 1981 Sch 1 para 5). Reassessment must in every case take place where a pupil is aged between thirteen and a half and fourteen and a half years, unless the child has been assessed since the age of twelve and a half years (Education (Special Educational Needs) Regulations 1983 reg 9). Where a child is also disabled, LEAs have a duty under the Disabled Persons (Services, Consultation and Representation) Act 1986 s 5 to keep under review the dates that statemented children are expected to finish their full-time education and give local authority social services departments the prescribed amount of notice of those dates (in force from 1 February 1988: SI 1988 No 51).

6. Reassessment at parents' request

In certain cases a parent can request an assessment. In a case where there is *no* statement in respect of the child under s 7, the LEA must comply with the request unless it is "unreasonable" (s 9(1)). If the child *is* made the subject of a statement, s/he must be reassessed, if the parents so request, provided there has been no assessment in the previous six months and unless the LEA is "satisfied that an assessment would be inappropriate" (s 9(2)).

7. Appeals and other forms of challenge

(a) Appeals

Parents have various appeal rights under the Act. First, there is a right of appeal in writing to the Secretary of State when the LEA, having made an assessment, considers that it is not required to determine that special educational provision should be made for a child (s 5(6)). The LEA must inform the child's parents of its decision and of their right of appeal (s 5(7)). On an appeal, the Secretary of State may, if he thinks fit, direct the LEA to reconsider its decision (s 5(8)).

Secondly, LEAs are required to make arrangements for parents to appeal against the special educational provision proposed in statements following a first or any subsequent assessment of a child, or against any amendment to an existing statement by the LEA (s 8(1)). The LEA must inform the parents of this right of appeal when serving them with a copy of the statement (s 7(9)(b)) or when amending an existing statement (Sch 1 para 6(4)). The appeal lies to an appeal committee—constituted under the Education Act 1980 and also having jurisdiction under that Act over school admissions appeals (see above, page 157). The committee's decisions on statements are *not* binding on LEAs, for the committee can only confirm the provision specified in the statement or remit the case to the LEA for reconsideration in the light of the committee's observations (s 8(4) and (5)). The committee must give adequate reasons for its decisions (*R* v *Surrey County Council ex parte H* (1985), *per* Waller LJ at 221). Parents have a further right of appeal, to the Secretary of State, if dissatisfied as a result of the committee's decision or the LEA's decision on the remitted case (s 8(6)). The Secretary of State can confirm, amend or order the cessation of a statement (s 8(7)). His decision cannot have retrospective effect. He can consider only the provision *to be made* (*R* v *Secretary of State for Education and Science ex parte Davis* (1988)).

(b) Complaint to the Secretary of State

A parent may also request the Secretary of State to use his powers under EA 1944 ss 68 and 99 (see above, pages 158–159) if the LEA decides not to assess a child under s 5.

(c) Judicial review

As many of the cases referred to in this chapter may illustrate, it is also possible for parents to invoke judicial review procedure (High Court) on the ground that the LEA or appeal committee has made an error of law or has acted unreasonably or in breach of natural justice (eg the appeal committee meeting was deliberately truncated in order to allow councillors to attend a council meeting later in the afternoon). Judicial review is not an appeal procedure as such, for the court can review only the legality of the decision taken, not its merits. For example, the court might consider whether the procedure was fair or whether the LEA acted in good faith.

(d) Wardship

The Family Division of the High Court may also make a child a ward of court, although as a way of supplementing the powers of the local authority rather than as a way of overturning an authority's decision over special educational provision (*Re D* (1988)).

8. Special needs and the National Curriculum

The government's policy is that *all* pupils, including those with special educational needs, should have the opportunity of benefiting from the National Curriculum. Exception from the National Curriculum is possible, although there can be no departure from the duty, in ERA 1988 s 1, to offer a balanced and broadly based curriculum to those with special educational needs (see National Curriculum Council *A Curriculum for All* (1989)).

(i) Under s 19 ERA 1988, temporary exception in individual cases may be ordered by head teachers, in circumstances prescribed by regulations: the Education (National Curriculum) (Temporary Exceptions for Individual Pupils) Regulations 1989. So far as SEN are concerned, a head teacher may make such an order, in the form of a "special direction", on the ground that it is for the time being inappropriate for a child to follow the prescribed National Curriculum, and that the National Curriculum should be modified in his case while he is being assessed for special educational needs or while a statement is being prepared. The Circular on these regulations states, however, that:

> ". . . a special direction will not always be necessary when a head teacher refers a pupil for assessment. Head teachers should consider in each case if there is a clear case for a direction, and should not assume that this will be the case or prejudge the outcome of the assessment procedures" (15/89 para 17).

(ii) Section 18 ERA 1988 provides:

"The special educational provision for any pupil specified

in a statement under section 7 of the 1981 Act of his special educational needs may include provision—
  (a) excluding the application of the provisions of the National Curriculum; or
  (b) applying those provisions with such modifications as may be specified in the statement."

(iii) The revised DES Circular on assessments and statements of special educational needs (22/89, *op cit*) states that the Secretary of State may consider using his power (in ERA 1988 ss 4 and 17) to prescribe modification or non-application of all or part of the National Curriculum in certain cases of special educational needs:

"For example, where the National Curriculum requirements would involve certain kinds of physical or practical work, alternative arrangements might be prescribed for those whose physical disabilities could put at risk their own safety or that of others. Such arrangements might apply to pupils with or without statements" (para 10).

9. Special needs in opted-out schools

Although a school may be taken out of local authority control and become "grant-maintained" under the ERA 1988 (see above, pages 15 and 16), the LEA will retain its duties in respect of pupils with special educational needs. This will be one of several continuing responsibilities which LEAs will be expected to carry out:

"in such a way that they treat the pupils at a grant-maintained school no less favourably than those at schools which they maintain" (see DES Circular 10/88, para 64).

10. LMS and special needs provision

Local management of schools (LMS) was considered in Chapter 1. Every LEA must prepare, and submit to the Secretary of State for approval, a financial delegation scheme (ERA 1988 s 33). Provision for children with special educational needs has certainly not been overlooked in the arrangements for financial delegation under ERA 1988.

The cost of provision for children in respect of whom there are statements may be excepted from delegation under the terms of a financial delegation scheme if the LEA so chooses (s 34) (as a "discretionary exception" in calculating the "aggregated schools budget"). If it *is* delegated, the LEA will:

> "retain responsibility for identifying, assessing and determining the provision required for individual pupils with statements, and will be able to allocate additional resources through the formula as additional children are so identified" (DES Circular 22/89, para 13).

Other special needs, and provision for statemented children which has not been delegated, should be taken into account in the formula for calculating a school's allocation of financial resources (DES Circular 7/88, para 104). Up to 25 per cent of the "aggregated schools budget" (the part of the general schools budget available for allocation to schools within a delegation scheme—see page 45 above) is determined with reference to the extent of special educational needs within a school, in addition to other factors (DES Circular 7/88, para 115; ERA 1988 s 38(3)(b)).

11. Staff training

The importance of specialised training for teachers of pupils with special educational needs was emphasised by the Warnock Report and is acknowledged by the DES (eg Circular 23/89, paras 30 and 31). Training for teachers and others working in this field constitutes four of the national priority areas covered by the LEA Training Grants Scheme (DES Circular 20/89, para 16 and Annex A, Nos 5–8). (See further pages 100–101 above.)

Chapter 9

Negligence, health and safety

1. Introduction

Although it is, perhaps, comforting to find an area relatively untouched by recent reforms in the law of education, the law governing health and safety of staff and pupils remains complex and, at times, less than clear-cut. The law has emanated from a number of sources. First there is the common law, deriving from the judgments of the courts over many years, which establishes negligence as a tort—a civil wrong giving rise to entitlement to compensation for the person wronged. Then there is statute law covering, for example, civil liability in respect of premises ("occupier's liability") and criminal liability in respect of unsafe or unhealthy working conditions. These areas of the law are of wide application. They apply to various workplaces, buildings and other places, and to people engaged in all kinds of activities. Thus, in order to describe the legal position as it applies to schools in particular, it is necessary to extract carefully the relevant principles from the general law. A substantial part of the task is to consider the wealth of relevant case law, on the care and supervision of pupils in particular, although it has to be appreciated that the teaching environment of the 1990s, like the current attitudes of many of the judges, is in many respects rather different from what it was when many of the cases were decided. For this reason, among others, it is not always possible to state with certainty the legal position in a particular situation. Although the principles on which liability may be determined can be stated, it would be a very brave (or foolish) person indeed that would attempt to state categorically whether a particular set of circumstances could give rise to liability! As Stephenson LJ said in *Porter* v *City of Bradford Metropolitan Council* (1985): "It is quite clear what the duty of an education authority and of its teachers is; the difficulty is to apply the law correctly to the facts of any particular case". The question of whether there has been negligence, and the appropriate remedy—be it damages or some other remedy—will often have to be resolved by way of litigation.

With this *caveat* stated, it is possible now to give consideration to the first of the relevant areas, negligence.

2. Negligence in the care and supervision of pupils

(a) Introduction

Negligence rests on three concepts: duty, breach and damage. Negligence arises when someone who owes a duty of care breaches that duty and as a result damage is occasioned to another person (known as the plaintiff). As negligence is based around the notion of reasonable care, it follows that an injury which no reasonable amount of care could have prevented and which was completely unforeseeable will not give rise to negligence. For example, in *Webb* v *Essex County Council* (1954), a pupil jumped from a stool being used as part of the "agility apparatus". Although the stool was surrounded by rubber mats, the boy, aged five, was injured. The court found that the apparatus itself was sound and that the teachers were not negligent: there was nothing further they could have done to prevent the injury, which resulted from a pure "accident".

It will be noted that the *Webb* case concerned an action brought against a local education authority. Under the principle of "vicarious liability" an employer is liable for, *inter alia*, the negligence of his/her employee occasioned while the employee is acting in the course of his/her employment. Where a teacher is concerned, this applies to anything undertaken as part of the teacher's contractual duties. There has always been some doubt about the application of the principle to voluntary duties—such as rugby coaching on a Saturday morning—and the teacher concerned should, in any event, always ensure that the employers have arranged insurance cover. The fact that a pupil assists with one or two routine tasks around the school does not make him or her an "employee" for the purposes of vicarious liability (*Smith* v *Martin and Kingston-upon-Hull Corporation* (1911); *Watkins* v *Birmingham City Council* (1975)).

In theory, the plaintiff may sue either the employer or the employee or both of them jointly—although it is rare for the teacher alone to be sued since the LEA's financial resources are far greater. If negligence is found, the employer may then be entitled to a contribution from the employee (for example, a teacher). In practice this might occur only rarely (see D Nice, *Education and the Law* (1986), page 194).

Although, under LMS, governing bodies will enjoy many of the rights of an employer, the LEA will retain the responsibility of an employer for the purposes of vicarious liability (except, as at present, in aided and special agreement schools). Nevertheless, as the DES Circular on local financial management explains (7/88, para 187):

"The number of decisions taken at school level will increase with local management, and heads and other staff will need to make sure that they follow the procedures set out in or under the LEA's scheme for securing adequate maintenance and meeting other relevant requirements, such as on health and safety".

(Governors, however, will, under LMS, acquire responsibilities in respect of certain activities under their remit, although they are exempted by ERA 1988 s 36(6) from liability for any harm resulting from their spending of the school budget (eg on faulty equipment)—see Chapter 3, pages 128–130.) In grant-maintained schools, the governors are the employers for the purposes of vicarious liability.

(b) The duty of care

The scope of the duty of care may be understood initially with reference to the "neighbour principle" enshrined in the *dictum* of Lord Atkin in the well-known case of *Donoghue* v

Stevenson (1932) at page 580). His Lordship stated that a person owes a duty of care to his/her "neighbours"—being "persons who are so closely and directly affected by my act that I ought reasonably to have them in contemplation when I am directing my mind to the acts or omissions that are called in question". The test for determining the existence of a duty of care is not found in this *dictum* alone, despite the approval given to it by the House of Lords in *Home Office* v *Dorset Yacht Co* (1970). The courts have struggled to develop this area in a clear and authoritative manner in recent years (see M Brazier, *Street on Torts,* 8th ed (1988), pages 161–163), but it now seems (*Caparo Industries plc* v *Dickman* (1990) *per* Lord Bridge) that the existence of a duty of care depends on various factors: (i) the foreseeability of harm, (ii) "proximity", or "neighbourhood" as per *Donoghue* v *Stevenson* (above) and (iii) that the court considers it just and reasonable to hold that there is a duty—although (ii) and (iii) were described by His Lordship as

> "little more than convenient labels to attach to the features of different specific situations which, on a detailed examination of all the circumstances, the law recognizes as giving rise to a duty of a given scope".

In any event, it is now well settled that among the "numerous and extensive categories of situations which are treated by the courts as imposing a duty of care . . . [is that whereby] a teacher owes a duty of care to his child-pupil" (*Street on Torts, op cit,* page 160).

Of course, it will still be necessary to show that the harm resulted from a breach of the duty of care which occasioned the damage.

(c) The standard of care

The general rule is that breach of the duty of care is judged by the standard of care expected of the reasonable person (eg *Blyth* v *Birmingham Waterworks Co* (1856), *per* Alderson B). In the case of a person performing professional duties, the classic view of Winfield, much cited, is that the law expects such a person to demonstrate the "average amount of competence associated with the proper discharge of the duties of that profession". But in *Wilsher* v *Essex Area*

Health Authority ((1986) (CA) and (1988) (HL)) the court held that the standard should be that which might be reasonably expected of a person in a particular *post* in question. This implies that a lower standard of care may not be expected of a probationer or other inexperienced teacher.

In the medical context, the doctor must also be acting in accordance with general and approved practice. If there are two conflicting opinions, the adoption of one practice will be justified if it is accepted as proper by a "responsible body of medical men skilled in that particular art" (*per* McNair J in *Bolam* v *Friern Hospital Management Committee* (1957)). Where teachers are concerned, a general and approved practice is easier to prove. In *Conrad* v *ILEA* (1967) it was recognized that there were two schools of thought as to appropriate initial instruction in judo. In *Chilvers* v *London County Council* (1916) a child was injured when a lance on a toy soldier he was playing with poked his eye. The court held the local authority not liable because it was common for children to be allowed to play with these toys. Similarly, when a child was injured taking part in gymnastic exercises, the fact that the teacher had been following general and approved practice in instructing other pupils to assist in the safety procedure led to a finding that he was not negligent (*Wright* v *Cheshire County Council* (1952)). But in *Fryer* v *Salford Corporation* (1937) Slesser LJ thought that the fact that it was educational practice at the time not to guard stoves used in domestic science was an insufficient reason for not installing a guard.

Where teachers are concerned, a special test governing the standard of care has been applied. The courts have held that a teacher is *in loco parentis*, which means that s/he acts in place of a parent. In an early decision, *Williams* v *Eady* (1893), the court held that the teacher should show the same standard of care as that of a "careful" parent. This test was applied in the case of *Rich* v *London County Council* (1953) when it was held that a LEA was under no obligation to take measures to keep boys away from an unfenced pile of coal in the school playground. Similarly, in *Martin* v *Middlesbrough Corporation* (1965), a child slipped on some ice and cut her hand on the pieces of a broken milk bottle which were lying on top of a drain in the playground. Willmer LJ felt that the risk of this injury occurring was foreseeable and that better arrangements for the disposal of empty milk bottles should have been made. His Lordship did "not think that the arrangements . . . made were such as would commend themselves to any reasonably prudent parent".

But the test has been modified. In *Lyes* v *Middlesex County Council* (1962), it was held to be important to apply the careful or prudent parent test in the context of the school rather than the home. In the school situation a teacher has the care of far more children than a parent ever has to deal with. In *Beaumont* v *Surrey County Council* (1968) Geoffrey Lane J (as he then was) preferred the "ordinary language of the law of negligence" to the test laid down in *Williams* v *Eady* (above). Thus a head teacher was bound to take "all reasonable and proper steps to prevent any of the pupils under his care from suffering injury from inanimate objects, the actions of their fellow pupils, or from a combination of the two. That is a high standard". It may be that nowadays the courts will incline more closely towards "the reasonable professional" standard, outlined earlier, although when *Van Oppen* v *Clerk to the Bedford Charity Trustees* (1989) (see below) was being heard in the High Court, the court adopted a similar approach to *Lyes* v *Middlesex* (above).

Returning to matters of general principle for a moment, another factor governing the standard of care concerns the social utility of the defendant's act. In *Daborn* v *Bath Tramways Motor Co Ltd* (1946) (at page 336) Lord Asquith said:

> "In determining whether a party is negligent, the standard of reasonable care is that which is reasonably to be demanded in the circumstances. A relevant circumstance . . . may be the importance of the end to be served in behaving in this way or that . . . [I]f all the trains in this country were restricted to a speed of five miles an hour, there would be fewer accidents, but our national life would be intolerably slowed down".

The importance of this need to balance the social utility of the act with the need to demonstrate care has been recognized by the courts when considering the standard of care required of a teacher. In the case of children, some

Negligence, health and safety

relaxation in supervision has been condoned on the grounds of its desirability in encouraging children to take increasing responsibility for their own actions as they grow up. In *Jeffrey* v *London County Council* (1954) McNair J said a balance had to be struck "between the meticulous supervision of children . . . and the very desirable object of encouraging their sturdy independence". Similarly, in another case Hilbery J dismissed an action brought against the governors and a teacher, following an incident in which boys who were using a cricket pitch roller caused it to roll on to one of their number, saying that "If boys were kept in cotton-wool, some of them would choke themselves with it" (*Hudson* v *Governors of Rotherham Grammar School* (1938)). In *Simkiss* v *Rhondda BC* (1983) the Court of Appeal confirmed that one had to balance the robustness which would make children take the world as they found it and the tenderness which would give them nurseries wherever they went.

(d) Children and negligence

(i) Liability of children

As we shall see below, teachers or LEAs/governors may be liable in negligence for failing to prevent harm caused by one pupil to another. Indeed, several of the cases referred to above were concerned with this. If the wrongdoing child is old enough to foresee the consequences of his behaviour the courts might find him/her to have been contributorily negligent, so damages against the LEA or governors would be reduced accordingly (see *Barnes* v *Bromley LBC* (1983) page 254 below). In other cases the pupil may be wholly liable, assuming there was no breach of duty by the teacher, if s/he fails to demonstrate the standard of care expected of a reasonable child of his/her age. In *Staley* v *Suffolk CC and Dean Mason* (26 November 1986, unreported but cited in *Street on Torts* 8th ed (1988), page 202 n 7) a boy aged twelve was held liable for throwing a tennis ball into a classroom at a boy and hitting the dinner lady.

251

(ii) Age and responsibility

A pupil's age is also relevant to the question of whether the supervision or instructions given to children in school are adequate. The courts are prepared to accept that as they get older, pupils may be assumed to be more responsible; and, as we have seen, the standard of care expected of a teacher may be influenced by the balancing of the need for careful supervision on the one hand with the encouragement of a pupil's progressive social and personal development on the other. Moreover, as the teacher is *in loco parentis*, the *dictum* of Lord Scarman (albeit in a different context) in *Gillick* v *West Norfolk and Wisbech AHA* (1985), that parental supervision is properly relaxed "gradually" in a child's transition to adulthood, is apposite.

In *Smerkinich* v *Newport Corporation* (1912) a youth aged nineteen was injured when using a circular saw at a technical institute. The local authority was held not to be liable but the judge (Lush J) said that the decision might have been different had the plaintiff been a child. In *Butt* v *Cambridgeshire and Ely CC* (1970) a large class of nine and ten year olds was using scissors, and one child accidently poked another child in the eye with his pair. The LEA was held not liable. But in *Black* v *Kent County Council* (1983) the court awarded over £31,000 in damages against the LEA when a child aged seven was jabbed in the eye by a pair of sharp pointed scissors he was using in an art class. Sir John Donaldson MR said that it was reasonably foreseeable that the use of sharp pointed scissors as compared with blunt ended ones involved quite a degree of risk where children of this age were concerned. The staff should avoid such risks.

The age of the pupil will also be relevant in determining whether any warning of risks involved in a particular activity may be effective to negate liability. It is difficult to apply the principle *volenti non fit injuria*—a willing party suffers no wrong—in a school situation since most activities are compulsory and it is hard to show that children were fully cognisant of the risks involved and were legally competent to accept them. (In the medical context, children under sixteen cannot, in general, validly consent to operations, and parental consent is generally required.) Clear warnings given to a class may absolve the teacher from liability, depending on the age of the class and on whether the class might be expected to be well-behaved or given to horse-play or carelessness (*Crouch* v *Essex County Council* (1966)). Warnings of the *specific* dangers involved in a particular activity should be given. For example, if a dangerous substance is being used in the laboratory, a more graphic and specific warning than simply "don't touch" is required (*Noonan* v *ILEA* (1974)).

(e) Circumstances involving intrinsically greater risks

> "It is fundamental to the relationship between school and pupil that the school undertakes to educate him in as wide a sense as it reasonably can. This involves the school having the pupils in its care and it involves the pupils in various activities in the classroom, in the chapel, in the gymnasium, on the sports field and so on. There are risks of injury inherent in many human activities, even of serious injury in some. Because of this, the school, having the pupils in its care, is under a duty to exercise reasonable care for their health and safety. Provided due care is exercised in this sphere, it seems to me that the school's duty is fulfilled" (*per* Ralph Gibson LJ in *Van Oppen* v *Clerk to the Bedford Charity Trustees* (1989) at page 291, cited with approval by Balcombe LJ in the Court of Appeal at pages 410–12).

The above judicial statement demonstrates that it is accepted by the courts that although various educational activities carry risks, they need not be avoided for this reason alone. Provided reasonable care towards pupils is shown, such activities may proceed. Indeed they are necessary if a pupil is to be educated in the widest sense (an aim towards which the "whole curriculum" concept in ERA 1988 s 1 (see Chapter 7) seems to be particularly directed). This is, once again, the social utility argument referred to earlier—the end justifying the means.

Nevertheless, even if the activity itself is acceptable regardless of the dangers, it is incumbent on teachers to minimise the risks by ensuring that the activity is carried out in a safe manner. They should do all that is reasonable to guard against any reasonably foreseeable risks. A run through some of the decided cases will give an indication of the standard of care which is expected.

In *Barnes* v *Bromley LBC* (1983) a male pupil was dismantling a rusty bicycle in the metal workshop. The bicycle was to be used as part of a sculpture. The boy was using an old and somewhat brittle riveting tool which slintered when he hit the bicycle with it, causing injury. There was held to be negligence, in view of the condition of the tool. But damages were reduced by one-third to take account of the boy's negligence in using the tool in that manner.

Fryer v *Salford Corporation* (1937) concerned an injury to an eleven year old girl whose apron was ignited by the flame on an unguarded cooker. It was held that it was perfectly natural for the children to crowd round the stove "having witnessed the final transfiguration of their own puddings" (*per* Slesser LJ). The danger was one which ought reasonably to have been anticipated and which reasonable precautions —in this case the provision of a guard—would have prevented.

In *Van Oppen* v *Clerk to the Bedford Charity Trustees* (1989) (*op cit*), the plaintiff was aged sixteen and a half at the time of the crippling injury he received in the course of a tackle while playing rugby at school. Initially he claimed damages both in respect of the school's negligence in coaching and in its failure to advise his father of the inherent risks in the game; the need to take out accident insurance for his son; and the fact that the school had no such cover. It was also alleged that there had been negligence in the school's failure to have such insurance cover at the material time. In the High Court the plaintiff's claim was unsuccessful on all counts. He pursued only the insurance aspect of the case in the Court of Appeal but was unsuccessful there as well. The Court of Appeal held that although it might be desirable for the school to arrange insurance and/or to inform parents of the need to take out independent personal accident insurance, this went beyond the school's duty in respect of the welfare of the pupils. Although the claim of negligent coaching was not taken to the Court of Appeal, Boreham J's comments in the High Court (at page 277) are instructive:

"It is accepted on all sides that the Bedford School, being *in loco parentis*, owed a general duty to the plaintiff and to all pupils to exercise reasonable care for his and their safety both in the classroom and on the games field. It is also accepted that injury is more likely if the correct techniques are not followed by the players, particularly in tackling. It follows therefore that it was the school's duty by teaching or by coaching or by correction to take reasonable care to ensure that the plaintiff in playing the game of rugby football applied correct techniques while tackling . . .

I am satisfied that the defendants, through staff 'taking' rugby, were well aware of the inherent risks in playing rugby football and of the need for the application of correct techniques and the correction of potentially dangerous errors and lapses. I am also satisfied that the standard of supervision was high, that the refereeing was vigilant and strict and that . . . there was at the school an emphasis on discipline, which meant playing the game correctly. There is therefore no substance in the allegations of negligence . . ."

In the context of rugby instruction, it may be noted that the participation by a teacher in a game with pupils, notwithstanding that it is for the purpose of demonstration, should be avoided, in the light of the decision in *Affutu-Nartoy* v *Clarke and ILEA* (1984). Here, the teacher tackled a teenage boy in a legitimate manner under the rules of the game, but, in law, unlawfully and dangerously. Hodgson J, in awarding damages, warned against teachers having physical contact with pupils in such circumstances.

In both *Conrad* v *ILEA* (*op cit*), where a student was injured during a judo session, and *Wright* v *Cheshire County Council* (1952), where a twelve year old boy was injured while vaulting—when the boy who was supposed to help him land left on hearing the school bell—the teachers concerned were following general and approved practice. In neither case was there negligence. The latter case contrasts with an earlier decision, *Gibbs* v *Barking Corporation* (1936), where a teacher who failed to assist a boy landing from a vault was held not to have taken reasonable care.

It is clear that if the pupil is told or encouraged to perform an activity which is beyond his/her reasonable capabilities and the teacher should have known this, and injury ensues, there is negligence. In *Moore* v *Hampshire County Council* (1981) the plaintiff, aged twelve, broke her ankle while attempting a handstand in a PE lesson at the secondary school she attended. She was awarded £500 in damages. She had a medical history of congenital dislocation of the hips and had wrongly persuaded the mistress that she was allowed to take PE. The teacher in question had in any event been told that the girl was not to take PE. The Court of Appeal unanimously held that although teachers' tasks of supervision were often very difficult there had not been adequate supervision of the girl. In *Tillotson* v *Harrow BC* (1984) £9,000 was awarded to a girl whose weight increased by fifty per cent following a leg fracture she sustained when jumping a hurdle. Negligence had been admitted by the LEA.

School trips and educational visits pose extra risks. These are considered under a separate heading below.

(f) Responsibility outside lessons

(i) Break-times/lunch-time

Lunch-time supervision is not part of a teacher's contractual duties. Head teachers are responsible, under the articles of government, for the internal organisation and management of the school. Under the Teachers' Pay and Conditions Document (see Chapter 2), head teachers are entitled to a break during the school day but must arrange for a suitable person to take responsibility for their functions during that break. In most schools at present the LEA employs assistants to carry out lunch-time supervision of pupils, under the control of the head teacher. It almost goes without saying that the LEA must provide suitable staff for this role. It appears that following financial delegation to schools under LMS, governors will be responsible for the appointment of these ancillary employees (ERA 1988 Sch 3 para 4), although they will be "employed" by the LEA in the majority of schools.

The level of supervision demanded during lunch-time and other breaks is less than that required during lesson times.

For example, in *Beaumont* v *Surrey County Council* (1968) a heavy-duty piece of elastic had been discarded into a bin in the playground and was discovered by some pupils who larked about with it. Unfortunately one pupil was struck in the eye and suffered a serious injury. Unusually, the two members of staff assigned to playground supervision were absent from the playground at the time of the incident. Various prefects were also required to assist in the supervision. But the defendants were held liable because supervision was lacking at the time. The courts found the *system* of supervision adequate, but felt that it had not been working properly at the relevant time. In *Ricketts* v *Erith Borough Council* (1943) a ten year old child left the school premises during the lunch break and returned with a bow and arrow which he fired causing injury. There was held to have been no failure of supervision. In *Pettican* v *Enfield LBC* (1970) Kilner-Brown J emphasised that where lunch-time supervision was concerned, staff could not be expected to perform as "policemen and security guards". His Honour rejected the plaintiff's suggestion that a teacher should have been on duty in each classroom when the children were sent indoors on wet days. The plaintiff had been injured on one such day when struck in the eye by a piece of chalk during horseplay. The LEA was found not liable. This case contrasts with another, reported in the *Times Educational Supplement* (13 November 1981) in which Sir Basil Neild J awarded a boy £6,500 damages after his eye was damaged by a paper clip fired at him by another pupil during a lunch-time in which the children were allowed indoors because of rain. One dinner lady had been given the task of supervising two classrooms, and this was found to have been inadequate supervision.

It is difficult to draw any firm guidance from these cases. As the courts say that in every case no more than "reasonable supervision" is required (eg *Clark* v *Monmouthshire County Council* (1954), *per* Denning LJ), all will depend on the particular circumstances involved.

(ii) Playground accidents before the start of school

The general rule is that there can be no responsibility for the supervision of pupils before the start of the school day; but where pupils are allowed on to the premises at a certain time there may be responsibility. The authority for the proposition that there is no liability before the school day begins is the decision of the Court of Appeal in *Ward v Hertfordshire County Council* (1969). Children were allowed into the playground before the start of the school day, but were unsupervised. One day an eight year old boy crashed into a wall during a race and injured his skull. The school staff knew that children frequently raced in the playground. The head teacher stated that he would not have prevented the racing had he been present. The trial judge decided that the jagged wall in the playground was inherently dangerous and that there should have been supervision. In a unanimous decision, the Court of Appeal found that there was no negligence. The accident had occurred in the ordinary course of play. Denning MR said: "It often happens that children run from one side of the playground to the other. It is impossible so to supervise them that they never fall down and hurt themselves. I cannot think that this accident shows any lack of supervision by the school authorities".

In *Mays v Essex County Council* (1975) a child was injured five minutes before the start of the school day when he fell while sliding on ice in the playground which had not been salted. The boy suffered permanent brain damage. The school gates were generally opened quite early, but most pupils arrived only about ten minutes before the start of school. The head teacher had sent a circular to parents requesting them not to send their children to school too early. The judge felt it perfectly reasonable for children of the plaintiff's age (fourteen) to be allowed to slide on the ice in an orderly fashion whilst unsupervised. No average prudent parent in the playground at that time would have thought it necessary to stop the children playing on the ice. Furthermore, it would have been impracticable to salt an area as large as the playground in question every time there was a frost. The judge also felt that parents could not impose responsibility on teachers outside the ordinary school hours. Only if the school voluntarily accepted responsibility for children arriving early (as opposed to opening the gates for the convenience of parents and in the interests of the safety of pupils) would it be under a duty to provide supervision. On the question of icy playgrounds, it could well be that a court today would take a stricter line. There may, in any event, be a duty owed to pupils as "visitors" (licensees) under the Occupiers' Liability Act 1957 (see below).

(iii) Responsibility after school hours

After school hours the school's responsibility is to ensure that there is an adequate system for handing children over to their parents. This is especially important where very young children are concerned. If the parents simply fail to collect or meet the child the school will not be liable (*Jeffrey* v *London County Council* (1954) *op cit*), although the position is, in reality, not all that clear cut. If a child remains on the premises after school hours, and if the parents cannot be contacted, the head teacher ought to ensure that the child is handed over to social services or the police to avoid any claim that s/he knowingly allowed a young child to wander out alone on to a public street with all its dangers. It must be emphasised, however, that in the absence of any decided case on the matter, this is a grey area in the law.

Barnes v *Hampshire County Council* (1969) concerned the situation where children are let out of school early. The normal procedure at the school in question involved handing pupils over to their parents or guardians at 3.30 pm. On one occasion pupils were released early, and one child, a five year old, wandered out into the street because her mother had not yet arrived at the school gate. She was injured on the road nearby at 3.29 pm. It was held that the risk of such injury was foreseeable, and the LEA was liable.

In *Good* v *ILEA* (1980) a child was injured when another pupil threw sand into his eye. The incident occurred after the end of the school day at 4.00 pm, but while both children were still on the school premises. The sand was in an area of the grounds which had been roped off and where a swimming pool was to be constructed. The children had been warned to keep away. It was normal for some children to be on the premises after school hours. Most children were collected by a parent at the end of the school day. But there was a play centre across the playground to which the remaining children could go while waiting for their parents. The children who were playing near the sand were unnoticed. The plaintiff claimed damages for negligence, arguing that the children should have been supervised. It was held that there was no breach of duty on the part of the school for not supervising the whole of the children's journey from the infants school building to the play centre.

It is important that if the arrangements at the end of the school day are to change—for example if the children are to be released early on a particular day—parents should be informed well in advance.

(iv) When a child wanders

When pupils absent themselves from school during the course of the school day it is not only their education that may suffer. There is also an increased risk of injury, especially where young children are concerned. While the duty to cause children to attend school rests with parents (see Chapter 6), the school has a responsibility to ensure that pupils are left in no doubt that they must not wander off. Moreover, supervision of pupils must be adequate so that the opportunities for straying are minimised.

In *Carmarthenshire County Council* v *Lewis* (1955), a boy aged four, who was a pupil at a nursery school, was made ready to go for a walk with one of the mistresses and another child. The mistress left the room to get herself ready, and while out of the room had to attend to an injured child. She was away for about ten minutes, and during her absence the two children left the classroom and wandered through an unlocked school gate and on to a busy road. A lorry driver had to swerve to avoid hitting one of the children, and as a result his vehicle collided with a telegraph pole. The driver was killed and his widow sought damages from the LEA. The case went eventually to the House of Lords where it was held that irrespective of the lack of negligence on the individual teacher's part, the LEA was liable for the failure to take adequate precautions to avoid what was a foreseeable accident. Lord Goddard said that if it was possible for these young children to escape into a busy street so easily when the teacher was not with them, this implied a lack of care and of precautions that might reasonably be required.

If the school has not been negligent, and a child escapes, and an injury to him/her or to a third party, away from the school, ensues, the teacher/LEA/governors should not be liable. However, the school should ensure that absences without permission are notified to parents or others as soon as possible. If a child complains of feeling ill, the school should endeavour to contact parents to collect the child rather than simply sending him/her home. What if the child, when crossing the road on his/her way home, collapsed and was injured? The parents would undoubtedly feel entitled to compensation for negligence on the part of the school, although once again this is, in many respects, a grey area.

(g) Responsibility for pupils outside school: educational visits and transport

(i) School trips

Where pupils are in their care, teachers and LEAs or governors are responsible for their safety. As the discussion above indicated, all reasonable steps to avoid foreseeable injury must be taken. When pupils are away from school on trips, the risk of injury may be greater. For example, hill-walking and sailing carry inherent risks.

But, as we have seen, the courts accept that activities of this nature are permissible, provided that reasonable safety can be ensured, because they help a child's proper development. Nevertheless, teachers must ensure that the arrangements for supervision of pupils during all visits is appropriate given the ages of the pupils concerned and other factors (for example if there are children with disabilities who need special care). When booking equipment or accommodation they should, wherever possible, keep to approved companies (usually the LEA will keep a list) and ensure that the appropriate authority has arranged appropriate insurance cover. Parents should be advised to arrange independent cover in appropriate cases.

The accidents in recent years at Land's End, when pupils from Stoke Poges school were swept into the sea and drowned, and in the Austrian Alps, when four teenage boys fell 300 feet off a mountain, have prompted a reappraisal of the precautions necessary for school trips. Many schools are now extremely wary of taking pupils away, especially abroad. But there seems no reason why trips should be curtailed, provided that sensible arrangements are made (including insurance) and proper precautions taken. Valuable guidance has been issued by various authorities and professional organisations (for example, the National Association of Head Teachers). Specific recommendations were made by the panel conducting the inquiry into the accident on the Austrian Alps (see *The Times*, 27 January 1989 for a summary).

The accident on the Austrian Alps occurred in 1988 during a visit by pupils from Altwood School, Maidenhead. Some pupils had been left by teachers to play in the snow in a "safe area" on top of a mountain which the party was visiting by cable car. Later, several unsupervised pupils wandered off to play in another area and four slid to their deaths. One of the surviving pupils said that they had been warned to keep to the paths and not to wander off. The coroner recorded a verdict of death by misadventure (reported in *The Times*, 7 July 1988). Berkshire Education Authority's report into the incident concluded: "Telling the pupils what to do and trusting them to obey was not enough . . ."; the teachers should not have allowed the pupils to go unsupervised for some fifty minutes; their presence might have discouraged the pupils from leaving the path (report in *The Times*, 27 January 1989).

A case in 1985 raised issues similar to those in the above case. The case, *Porter* v *City of Bradford Metropolitan Council* (14 January 1985 (CA) unreported, but available from *Lexis*), arose out of an incident occurring during an outing by a dozen fifteen and sixteen year old pupils, and their geology teacher, to Shipley Glen. One boy, X, had been rolling large stones down a slope at the bottom of which were five pupils from the group. No one was hurt, but the teacher saw the boy and told him to desist. Later, the teacher proceeded up the glen with a number of pupils who had a keener interest in geology, and was out of sight and sound of the children who were involved in the first incident. X started to drop or throw stones from a bridge. After perhaps fifteen minutes of doing this he dropped a stone which landed on the head of a girl pupil, fracturing her skull. In the High Court, Bennett J held that the teacher had been negligent. In the light of the earlier incident in which he had learnt of X's propensities, there was a foreseeable danger and he should have used his best endeavours to keep the party together.

The LEA appealed to the Court of Appeal. Giving the court's judgment, Stephenson LJ said that he did not wish to impose on teachers a duty of supervision which went beyond that of a reasonable parent (in the context of a school trip of this nature); but

". . . looking at the admitted facts of this case and looking at what [X] did such a short time before, I think . . . that on this occasion [the teacher], faced with the difficult task of trying to instruct pupils, some of whom were keen and some of whom were obviously not, failed in his duty to supervise this particular set of pupils. In my judgement he ought not to have relied on the obedience of [X] as negativing any reasonable possibility that he might try something of the same sort again; he ought to have kept the pupils, willing and unwilling, together and he ought not to have gone out of sight and sound of this group, including as it did the boy [X], although I sympathise with him and appreciate the difficulty of his task . . ."

(ii) Transport

There have been various cases concerned with liability for injuries sustained on transport provided by the LEA. It is clear that children on school buses must be supervised (*Shrimpton* v *Hertfordshire County Council* (1911)) and that the careful/prudent parent test (above) is relevent to determining the standard of care required (*Ellis* v *Sayers Confectioners* (1963)). In *Jacques* v *Oxfordshire County Council* (1967), a child was injured by a pellet fired at him by another pupil while they were both travelling on a school bus. The LEA was held not to be negligent, even though supervision had been left to prefects. Where pupils are using public transport to get to and from school the bus company/transport executive will be responsible for ensuring the safety of passengers.

Where teachers transport pupils in their own vehicles, they should ensure that they are covered by their own insurance policies for doing so. Many a teacher has rushed a child with a serious cut to hospital in total ignorance of whether s/he is covered by his/her insurance policy should an injury to the passenger ensue during transportation. LEAs or governors generally give instructions to staff on such matters and may arrange cover.

When the school or authority's own vehicles are used there must be comprehensive insurance cover. Teachers must make sure that the particular use to which the vehicle is to be put is covered by the policy and that the teacher concerned is authorised to drive the vehicle.

If the vehicle in question is a school minibus, the provisions of the Transport Act 1985 may apply. Under the Act, vehicles seating between eight and sixteen passengers (excluding the driver) ("small buses") and larger vehicles, ie those adapted to carry more than sixteen passengers, may be excluded from the requirement (in the Transport Act 1981 ss 12(1) and 22) that the driver has a public service vehicle licence (Transport Act 1985 s 18(a)). The vehicle must, *inter alia*, not be used for carrying members of the public at large or with a view to profit (Transport Act 1985 s 19(2)). In the case of a "small bus", a permit may be granted by the local education authority (s 19(3) and (7)) or traffic commissioners (s 19(4)) to a school (or others). In the case of a "large bus", a permit may be granted by the traffic commissioners to a LEA or co-ordinating body for religion, social welfare etc, (s 19(6))—provided that there will be "adequate facilities or arrangements for maintaining any bus under the permit in a fit and serviceable condition". A permit holder may hold more than one permit—but needs a separate permit in respect of each vehicle (s 19(9)). Restrictions may be imposed on the use of the vehicle, by way of conditions attached to the granting of a permit (s 19(7)(a) and 20(4)). Conditions of fitness for use (small bus) and other matters relating to the driving of buses (small and large) are as prescribed by regulations under s 21.

3. School premises and environment

(a) The Occupiers' Liability Act 1957

The Occupiers' Liability Act 1957 imposes a duty of care on

the occupier of premises (s 1(1)). An occupier is the person in control of the premises. In the case of a public sector school, it appears that the occupiers will generally be the governing body and/or LEA (for it is possible for there to be more than one occupier for the purposes of the Act). Under LMS (see Chapter 1) the LEA will generally retain ownership of school buildings and be responsible for major repairs, whereas governing bodies will be responsible for management of the premises and routine maintenance (see Appendix 2). In *Wheat* v *E Lacon & Co Ltd* (1966) (HL)), both the owners and the manager of a public house were held to be occupiers; LEAs and governors are, therefore, likely to be occupiers of a school.

There is also a duty owed not only by occupiers of premises *per se* but also by those "occupying or having control over any fixed or movable structure, including any vessel, vehicle or aircraft" (s 1(3)). According to *Street on Torts* (8th ed, 1988, by M Brazier, page 265) this subsection probably applies to playground swings. If a "portakabin" is not covered by s 1(1), it is surely covered by s 1(3).

The duty is owed to "visitors"—basically persons entitled to enter the premises by express or implied licence. (On liability in respect of trespassers and non-invited entrants, see the Occupiers' Liability Act 1984 and *Street on Torts, op cit*, pages 270–271.) So far as a school is concerned, "visitors" include pupils (*Woodward* v *Mayor of Hastings* (1944)) and *Ward* v *Hertfordshire County Council* (1969)), parents (*Griffiths* v *Smith* (1941)) and teachers. The duty applies to the state of the premises and "things done or omitted to be done on them". For example, in *Woodward* v *Mayor of Hastings* (1944) there was liability when a pupil slipped on frozen snow on a school step which had not been cleared. The case was decided under the previous common law, but today would be covered by the 1957 Act. In *Gillmore* v *London County Council* (1938) a child slipped on a highly polished school hall floor. The injury was held to have been foreseeable. The floor had been polished to such an extent that there was a serious risk of injury.

The duty that is owed is "the common duty of care". This is:

"a duty to take such care as in all the circumstances of the case is reasonable to see that the visitor will be reasonably safe in using the premises for the purpose for which he is invited or permitted by the occupier to be there" (s 2(2)).

Among the factors to be considered in determining whether or not the duty has been fulfilled, is the degree of care which might be expected of the visitor. The Act specifically states that "an occupier must be prepared for children to be less careful than adults" (s 2(3)(a)). Thus in *Williams* v *Cardiff Corporation* (1950) (decided under the previous common law but still relevant) it was held that a child aged four might be at risk of damage where there was a grassy slope with broken glass at the bottom. If the child is unaccompanied by a parent or guardian, the fact that the occupier might reasonably have expected the child to have been accompanied might be taken into account (*Bates* v *Parker* (1954)). This principle might be relevant if a school has a system for the delivery of children to school by their parents which envisages the parents accompanying the childen to a certain place on the premises, and an injury occurs to a child who is unaccompanied. A further point to note is that an occupier is entitled to expect that a person entering in the exercise of his/her calling will appreciate and guard against any special risks ordinarily incident to his work (s 2(3)(b)).

A warning may be given to visitors, but it will not be sufficient to absolve the occupier from liability unless it was specific as to the danger or could reasonably be acted upon (s 2(4)(a)). If a risk is willingly accepted as his by the visitor concerned the occupier will not be liable (s 2(5)); where pupils are concerned there may be doubts about their capacity to accept risks in view of their age.

If the damage is caused by a danger resulting from the faulty execution of work by contractors, the occupiers will not be liable if s/he can show that s/he acted reasonably in entrusting the work to an independent contractor, took reasonable steps to ensure that the contractor selected was one who was competent, and checked that the work was properly done (s 2(4)(b)).

(b) The Education (School Premises) Regulations 1981

These regulations (as amended) impose minimum standards

for school premises. The regulations are made under EA 1944 s 10, and apply to all LEA-maintained schools and (by virtue of amendment regulations (SI 1989 No 1277)) grant-maintained schools. Sixth form colleges count as schools for this purpose (reg 3(1)). It may be argued that despite the existence of these minimum standards, many school buildings are in a very poor condition and facilities are sometimes lacking, as the National Association of Inspectors and Educational Advisers recently reported (*The Times* 25 September 1989).

The regulations apply to all aspects of school premises, starting with the land itself—which must be "adequate" to permit the provision not only of buildings, recreation areas and playing fields of the required standard, but also of ancillary facilities such as service roads, delivery bays and vehicle parks (reg 4). Recreation areas (ie outdoor areas for "recreation, play and outdoor education") and playing fields (outdoor areas suitable, and laid out, for team games) must conform to the requirements of size (area) determined under Schedules 2 and 3 (regs 5 and 6). These contain formulae which take account of the various ages of the pupils who may use the facilities and the kind of school involved. Recreation areas must consist partly (eg at least one-third of the total recreation area, in the case of infants schools) of paved areas and/of areas with hard porous surfaces. Unfortunately, many school playing fields (and gymnasia) are badly maintained and pose a threat to pupil safety, according to a report by HMI (*A Survey of Work in Physical Education in 16 Secondary Schools* (1990) DES).

School buildings must be adequate to permit (reg 7):

(a) the convenient passage of persons and movement of goods within the buildings;
(b) the storage, in or near teaching accommodation, of apparatus, equipment and materials used in teaching;
(c) the storage, elsewhere than in the teaching accommodation, of furniture and certain other items not presently required;
(d) the separate storage of any fuel required for the purposes of the school;
(e) the storage and drying of pupils' outdoor clothing and for storing their other belongings; and

(f) the preparation of food and drinks and the washing of crockery and other utensils.

The school buildings must also provide not less than the prescribed minimum area of teaching accommodation (which, in the case of a nursery class or school, includes playroom area) (reg 8). The minimum is calculated with reference to, in essence, the ages of the pupils at the school (Sch 4). Where the school has pupils who are aged sixteen or over, accommodation must be provided for "private study and social purposes" (reg 9). School buildings must also contain not less than the prescribed minimum washroom facilities (reg 10(1)–(3)), with washbasins and sanitary fittings of a prescribed number and type (eg two-thirds of those provided for boys should be urinals). In some cases there must be changing facilities for the over-eights, including showers for the over-elevens (reg 9(5)–(7)). Staff washrooms and cloakrooms, and changing facilities for staff teaching PE to the over-eights, must also be provided (reg 11(2) and (3)).

There should be suitable accommodation at the school for medical and dental examination and treatment of pupils, and for the care of pupils during schools hours (reg 12).

So far as staff accommodation is concerned, schools are to have a head teacher's room and room for use by staff "both for the purposes of work (otherwise than in teaching accommodation) and for social purposes" (reg 13). In a special school, and in a school with more than 250 pupils (which number is to be calculated with reference to reg 3) or where the majority of pupils are aged eleven or over, there is also to be a room for the senior assistant teacher.

(Note that Part IV of the regulations (regs 14–21) prescribes minimum accommodation (including sleeping accommodation) for staff and pupils at boarding schools.)

School buildings must be of a design and construction that reasonably assure the safe escape of occupants in the case of fire, and their health and safety in other respects (reg 24(1) and (2)). In fulfilling this requirement, regard must be had to the likely rate at which flames might spread, the resistance to fire of materials and structures, and the means of escape in case of fire (reg 24). The design and construction of the buildings should be of an approved standard with regard to acoustics, lighting, thermal environment and, where new buildings are concerned, energy conservation (reg 25). The standard is that laid down in Design Note 17 (2nd ed), *Guidelines for Environmental Design and Fuel Conservation in Educational Buildings*. (Note that these requirements are additional to others, eg under the Health and Safety at Work Etc Act 1974—see below.)

Other provisions are concerned with: load bearing structures (reg 22); weather protection ("reasonable resistance to penetration by rain, snow and wind and . . . moisture rising from the ground") (reg 23); water supplies (so far as practicable to be drawn from the mains) (reg 26); and drainage (reg 27).

Under transitional arrangements introduced on 1 August 1981 (Sch 1), a small number of the provisions do not come into effect until 1 September 1991 (eg changing accommodation for staff (reg 11(3)) and head teacher's room (reg 13(1))) (except in nursery schools, schools with more than 120 pupils, and special schools)).

If injury results from a breach of these regulations, parents may have a claim for breach of statutory duty (eg *Reffell* v *Surrey County Council* (1964)—girl badly cut when her hand went through a glass panel of a swing door in a school corridor—the glass had not been of an appropriate standard; *Ching* v *Surrey County Council* (1910)—hole in school playground surface—child injured—damages awarded for breach of statutory duty; *Morris* v *Caernarvon County Council* (1910)—child caught hand in door which was too tightly sprung and represented a danger—authority held liable).

Finally, it may be noted that a private members' bill, which if passed would have made provision (through regulations) for compulsory safety standards for equipment, layout and surfaces in children's playgrounds, was unsuccessfully put forward under the "ten minute rule" in 1989 (the Safety in Children's Playgrounds Bill). It is not clear whether this three clause bill would have applied to playgrounds in, or attached to, schools.

(c) Chronically Sick and Disabled Persons Act 1970

The Chronically Sick and Disabled Persons Act 1970

contains several provisions of particular relevance to disabled persons. The Act provides for access to and within, parking at and toilets in, universities, schools and colleges (s 8) and workplaces (s 8A—inserted by Chronically Sick and Disabled Persons (Amendment) Act 1976). Notices must be displayed for facilities provided under, *inter alia*, ss 8 and 8A of the 1970 Act (Disabled Persons Act 1981 s 5).

The requirements concerning the standard to which the facilities referred to in ss 8 and 8A should conform will change once s 6 of the 1981 Act (above) is brought into effect (by statutory instrument). Under the 1970 Act the facilities are to be provided "in so far as it is in the circumstances both practicable and reasonable". Under the amendment, these words are replaced with the words "appropriate provision". Facilities in schools and other educational institutions required under s 8 must conform to the standard laid down in Design Note 18, published by the Secretary of State for Social Services and entitled *Access for the Physically Disabled to Educational Buildings*.

(d) The Health and Safety at Work Etc Act 1974

The Act and its enforcement: Only a brief résumé of this important piece of legislation can be accommodated here. The Act aims, *inter alia*, to secure the health, safety and welfare of persons at work and to protect persons who are not at work against risks to their health and safety arising out of or in connection with the activities of workers (see s 1(1)). The Secretary of State may make regulations (s 15) dealing with, for example, particular hazards. For example, the Control of Substances Hazardous to Health Regulations 1988 impose safety standards and procedures in respect of chemical substances, including (so the author is reliably informed(!)) photocopier toner. The Health and Safety Information for Employees Regulations 1989 require, *inter alia*, an employer to ensure that an "approved" poster is displayed, in a readable condition, at a place which is reasonably accessible to an employee while at work (regs 4 and 5). The "approved" poster outlines the provisions of the 1974 Act as they affect employees, and gives other relevant information.

Under the 1974 Act, a Health and Safety Commission and Executive have been appointed. The Commission can issue approved Codes of Practice (s 16). It can carry out research into health and safety matters and is responsible for the provision of information to employers, government departments and others (s 11). The Executive is responsible for the administration and enforcement of the law (s 18). Suitably qualified inspectors are to be appointed (s 19), with a wide variety of powers to enter premises, take measurements and samples and seize anything likely to cause imminent danger and render it harmless (ss 20 and 25). It is an offence to hinder an inspector (s 33). If they find that the Act has been broken, inspectors may prosecute. The court can impose a large fine and, in some cases, a term of imprisonment not exceeding two years (*ibid*). What inspectors are most likely to do is to issue either an "improvement notice", requiring the wrongdoer to carry out specified action to remedy the contravention within a specified period (s 21), or, where there is, or potentially is, a risk of serious personal injury, a "prohibition notice", ordering that a certain activity ceases until the contravention is remedied.

Duties under the Act: Duties are owed under the Act by employers to their employees and others (ss 2 and 3) and by employees to themselves and others (s 7). Manufacturers, designers, importers and suppliers are also under duties as regards the design, construction, and testing of any article for use at work and information as to use provided with it (s 6).

For the purposes of ss 2 and 3, the LEA, or, in aided schools, the governing body, is the employer and will remain so after financial delegation (see Chapter 1). The financial delegation Circular (7/88, para 189) states that certain aspects of health and safety provision will fall to governing bodies as part of their delegated budget, such as purchase and maintenance of equipment (including fire fighting equipment). As controllers of school premises, governing bodies will be subject to the requirements in s 4 of the 1974 Act. The Act states that such persons should make sure that the premises, means of access to or egress from buildings, and any plant or substance in the premises, are safe for persons other than their employees (see s 4(1), and see also s 4(4)).

An employer must also "ensure, so far as is reasonably practicable, the health, safety and welfare at work of all his employees" (s 2(1)). Particular regard must be had to various matters (in s 2(2)). These include the need to provide, "so far as is reasonably practicable": plant, workplaces and systems of work, and arrangements for handling, transporting and storing substances and articles, that are safe and without risk to health; and information, instruction, training and supervision to ensure health and safety of employees. The employer must also provide a working environment which is, so far as is reasonably practicable, safe, without risks to health, and has adequate facilities for employees' welfare at work. The phrase "so far as is reasonably practicable" means that the employer may balance the degree of risk against the employer's sacrifice in money, time or trouble (*Edwards* v *National Coal Board* (1949); *West Bromwich Building Society* v *Townsend* (1983)).

In prescribed cases, safety representatives may be appointed by recognized trades unions from amongst the employees (s 2(4)), and safety committees may be established to keep under review the measures taken by the employer to ensure the health and safety of the employees (s 2(7)). (See further the Safety Representatives and Safety Committees Regulations 1977.) Save in certain exceptional cases, the employer must also prepare a health and safety policy statement and bring it to the notice of the employees (s 2(3)).

Similar, although less specifically stated, duties concerning health and safety are owed by employers to persons other than their employees (s 3). This brings pupils within the scope of the Act.

Teachers and other staff are, as employees, under a duty, while at work, to take reasonable care for their own safety and that of others who may be affected by their acts or omissions (s 7(a)). They must also co-operate with an employer as regards the performance of the employer's duties concerning health and safety (s 7(b)). An employer may not charge its employee for anything provided in furtherance of its statutory duties *vis-à-vis* health and safety (s 9).

The Act also states that "any person", which would include a pupil (although if aged under ten s/he is irrebuttably presumed to be *doli incapax*—under the age of criminal responsibility), must not "intentionally or recklessly interfere or misuse anything provided in the interests of health, safety or welfare" (eg safety notices, fire extinguishers, first aid kits) (s 8).

Section 47 of the Act specifically precludes any right of action in *civil* proceedings arising from a breach of ss 2–8. So breaches of these duties do not create statutory torts (see Wedderburn, *The Worker and the Law* (1986), page 417).

Work placements: Trainees on government training schemes, such as the Youth Training Scheme, may be "employees" for the purposes of the Act (SI 1983 No 1919; Health and Safety (Training for Employment) Regulations 1988 reg 4). Although pupils in their final year of compulsory schooling may be given work experience (Education (Work Experience) Act 1973), such pupils are not "employees" for the purposes of s 2, although they may be protected by the duty in s 3. (See also *(e) Miscellaneous* below.) Regarding the employment of children and young persons, see the Employment Act 1989.

(e) Miscellaneous

Reporting of injuries etc: Regulations (the Reporting of Injuries, Diseases and Dangerous Occurrences Regulations 1985) require employers to notify the Health and Safety Executive as quickly as possible of a death or prescribed category of serious injury to an employee (for example, bone fracture other than in the hand or foot, burn from electric shock, amputation of a finger, loss of sight in an eye) (reg 3). Dangerous occurrences (set out in Sch 1 and referring to such matters as the unintended collapse of a wall or floor in a workplace) must be reported by the person having control of the premises (which, in schools, probably means the governing body or head teacher) (regs 2 and 3). A record of all reportable injuries must be kept by the employer; and a record of dangerous occurrences must be kept by the person in control of premises (reg 7). The record must generally be kept at the workplace. Schedule 3 prescribes the information which must be recorded.

Certain diseases suffered by employees carrying out prescribed categories of work must also be notified (reg 5). Few of these are relevant to teaching, but certain infections such as tuberculosis have to be notified.

Compulsory insurance of employees; liability for defective equipment: Employers have a common law duty to take reasonable care for the safety of their workers, by providing competent co-workers, adequate premises and equipment and a proper system of working (see M Brazier, *Street on Torts*, 8th ed (1988), Chapter 17). Regardless of this, there is a statutory duty on an employer to have insurance cover in respect of liability for injuries to, or diseases suffered by, employees arising out of or in the course of their employment (Employers' Liability (Compulsory Insurance) Act 1969). Pupils on work experience are not employees for this purpose, and LEAs or governors should ensure that if the employer is not willing to take out insurance cover for such pupils, they (ie the LEA or governors) do.

Where the employer provides any plant, equipment or vehicle for his employees to use in their work, and the employee is injured because the equipment etc is defective, the employer may be liable (Employers' Liability (Defective Equipment) Act 1969). The employee must show that the fault in the equipment resulted from the negligence or other tort of a third party (for example, the supplier or manufacturer).

Danger from unwelcome visitors to school premises and others: Schools may be under a duty to take reasonable precautions to protect teachers and pupils from the unlawful intentions of unwelcome visitors to school premises. In *West Bromwich Building Society* v *Townsend* (1983) McNeill J rejected counsel's argument that the risk of injury from criminals was outside an employer's obligations under the Health and Safety at Work Etc Act 1974 (above), although that was in relation to the lack of a "bandit screen" at a building society office. Generally, if a parent or pupil is violent towards a teacher, the teacher, almost certainly backed by his/her trade union, would be able to bring a suit for trespass to the person.

To avoid any possible claim of negligence against a school for the theft of belongings from the premises (in practice, unlikely to succeed), parents and pupils should be advised that valuables and more than small amounts of money should not be brought on to the premises. LEAs will generally not accept responsibility for loss of or damage to pupil's property and they should advise parents and pupils of this.

A person who causes a nuisance or disturbance on school premises commits a summary offence under the Local Government (Miscellaneous Provisions) Act 1982 s 40 (as amended). A police constable or person authorised by the LEA may enter school premises to remove such a person.

Interference with equipment: The case of *DPP* v *K* (1990) offers a salutary lesson to pupils who enjoy tampering with equipment. A fifteen year old pupil, K, had been attending a chemistry lesson at which sulphuric acid was being added to chlorine, water and ammonia to test its effects. The pupils had been given an instruction sheet advising great care when working with acid. K asked to go to the toilet, and, unbeknown to the teacher, took a test-tube of concentrated acid with him. He tested it on some toilet paper, and then, hearing footsteps approaching, panicked and poured the acid into the hot-air hand dryer, the nozzle of which was pointed upwards. K left, intending to return to the toilet after his lesson to wash out the drier. However, before he could return another pupil turned on the drier and acid was ejected on to his face, causing a permanent scar. It was alleged that K's behaviour had been reckless and that he was guilty of committing an assault occasioning actual bodily harm contrary to s 47 Offences Against the Person Act 1861. In the Divisional Court, Parker LJ said that K knew either that there was a risk that someone might use the machine before he could return to remove the acid, or he gave no thought to that risk. K's conviction stood, although it now seems that the wrong test of reasonableness was applied: *R* v *Spratt* (1990).

The injured boy would probably also have had a strong case for compensation in a civil court. Although injuries caused by a pupil to a fellow pupil rarely give rise to criminal liability, injuries resulting from either equipment that has been tampered with, or misused substances are all too common, and K's prosecution should, perhaps, be cited by teachers in order to discourage such behaviour.

Appendix 1

Procedures for acquisition of grant-maintained status

(See ERA 1988 ss 60–72; DES Circular 10/88 paras 14–40; DES booklet *School Governors : How to become a Grant-Maintained School*)

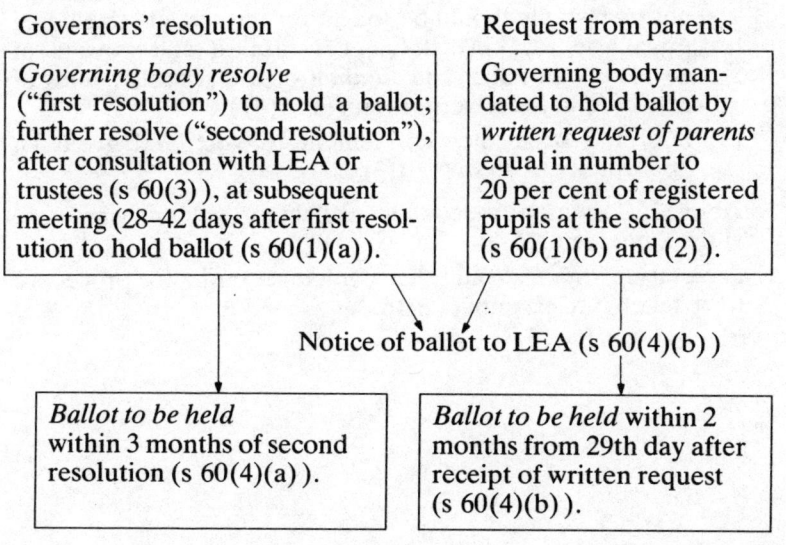

Governors' resolution	Request from parents
Governing body resolve ("first resolution") to hold a ballot; further resolve ("second resolution"), after consultation with LEA or trustees (s 60(3)), at subsequent meeting (28–42 days after first resolution to hold ballot (s 60(1)(a)).	Governing body mandated to hold ballot by *written request of parents* equal in number to 20 per cent of registered pupils at the school (s 60(1)(b) and (2)).

Notice of ballot to LEA (s 60(4)(b))

Ballot to be held within 3 months of second resolution (s 60(4)(a)).	*Ballot to be held* within 2 months from 29th day after receipt of written request (s 60(4)(b)).

Notes:
1. Written request from parents to be delivered to chair or clerk of governors (s 60(6)).
2. No ballot may be held within twelve months of a previous ballot unless Secretary of State gives written consent (s 60(5)).
3. Parent entitled, on request – in connection with ballot – to list of all parents of registered pupils (s 60(7)) unless parent on list requests non-disclosure in writing (s 60(8)).

Charge, not exceeding cost, may be made by the governors.
4. Governors to decide who is/is not a parent of a pupil at the school (s 60(10)).

* * * * *

Before the ballot

1. Arrangements to be made for ballot to be secret and postal (s 61(2)).
2. Governors required to "take such steps as are reasonably practicable to secure that every person eligible to vote in the ballot" is:
    (a) given sufficient information about the procedure and consequences of GM status "as may reasonably be expected to enable him to form a proper judgement as to whether or not such status should be sought for the school" (including procedure for GM status, constitution and powers of governors, conduct and funding of the school, names of proposed initial governors etc) (s 61(4));
    (b) informed of his/her entitlement to vote and given an opportunity to do so (s 61(3)).
3. Above information to be made available to persons who work at the school (s 61(5)).
4. Secretary of State's (published) guidance on ballot procedure to be taken into account (s 61(6)).

Appendix 1

The ballot

(Note: Ballot is to be carried out by Electoral Reform Society: Education (Parental Ballots for Acquisition of Grant-maintained Status) (Prescribed Body) Regs 1988 (SI 1988 No 1474). The costs of conducting the ballot are recoverable from the Secretary of State (s 61(12)). The DES has issued guidance on the conduct of these ballots.

"First ballot"

Total no. of votes cast by persons eligible to vote is *less than 50 per cent* of number of such persons (s 61(8)).	Total no. of votes cast by persons eligible to vote is *50 per cent or more* of number of such persons.

"Second ballot" (must be within 14 days of "first ballot")

Vote decided *by simple majority of those voting* (NB result of first ballot disregarded s 61(9)(a)).

Note: *Publication of proposals*
To be published:

    (i) by being posted at or near school's main entrance; and

    (ii) at at least one "conspicuous place within the area served by the school";

    (iii) by being available for public inspection at the school or other convenient (to the public) place in area (s 63(1)).

Also, a summary to be published in at least one newspaper circulating in the area (s 63(2)).
(Prescribed contents of summary in s 63(3).)

Within 6 months of ballot

Governors to *publish proposals* and submit them to Secretary of State (s 62(2)). Annexed to proposals must be: result of ballot (votes for and against); classification of school; description of character of school, number of pupils for whom accommodation can be provided at the school, other prescribed information; details of initial governors etc (as per s 62(7)); proposed admission and special needs arrangements, and arrangements for induction and INSET of teachers (further details in 10/88).

After publication of proposals

Within two months of publication of proposals:

Objections submitted to Secretary of State by:
(i) 10 or more local electors; or
(ii) the trustees (if any) of the school; or
(iii) the governing body of the school; or
(iv) the LEA (s 62(10)).

No objections from categories (i)–(iv) opposite (Secretary of State *not* obliged to consider objections from others – except perhaps under public law duty to consult).

↓

Secretary of State

↓

Rejects the proposals but may ask governors to submit further proposals within a specified time (s 62(11)(a), (12) & (13)).

Approves proposals – but may ask for modifications, and may then approve them with modifications (s 62(11)(b)).

Note: transition arrangements for the period between approval and incorporation are laid down in ERA 1988 Sch 5.

Initial governing body becomes *body corporate* under proposed corporate name – on proposed date of implementation (s 62(14)).

↓

Within 6 months, *instruments and articles of government to be made* – in the interim Secretary of State may give direction on matters covered by instruments and articles (s 72(1) and (2)).

Appendix 2

DES Circular 7/88 Education Reform Act: Local Management of Schools (Annex A)

DIVISION OF RESPONSIBILITY FOR BUILDING AND GROUNDS MAINTENANCE BETWEEN LEAs AND SCHOOLS

This Annex sets out a possible division of responsibilities for building and grounds maintenance between LEAs and schools. It draws upon helpful work by the Royal Institution of Chartered Surveyors (see paragraph 70 of this Circular). LEAs will not be required to adhere to this division in detail, but the Secretary of State will expect that in general the responsibilities of schools should cover the main items indicated below as a minimum. As stated in paragraph 69, schemes should provide for schools to be able to arrange for minor emergency repairs to items which otherwise fall within the LEA's area of responsibility (eg minor repairs to leaking pipes). LEA responsibilities are described by overall headings for each item, with school responsibilities described in more detail.

LEA Responsibility	School Responsibility
A. STRUCTURE	
– Foundations	
– Structural frames	
– Floor structures (including ground floor slabs)	Repair or replacement of floor finishes
– Roof structures (including weather-proof coverings and insulation)	Repair of ceiling finishes
– Skylights, rooflights and verandahs	Minor repairs and repairs of glazing
– Rainwater goods	Clearing out gutters and downpipes

281

- Staircase and landing structures (including handrails and balustrades)
- External walls and surfaces (including insulation)
- Internal walls, partitions and glazed screens
- Windows and fittings (including window walls)
- Doors and fittings

- Ceiling structures (including suspension systems)

Timber preservation

Repair of finishes and coverings
Repair of exposed internal finishes
Repair of surface finishes and glazing
Minor repairs, adjustment and glazing
Minor repairs, adjustment and glazing
Ceiling tiles/finishes and minor plaster repairs
Glazing: to include all glazing throughout as indicated above

B. DECORATION
- All external decoration

All **internal decoration:** including cleaning and preparation

C. WATER AND DRAINAGE SERVICES
- Internal water supply services (including pumps, pipes, tanks and insulation)

- Replacement of water supply including sanitary equipment

Minor repair and adjustment including taps and other fittings

- Waste and soil drainage services

Cleaning of pipes and maintenance of traps, wire guards etc

D. ELECTRICAL SERVICES
- Servicing, repair and replacement of general electrical installations including switchgear, cables and conduits up to and including switches, sockets and other outlets
- All external lighting, including columns, floodlights and road lighting

Replacing lamps, tubes and plugs

Appendix 2

- Steel chimneys
- Alarm, emergency and time systems (except for any systems purchased at school cost)

Reset of alarms and fire detection systems; minor repairs to clocks and bells; maintenance of any systems purchased at school cost

- Fan convectors and other fixed space and water heating equipment; fixed ventilation units

Portable heating and ventilation equipment; general cleaning; maintenance and replacement of fittings on all items
Kitchen equipment: servicing and repair of fixed cooking equipment including ovens, ranges, fryers, boilers, steamers, grills and mixers. Heated trolleys, refrigerators, cold rooms, fixed water boilers and sterilising sink heaters
Laundry equipment: servicing and repair of washing machines, tumble driers, spin driers, extractors and irons (excluding drainage systems)

- Lifts, hoists, barriers and electric door motors and controls
- Specialist external equipment (eg earthing, lightning conductors)
- Standby generators
- Temporary accommodation: all power supply and wiring

E. MECHANICAL SERVICES
- Servicing, repair and replacement of mechanical installations and plant including:
    - Boilers, including automatic controls and electrics

- Ancillary boiler equipment: pumps and tanks
- Heating and domestic hot water distribution systems, including replacement of radiators and other heat emitters, taps and shower fittings
- Gas distribution systems
- Fixed air-conditioning and ventilation equipment
- Direct oil and gas fired heater units
- Sewage pumps and chambers

Minor repairs and adjustments to heat emitters, taps and shower fittings

- Swimming pools: including filtration plant, pumps pipes and boilers

Kitchen equipment: servicing and repair of gas cooking equipment including motors and burners etc
Chemical dosing, cleaning and minor maintenance

Fire fighting equipment: extinguishers, fire blankets and fixed hoses

- Fume cupboards, including extractor fans and ductwork

F. FURNITURE & FITTINGS

Internal joinery fixtures: including cupboards, shelves, display boards, fixed benches and other internal seating with its coverings
Gymnasium equipment: repairs of all fixed sports and gymnasium equipment and markings
Supply, fixing and maintenance of all internal signs, blinds, curtain tracks etc
Fires and fireplaces

Appendix 2

G. EXTERNAL WORKS
   - Demolition of buildings and clearance of sites; sealing of services
   - Major repairs to hard-paved areas including roads, playgrounds, car parks and courts

     Minor repairs to hard-paved areas
   - Perimeter and retaining walls; perimeter fencing and gates

     Minor repairs to walls, fencing and gates
   - Major external fixtures

     Minor external fixtures eg signs and notices
   - Mature trees

     Upkeep of grounds: maintenance of grounds, playing fields, amenities land, landscaped areas and boundary hedges (except mature trees)
   - Mains drainage including traps, gullies and manholes

     Cleaning and unblocking drainage systems
     Refuse containers and bins
     Pest control
   - Gas, electric, water and heating mains
   - Maintenance of ancillary buildings, including garages and huts, constructed at LEA cost

     Maintenance of ancillary buildings constructed at school cost

H. MISCELLANEOUS
   - Asbestos removal or treatment
   - External maintenance on temporary buildings

     Internal maintenance on temporary buildings; all glazing repairs

Appendix 3

Conditions of employment of teachers
(Extract taken from The School Teachers' Pay and Conditions Order 1989 (ISBN 0 11 270672 X) and reproduced with the permission of the Controller of Her Majesty's Stationery office. The 1990 Document is expected to make very few changes on conditions.)

PART VIII—Conditions of employment of head teachers

Overriding requirements

27. A head teacher shall carry out his professional duties in accordance with and subject to—

    (1) the provisions of the Education Acts 1944 to 1988;

    (2) any orders and regulations having effect thereunder;

    (3) the articles of government of the school of which he is head teacher, to the extent to which their content is prescribed by statute;

    (4) where the school is a voluntary school or a grant-maintained school which was formerly a voluntary school, any trust deed applying in relation thereto;

    (5) any scheme of local management approved or imposed by the Secretary of State under section 34 of the Education Reform Act 1988;

    and, to the extent to which they are not inconsistent with these conditions—

Appendix 3

   (a) provisions of the articles of government the content of which is not so prescribed;
   (b) in the case of a school which has a delegated budget,
       (i) any rules, regulations or policies laid down by the governing body under their powers as derived from any of the sources specified in sub-paragraphs (1) to (5) and (a) above; and
       (ii) any rules, regulations or policies laid down by his employers with respect to matters for which the governing body is not so responsible;
   (c) in any other case, any rules, regulations or policies laid down by his employers; and
   (d) the terms of his appointment.

General functions

28. Subject to paragraph 27 above, the head teacher shall be responsible for the internal organisation, management and control of the school.

Consultation   29. In carrying out his duties the head teacher shall consult, where this is appropriate, with the authority, the governing body, the staff of the school and the parents of its pupils.

Professional duties

30. The professional duties of a head teacher shall include—

School aims
   (1) formulating the overall aims and objectives of the school and policies for their implementation;

Appointment of staff
   (2) participating in the selection and appointment of the teaching and non-teaching staff of the school;

Management of staff
   (3) (a) deploying and managing all teaching and non-teaching staff of the school

and allocating particular duties to them (including such duties of the head teacher as may properly be delegated to the deputy head teacher or other members of the staff) in a manner consistent with their conditions of employment, maintaining a reasonable balance for each teacher between work carried out in school and work carried out elsewhere.

(b) ensuring that the duty of providing cover for absent teachers is shared equitably among all teachers in the school (including the head teacher), taking account of their teaching and other duties;

Liaison with staff unions and associations

(4) maintaining relationships with organisations representing teachers and other persons on the staff of the school;

Curriculum

(5) (a) determining, organising and implementing an appropriate curriculum for the school, having regard to the needs experience, interests, aptitudes and stage of development of the pupils and the resources available to the school; and his duty under sections 1(1) and 10(1)(b) and (2) of the Education Reform Act 1988;

(b) securing that all pupils in attendance at the school take part in daily collective worship in pursuance of his duty under section 10(1)(a) of the Education Reform Act 1988;

Review

(6) keeping under review the work and organisation of the school;

Standards of teaching and learning

(7) evaluating the standards of teaching and learning in the school, and ensuring that proper standards of professional performance are established and maintained;

Appraisal, training and development of staff

(8) (a) supervising and participating in any arrangements within an agreed national framework for the appraisal of the performance of teachers who teach in the school;

Appendix 3

	(b) ensuring that all staff in the school have access to advice and training appropriate to their needs, in accordance with the policies of the maintaining authority or, in the case of a grant-maintained school, of the governing body, for the development of staff;
Management information	(9) providing information about the work and performance of the staff employed at the school where this is relevant to their future employment;
Pupil progress	(10) ensuring that the progress of the pupils of the school is monitored and recorded;
Pastoral care	(11) determining and ensuring the implementation of a policy for the pastoral care of the pupils;
Discipline	(12) determining, in accordance with any written statement of general principles provided for him by the governing body, measures to be taken with a view to promoting, among the pupils, self-discipline and proper regard for authority, encouraging good behaviour on the part of the pupils, securing that the standard of behaviour of the pupils is acceptable and otherwise regulating the conduct of the pupils; making such measures generally known within the school, and ensuring that they are implemented;
	(13) ensuring the maintenance of good order and discipline at all times during the school day (including the midday break) when pupils are present on the school premises and whenever the pupils are engaged in authorised school activities, whether on the school premises or elsewhere;
Relations with parents	(14) making arrangements for parents to be given regular information about the school curriculum, the progress of their children and other matters affecting the school, so as to promote common understanding of its aims;

Relations with other bodies	(15) promoting effective relationships with persons and bodies outside the school;
Relations with governing body	(16) advising and assisting the governing body of the school in the exercise of its functions, including (without prejudice to any rights he may have as a governor of the school) attending meetings of the governing body and making such reports to it in connection with the discharge of his functions as it may properly require either on a regular basis or from time to time;
Relations with authority	(17) (except in the case of grant-maintained schools) providing for liaison and co-operation with the officers of the maintaining authority; making such reports to the authority in connection with the discharge of his functions as it may properly require, either on a regular basis or from time to time;
Relations with other educational establishments	(18) maintaining liaison with other schools and further education establishments with which the school has a relationship;
Resources	(19) allocating, controlling and accounting for those financial and material resources of the school which are under the control of the head teacher;
Premises	(20) making arrangements, if so required by the maintaining authority or the governing body of a grant-maintained school (as appropriate), for the security and effective supervision of the school buildings and their contents and of the school grounds; and ensuring (if so required) that any lack of maintenance is promptly reported to the maintaining authority or, if appropriate, the governing body;
Appraisal of head teacher	(21) (a) participating in any arrangements within an agreed national framework for the appraisal of his performance as head teacher; (b) participating in the identification of areas in which he would benefit from further training and undergoing such training;

Appendix 3

Absence   (22) arranging for a deputy head teacher or other suitable person to assume responsibility for the discharge of his functions as head teacher at any time when he is absent from the school;

Teaching   (23) participating, to such extent as may be appropriate having regard to his other duties, in the teaching of pupils at the school, including the provision of cover for absent teachers.

Daily break   31. A head teacher shall be entitled to a break of reasonable length in the course of each school day, and shall arrange for a suitable person to assume responsibility for the discharge of his functions as head teacher during that break.

PART IX—Conditions of employment of deputy head teachers

Professional duties

32. A person appointed deputy head teacher in a school, in addition to carrying out the professional duties of a school teacher, including those duties particularly assigned to him by the head teacher, shall—

  (1) assist the head teacher in managing the school or such part of it as may be determined by the head teacher;
  (2) undertake any professional duty of the head teacher which may be delegated to him by the head teacher;
  (3) undertake, in the absence of the head teacher and to the extent required by him or the relevant body or, in the case of an aided school, the governing body, the professional duties of the head teacher;
  (4) be entitled to a break of reasonable length in the course of each school day.

PART X—conditions of employment of school teachers

Exercise of general professional duties

33. A teacher who is not a head teacher shall carry out the professional duties of a school teacher as circumstances may require—

   (1) if he is employed as a teacher in a school, under the reasonable direction of the head teacher of that school;
   (2) if he is employed by an authority on terms under which he is not assigned to any one school, under the reasonable direction of that authority and of the head teacher of any school in which he may for the time being be required to work as a teacher.

Exercise of particular duties

34. (1) A teacher employed as a teacher (other than a head teacher) in a school shall perform, in accordance with any directions which may reasonably be given to him by the head teacher from time to time, such particular duties as may reasonably be assigned to him.
   (2) A teacher employed by an authority on terms such as those described in paragraph 33(2) above shall perform, in accordance with any direction which may reasonably be given to him from time to time by the authority or by the head teacher of any school in which he may for the time being be required to work as a teacher, such particular duties as may reasonably be assigned to him.

Professional duties

35. The following duties shall be deemed to be included in the professional duties which a school teacher may be required to perform—

Appendix 3

Teaching	(1) (a) planning and preparing courses and lessons;
	(b) teaching, according to their educational needs, the pupils assigned to him, including the setting and marking of work to be carried out by the pupil in school and elsewhere;
	(c) assessing, recording and reporting on the development, progress and attainment of pupils;
	in each case having regard to the curriculum for the school;
Other activities	(2) (a) promoting the general progress and well-being of individual pupils and of any class or group of pupils assigned to him;
	(b) providing guidance and advice to pupils on educational and social matters and on their further education and future careers, including information about sources of more expert advice on specific questions; making relevant records and reports;
	(c) making records of and reports on the personal and social needs of pupils;
	(d) communicating and consulting with the parents of pupils;
	(e) communicating and co-operating with persons or bodies outside the school;
	(f) participating in meetings arranged for any of the purposes described above;
Assessments and reports	(3) providing or contributing to oral and written assessments, reports and references relating to individual pupils and groups of pupils;
Appraisal	(4) participating in any arrangements within an agreed national framework for the appraisal of his performance and that of other teachers;

Review: further training and development	(5) (a) reviewing from time to time his methods of teaching and programmes of work;
(b) participating in arrangements for his further training and professional development as a teacher;
Educational methods	(6) advising and co-operating with the head teacher and other teachers (or any one or more of them) on the preparation and development of courses of study, teaching materials, teaching programmes, methods of teaching and assessment and pastoral arrangements;
Discipline, health and safety	(7) maintaining good order and discipline among the pupils and safeguarding their health and safety both when they are authorised to be on the school premises and when they are engaged in authorised school activities elsewhere;
Staff meetings	(8) participating in meetings at the school which relate to the curriculum for the school or the administration or organisation of the school, including pastoral arrangements;
Cover	(9) supervising and so far as practicable teaching any pupils whose teacher is not available to teach them:

provided that no teacher shall be required to provide such cover—

(a) after the teacher who is absent or otherwise not available has been so for three or more consecutive working days; or

(b) where the fact that the teacher would be absent or otherwise not available for a period exceeding three consecutive working days was known to the maintaining authority or in the case of a grant-maintained school or a school which has a delegated budget and whose local management scheme delegates the relevant responsibility for the pro- |

Appendix 3

vision of supply teachers to the governing body, for two or more working days before the absence commenced; unless –

(i) he is a teacher employed wholly or mainly for the purpose of providing such cover ("a supply teacher"); or

(ii) the authority or the governing body (as the case may be) have exhausted all reasonable means of providing a supply teacher to provide cover without success; or

(iii) he is a full-time teacher at the school but has been assigned by the head teacher in the time-table to teach or carry out other specified duties (except cover) for less than 75 per cent of those hours in the week during which pupils are taught at the school;

Public examinations
(10) participating in arrangements for preparing pupils for public examinations and in assessing pupils for the purposes of such examinations; recording and reporting such assessments; and participating in arrangements for pupils' presentation for and supervision during such examinations;

Management
(11) (a) contributing to the selection for appointment and professional development of other teachers and non-teaching staff, including the induction and assessment of new and probationary teachers;

(b) co-ordinating or managing the work of other teachers;

(c) taking such part as may be required of him in the review, development and management of activities relating to the curriculum, organisation and pastoral functions of the school;

THE LAW RELATING TO SCHOOLS

Administra-
tion

(12) (a) participating in administration and organisational tasks related to such duties as are described above, including the management or supervision of persons providing support for the teachers in the school and the ordering and allocation of equipment and materials;

(b) attending assemblies, registering the attendance of pupils and supervising pupils, whether these duties are to be performed before, during or after school sessions.

Working time

36. (1) (a) a teacher employed full-time, other than in the circumstances described in sub-paragraph (c), shall be available for work for 195 days in any year, of which 190 days shall be days on which he may be required to teach pupils in addition to carrying out other duties; and those 195 days shall be specified by his employer or, if the employer so directs, by the head teacher;

(b) such a teacher shall be available to perform such duties at such times and such places as may be specified by the head teacher (or, where the teacher is not assigned to any one school, by his employer or the head teacher of any school in which he may for the time being be required to work as a teacher) for 1265 hours in any year, those hours to be allocated reasonably throughout those days in the year on which he is required to be available for work;

(c) sub-paragraphs (a) and (b) do not apply to such a teacher employed wholly or mainly to teach or perform other duties in relation to pupils in a residential establishment;

(d) time spent in travelling to or from the place of work shall not count against the 1265 hours referred to in sub-paragraph (b);

(e) such a teacher shall not be required under his contract as a teacher to undertake midday supervision, and shall be allowed a break of reasonable length either between school sessions or between the hours of 12 noon and 2.00 pm;

(f) such a teacher shall, in addition to the requirements set out in sub-paragraphs (a) and (b) above, work such additional hours as may be needed to enable him to discharge effectively his professional duties, including in particular the marking of pupils' work, the writing of reports on pupils and the preparation of lessons, teaching material and teaching programmes. The amount of time required for this purpose beyond the 1265 hours referred to in sub-paragraph (b) and the times outside the 1265 specified hours at which duties shall be performed shall not be defined by the employer but shall depend upon the work needed to discharge the teacher's duties.

(2) In this paragraph, "year" means a period of 12 months commencing on 1st September unless the school's academic year begins in August in which case it means a period of 12 months commencing on 1st August.

Appendix 4

(Sections referred to are from the Education (No 2) Act 1986.)
DES Circular 7/87 The Conduct of Governor Elections (Annex 9)

PRE-ELECTION PUBLICITY

15. By virtue of section 30(2)(g) (see paragraphs 6 to 12 of Circular 8/86), the governors' annual report to parents is required to provide such information as is available about arrangements for the next election of parent governors.

16. Beyond that, section 15(6) (reproduced in paragraph 4 of this Annex), requires the responsible authority to give appropriate publicity to the election process when a vacancy needs to be filled. It is suggested that a letter should be sent to each household, perhaps using pupil post, (see paragraph 26 of this Annex) enclosing nomination forms and setting out the timetable for each stage. Where a substantial number of parents have a language other than English as their mother tongue, the letter (and all other documents relating to elections) should be translated into other languages.

17. Responsible authorities should frame their publicity to maximise participation, emphasising the importance conferred on school government by the Act. LEAs may also wish to consider measures, such as an authority-wide parent governor election week, in which governing bodies of aided and special agreement schools might also choose to participate.

NOMINATIONS

18. Responsible authorities are to decide how nominations are to be made, for example, whether a proposer and a seconder are required, or a larger number of sponsors. This should be explained clearly in the preliminary letter. Where participation has been low in the past, responsible authorities may wish to consider allowing self-nomination and nomination by a spouse. In any case, those nominated should signify in writing their willingness to stand for election. It is recommended that they should be invited to supply, with their nomination, a short personal statement for circulation to

Appendix 4

parents, either on the ballot paper or separately, if an election is required.

19. Proposers, seconders and other sponsors should, like the nominee, all be parents of registered pupils at the school. No parent should participate in more nominations than there are vacancies.

20. If the number of qualified nominees (see paragraphs 12 to 14 of this Annex) is smaller than or equal to the number of vacancies no voting is required: those nominated are simply declared to be governors. If there are vacancies remaining, the governing body is to appoint parent governors, see paragraph 5.3.5 of this Circular.

CONDUCT OF THE ELECTION

21. It is suggested that responsible authorities should appoint a PRESIDING OR RETURNING OFFICER for each school. In many cases this will be the head teacher, but the clerk to the governors or the chairman of the governors might also be appropriate.

22. The responsible authority is to select the ELECTORAL METHOD to be employed. This might be first-past-the-post or some form of proportional representation. If the latter is chosen, the responsible authority needs to ensure that the presiding/returning officer is familiar with the intricacies of the system.

23. It is for the responsible authority to determine whether a parent is to have one vote per child per vacancy or only one per vacancy. They should ensure that, whatever basis is chosen, it is made clear to the electorate.

24. The ballot paper should list the names of all the candidates, either in alphabetical order or at random. It may also include the short personal statement supplied by each candidate (see paragraph 18 of this Annex). Clear instructions for voting should be given, especially if proportional representation is to be used, and it should be stressed that no other mark should be made on the ballot paper. There must be at least one ballot paper per parent.

25. In operating the SECRET BALLOT required by section 15(4), it is necessary to ensure secrecy whilst also including some safeguards against voting in duplicate or by those not eligible to participate. A register of electors would in many cases be too time-consuming and complicated to make it worthwhile.
A REQUIREMENT THAT THE BALLOT PAPER BE SIGNED BY THE VOTER IS NOT CONSISTENT WITH A SECRET BALLOT. One possible method would be the use of a double envelope system.
The ballot paper would be sealed in the inner unmarked envelope

which would be sealed in an outer envelope signed on the back by the voter. To ensure confidentiality, such a method would require a proper two-stage system of recording votes cast and opening ballot papers. The procedure might be that, on receipt of the ballot papers, the presiding/returning officer would check the name on the outer envelope for entitlement to vote and note the return of the ballot paper. The inner envelope containing the ballot paper would then be placed in the ballot box for counting at the appointed time later.

26. By virtue of section 15(5), parents have to be afforded the opportunity to vote by post. It will be for the responsible authority to decide how this requirement is to be combined with personal and proxy voting (if any). Any ballot where both postal and personal voting are allowed should be approached with caution since administration and verification could be complicated. In many cases, the responsible authority will no doubt wish to get ballot papers to and from parents by means of the pupils. However, where parents have more than one child in a school and voting is to be on the basis of one vote per parent per vacancy, some system will need to be devised to ensure that no parent receives more than one ballot paper. Ballot papers will also need to be posted or otherwise delivered, to parents whose child is absent from school when the ballot papers are issued.

27. It is suggested that ballot papers could be returned to the school, to a specified central point, over a period of days. During that period, candidates might also hold meetings for parents and the opportunity given for voting to take place in person. (This might coincide with the parents' annual meeting.)

28. The responsible authority should decide whether PROXY VOTING is to be allowed and, if so, who is to be entitled to act as proxy and how this is to be notified to the presiding/returning officer. The case for proxy voting is diminished by the requirement that postal voting be allowed, but it might be considered in schools where it is common for parents to be away for long periods of time, as for example in the case of service families.

29. If a ballot paper is inadvertently spoilt (or lost by the pupil) a duplicate may be issued by the presiding/returning officer. An election is not invalidated by an individual's failure to receive or to return a ballot paper.

THE COUNT

30. The count should be conducted by the presiding/returning officer at a time and place determined by the responsible authority. He may allow the candidate or their nominated representatives to be present. He should have responsibility for

deciding the validity of dubious or spoilt ballot papers, but should be able to refer to a nominee of the responsible authority in difficult cases.

31. The responsible authority should decide, and announce well before the election, the method for deciding an election in the event of a tie. As a first step, the votes should be recounted. If the votes are then still equal, possible methods of deciding who is to become the governor include drawing lots, tossing a coin, or choosing the candidate with the youngest child at the school.

POST ELECTION

32. The result of the election (including any appointments – see paragraph 20 of this Annex) should be notified by the responsible authority to all parents, to the LEA and to the other members of the governing body. The ballot papers should be retained securely for, say, six months, in case the election result is challenged. The number of ballot papers issued and the number returned at each election should be noted in order to monitor participation.

33. The responsible authority should review their election procedures from time to time, and particularly in the light of any problems found in their use.

Index

page

Absence from school 252–253
Accidents—see *Negligence*
Admission(s):
    discrimination in 168
    limits of numbers of 35–36, 148–153
    parental preference in 153–159
    powers of Secretary of State in respect of 158–159
    publication of information about 135–136, 152–153, 156
    single sex schools, to 164
Admissions register 177
Aggregated schools budget 148–153
Aided school, governing body of 109
Allocation of school places—see *Admission(s)*
Alteration of schools 33–36
Amalgamation of schools 36–40
Annual report of governors 128, 140
Anti-discrimination—see *Equal opportunities*
Appeals:
    admission decisions, in respect of 156–158
    failure to reinstate pupil, in respect of 191–192
    pupil records, in respect of 146
    special educational needs, in respect of 240–242
Appointment of staff 71–80
Articled teacher scheme 69
Articles of government 104–106, 187–188, 189, 191, 192
Assisted places scheme 25–26
Attendance:
    register 177–178
    school, at 178–186

Ballot
    chairmanship of governors, for 117–118
    conversion to grant-maintained status, for 15–16, 17–18
    place on governing body, for 298–301
Board and lodging, provision of by LEA 175–176
Break-time supervision 156–157
Broadcast, copyright in 223–230

303

page

Budget share	50–53
Budgeting—see *Local management of schools*	
Capital grant	20–21
Care proceedings	185–186
Catering, competitive tendering in respect of	48–50
Character of school, change of	33–34
Charges for education	219–222
City colleges for the technology of the arts, constitution of	22
City technology colleges, constitution of	22
Cleaning, competitive tendering in respect of	48–50
Closure of school	3, 36–40
Clothing, provision of by LEA	175
Collective worship	212–216
Committees, delegation of powers of governors to	123–128
Community school, meaning of	80
Competitive tendering	48–50
Complaints	222–223
Compulsory school age, definition of	179
Computerised data	146–147
Confidentiality	144–145
Confiscation of property	195
Consultation by LEA	27–30
Controlled school, composition of governing body of	108
Copying—see *Copyright*	
Copyright	223–230
infringement of	226–227
meaning of	224–225
Corporal punishment	226–227
Council for Accreditation of Teacher Education	63
County school:	
closure of	36–37
control of	11
definition of	10–11
establishment of	30–31
governing body of	108
Curricular record—see *Pupil(s), records*	
Curriculum	196–230
basic	198–199, 231–234
complaints about	206
National—see *National Curriculum*	
philosophy of	196–197
secular	197–198
Curriculum Council for Wales	206
Data protection	146–147
Defamation	146

Index

page

Delegation:
   governors, by 123–128
   scheme—see *Financial delegation scheme*
Detention 194–195
Disabled pupil(s) 240
Discipline:
   pupils, among 187–195
   staff, among 80–90
Discrimination:
   meaning of 161–162
   See also *Equal opportunities*
Dismissal, member of staff, of 80–90
Displaced person, education of 58
Dramatic work—see *Copyright*
Dress 169–170
Dyslexia 232

Education Assets Board 17
Education support grant scheme 102
Educational Maintenance Allowance 176
Educational policy, publication of information about 136–142
Election:
   chairmanship of governors, for 117–118
   conversion to grant-maintained status, for 15–16, 17–18
   place on governing body, for 298–301
Equal opportunities 5, 72–73, 80–81, 160–176
Equipment, insurance in respect of 274
Establishment of schools 30–33
Examination fees, circumstances in which recoverable from parent 220
Exclusion from school 188–192
Expenses of pupil, payment of by LEA 174
Expulsion from school 188–192
External qualifications 218–219

Film—see *Copyright*
Financial assistance for pupils 172–176
Financial delegation scheme:
   budget share formula in 50–53
   conditions attached to 53–54
   duty to implement 43–44
   governors' liability in respect of 55–56
   implementation of 55
   monitoring of 56–58
   provision for budget share in 44–53
   provision for special educational needs in 243–244
   publication of 54–55
   suspension of 56–57

page

Funding:
  grant-maintained schools, of 19–21
  nursery schools, of 27
  see also *Local management of schools*
Further education:
  definition of 7
  duties of LEAs in respect of 6–8

General schools budget 44
Governing body:
  composition of 106–111
  election to, procedure for 298–301
Government:
  articles of 104–106, 187–188, 189, 191, 192
  instrument of 104–106
  schools, of 103–134
  See also *Governor(s)*
Governor(s):
  annual report of 128, 140
  delegation of functions by 123–128
  disputes between and LEA 130–132
  disqualification of 114–115
  election to chairmanship and vice chairmanship of 117–118
  expenses of 132
  financial delegation to—see *Financial delegation scheme*
  meetings of 116–123
  personal liability of 55–56, 128–130
  pecuniary interest of 119–120
  removal of from office 115–116
  resignation of 115
  term of office of 113–114
  training of 132–133
  withdrawal of from meetings, when necessary 119–122
Grant-maintained schools
  acquisition of status of 16–17, 277–280
  autonomous nature of 15
  closure of 37–39
  conversion to, consideration of 27–30
  duties of LEAs in respect of 21–22
  funding of 19–21
  governing body of 107, 110
  maintenance of 2
  significant change to 34–35
  transfer of property to 17
  transfer of staff to 18–19, 100

Head teacher(s) and deputy head teacher(s):
  appointment of 74–75, 77–78

Index

page

pay of 91–92
   responsibility of in respect of secular curriculum 197–198
Health and safety 270–273
Higher education, role of LEAs in respect of 7–8
Holiday dates 133
Home, schooling at 179
Homosexuality 210–211
Hours 133–134

ILEA:
   abolition of 1
In loco parentis 249–250
Incentive allowances 95–96
Independent school(s):
   assisted places at 25–26
   autonomous nature of 23–24
   complaint about 24
   controls on 23–24
   definition of 23
   registration of 23
Information, publication of 135–147, 198, 208
Injury, recording of 273
   See also *Negligence*
Instrument of government 104–106

Junior pupil, definition of 6

LEA(s):
   consultation by 27–30
   definition of 1
   diminution of influence of 103–104
   disputes with governor(s), resolution of 130–132
   duty of to provide education 2–8
   grant-maintained schools, duties of in respect of 21–22
   information to be given by 137–139
   learning difficulties, provision by in respect of 8, 231–234
   vicarious liability of for act(s) of teacher(s) 246–247
Learning difficulty
   meaning of 8, 232
Lessons, charging for 219–220
Local education authority—see *LEA(s)*
Local management of schools ("LMS") 40–58
   philosophy of 40–42
   See also *Financial delegation scheme*
London weightings 94–95
Lunch time supervision 256–257

Maintained special school, governing body of 108

307

Maintenance, competitive tendering in respect of 48–50
Materials, charging for 219–220
Maternity leave 89–90
Meals, provision of 172–173
Middle school, meaning of 9
Milk 172–173
Music tuition, charge for 219

National Curriculum 199–206
   assessment of pupils under 199
   content of 200–202, 205–206
   Council 205–206
   exception from 202–204, 242–243
   implementation of 204–205
Negligence
   care and supervision of pupils, in 246–264
   governor(s), by 128–130
   meaning of 246–251
   See also *Health and Safety*
Non-attendance 180–186
Numbers admissible to a school 148–153
Nursery education 6, 26, 27

Optional extras, charges for 221–222
Outings 221, 261–263

Parent(s):
   duty of to ensure attendance 178–179, 181, 184
   governors 106
   meetings of 147
   preference of 153–159
   prospective pupils(s), of, information to be given to 137
      See also *Prospectus*
   reports to 202
Play (dramatic)—see *Copyright*
Political issues 206–207
Preference about school to be attended 153–159
Pregnancy—see *Maternity leave*
Premises:
   approval of 32–33, 35
   provision for the disabled in 169–170
   responsibility for 281–285
   safety of 264–269
   See also *Health and Safety; Negligence*
Primary education
   definition of 6
   duty of LEA to provide 2–6
Probationary period 70–71

Index

page

Prospectus 137–139
Public information about schools 140–142
Punishment—see *Corporal punishment; Confiscation; Detention*
Pupil(s):
    assessment of 199
    attendance of 178–186
    care and supervision of 246–264, 257–264
    disabled 240
    discipline of 187–195
    dress of 169–170
    exclusion of from school 188–192
    financial assistance for 172–176
    negligence of 251
    non-attendance of 180–186
    records 142–146
        confidentiality of 144–145
        disclosure of 143–144, 147
        transfer of 145–146
    reinstatement of following exclusion 189–191
    registration of 177–178
    special educational needs of 231–244

Race relations—see *Equal opportunities*
Records 143–147, 168–172
Redundancy 87
Registrar of Independent Schools 23–24
Registration of pupils 177–178
Religious education 216–218
Removal of school to a new site 35
Repairs, competitive tendering in respect of 48–50
Reports to parents 202

School(s):
    amalgamation of 36–40
    closure of 3, 36–40
    leaving age 179
    prospectus 137–139
School Examinations and Assessment Council 206, 218–219
Secondary education:
    definition of 6
    duty of LEA to provide 2–5, 6
Secular Curriculum 197–198
Senior pupil, definition of 6
Session times 133–134
Sex:
    discrimination 161–168
    See also *Equal opportunities*
    education 207–210

	page
Single sex schools	164–165
Sound recording—see *Copyright*	
Special:	
agreement school:	
definition of	15
governing body of	109
educational needs	231–244
appeals concerning	240–242
financial delegation scheme, provision for in	243–244
identification of	234–237
meaning of	232–233
ordinary schools, provision for in	233–234
statement of	237–240
purpose grant	20–21
school:	
meaning of	9
Speech therapy	232
Staff	59–102
appointment of	71–80
contract of employment of	84
discipline	80–90
dismissal of	80–90
grant-maintained school, transfer of to	18–19
maternity leave for	89–90
negligence of—see *Negligence*	
non-teaching, pay and conditions of	98–100
redundancy of	87
suspension of from employment	82–84
training	100–102, 244
unfair dismissal of	84–88
See also *Teacher(s)*	
Stages in education	2
"Standard National Scale"	92–94
Statistics, compilation of	142
Statutory advisory council on religious education ("SACRE")	212
Subject choices, sex discrimination in	165–166
Supervision order(s)	185–186
Supply teacher(s)	97
Suspension from school	188–192
Teacher(s):	
accommodation for	268
appraisal of	102
articled	69
collective worship and	214, 216
conditions of employment of	286–297
duties of	98
health and safety of	270–273

Index

page

hearing and visual impaired, of 64, 65, 69
"licensed" 61–62, 63, 64, 66–69
mainland Europe, qualified in 62
mentally handicapped, of 64, 65, 66
Northern Ireland, qualified in 62
pay of 90–97
probationary period 70–71
qualification as 61–71
Scotland, qualified in 62
shortage of 4, 60, 61
supply 97
unqualified 65–66
working conditions of 90–91, 97–98
See also *Head teacher; Staff*
Teaching hours 133–134
Term dates 133
Training:
  governor(s), of 132–133
  staff, of 100–102, 244
  teacher(s), of 61–71
Transport:
  provision of 173–174, 181, 184
  safety of 263–264
Travellers, education of 58
Trips:
  charges for 221
  safety of pupils on 261–263
Truancy 180–186
Trust deed 105–106

Unfair dismissal 84–88

Voluntary aided schools, nature of 13–14
Voluntary controlled schools, definition of 12–13
Voluntary schools:
  categories of 11–15
  closure of 36–37
  establishment of 31–32

Wardship proceedings 186, 242
Working conditions 90–91, 97–98
Worship 212–216

311